THE ARAB REVOLUTIONS AND AMERICAN POLICY

FOREWORD BY JOSEPH S. NYE & BRENT SCOWCROFT

EDITED BY NICHOLAS BURNS & JONATHON PRICE

The Aspen Institute
One Dupont Circle, N.W.
Suite 700
Washington, DC 20036

Published in the United States of America in 2013 by The Aspen Institute

ISBN: 0-89843-579-X
Wye Publication Number: 13/008

Cover Design by: Steve Johnson
Interior Layout by: Sogand Sepassi

aspen strategy group

CO-CHAIRMEN

Joseph S. Nye, Jr.
University Distinguished Service Professor
John F. Kennedy School of Government
Harvard University

Brent Scowcroft
President
The Scowcroft Group, Inc.

DIRECTOR

Nicholas Burns
Professor of the Practice of Diplomacy
and International Politics
John F. Kennedy School of Government
Harvard University

DEPUTY DIRECTOR

Jonathon Price
Deputy Director
Aspen Strategy Group

ASSOCIATE DIRECTOR

Jennifer Jun
Associate Director
Aspen Strategy Group

MEMBERS

Madeleine Albright
Chair
Albright Stonebridge Group

Graham Allison
Director, Belfer Center
John F. Kennedy School of Government
Harvard University

Zoë Baird Budinger
President
Markle Foundation

Samuel R. Berger
Chair
Albright Stonebridge Group

Stephen E. Biegun
Vice President
Ford Motor Company

Robert D. Blackwill
Henry A. Kissinger Senior Fellow for
U.S. Foreign Policy
Council on Foreign Relations

James E. Cartwright
Harold Brown Chair in Defense Policy Studies
Center for Strategic and International Studies

Eliot Cohen
Robert E. Osgood Professor of Strategic Studies
Johns Hopkins SAIS

Susan Collins
Senator
United States Senate

Richard Cooper
Maurits C. Boas Professor of International
Economics
Harvard University

Acknowledgements

Nicholas Burns
Director, Aspen Strategy Group

Jonathon Price
Deputy Director, Aspen Strategy Group

With the Arab revolutions still underway, the Aspen Strategy Group convened for a four day workshop in Aspen, Colorado from August 3-7, 2012, to examine the urgent strategic, political and economic challenges confronting the United States in the Middle East today. This publication contains a collection of policy papers written by renowned Middle East experts that served to guide our discussions in Aspen, and more broadly, reflect the diversity of thoughts and depth of expertise that characterizes our meeting. Participants included a bipartisan and tri-generational group of ASG members and invited guests, ranging from current government officials and policymakers to corporate leaders, all of whom gathered in Aspen with the singular aim of focusing on the question of U.S. policy in the Middle East. Only by ensuring such a diversity of voices could we achieve a meaningful dialogue on the transformations under way in Syria, Egypt, Iran, and Israel. We were honored to have the President of the Council on Foreign Relations, Dr. Richard N. Haass, open the meeting with the fourth annual Ernest May lecture.

The Aspen Strategy Group would not be possible without the generous and constant support of our partners. These are organizations and individuals who invest time and resources in our mission to provide a forum for open and bipartisan dialogue on matters of national security and foreign policy. We owe our sincerest gratitude to Mr. Howard Cox, Exxon Mobil Corporation, Dr. Daniel Feldman, Mr. Moses Feldman, the Bill & Melinda Gates Foundation, the Markle Foundation, McKinsey & Company, Mr. Simon Pinniger and Ms. Carolyne Roehm, the Margot & Thomas J. Pritzker Family Foundation, the Resnick Family Foundation, the Stanton Foundation, and Ms. Leah Joy Zell.

We would also like to thank our Associate Director Jennifer Jun and our Brent Scowcroft Award Fellows Kevin Jones, Khaled Fayyad and Kimberly Aagaard for their important contributions to this initiative. We look forward to following their careers as the next generation of leaders and experts. We appreciate the service of Missy Daniels in proofreading and editing this publication.

This was certainly one of our most vigorous and interesting summer workshops the ASG has held. The dynamism, frankness, and openness of our debate would not be possible without the invaluable contribution of our distinguished members, to whom we are sincerely grateful. We are also thankful to the experts whose papers and presentations guided and enriched our discussions, as well as the government officials who took the time to be with us and share their thoughts during this precarious time of evaluating U.S. strategy.

Finally, our highest regards go to our co-chairmen, Joseph Nye and Brent Scowcroft, whose vision and expertise provide the founding merits of the Aspen Strategy Group. Only through their leadership has the ASG been able to serve as an ongoing forum of innovative strategic thinking on the most complex foreign policy and national security issues of the day.

Contents

Part 1

U.S. POLICY ON THE ARAB REVOLUTIONS 18 MONTHS IN:
WHAT HAVE WE ACCOMPLISHED?

CHAPTER 1

Part 2

THE OBAMA RESPONSE: HAS IT BEEN EFFECTIVE?

CHAPTER 2

CHAPTER 3

Foreword
by ASG Co-Chairmen

Joseph S. Nye, Jr.
ASG Co-Chairman

Brent Scowcroft
ASG Co-Chairman

On December 17, 2010, the self-immolation of a 26 year-old street vendor in Sidi Bouzid, Tunisia sparked a revolution across the country, inciting demonstrations and riots throughout Tunisia and catalyzing a wave of revolutions across the Arab world. In the two years that have passed since, authoritarian regimes that were decades-in-power have been overthrown in four countries—Tunisia, Egypt, Libya, and Yemen—and momentous civil uprisings have erupted in Bahrain and Syria. Although the long-term outcomes remain hard to predict, this is a critical time for the United States to examine the various drivers and immediate outcomes of the Arab revolutions and their influence on the formulation of American strategy in a region reborn. Recent attacks on American embassies in the Middle East, including the tragic killings of Ambassador Chris Stevens and three Foreign Service officers in Libya, serve as a poignant reminder of the complicated task of crafting a foreign policy toward a region historically marred by deep religious and sectarian strife.

In assessing U.S. strategic decisions, we should be mindful that our policymakers are operating in a context of extreme uncertainty arising from regional instability in the Middle East. Our most recent American experiences in the region remind us that wielding American power by making big bets on long term outcomes has largely ignored the fragmented nature of the Middle East, both in regional and country-specific contexts. Some experts have been quick to point out parallels of the Arab revolutions with the collapse of the Soviet empire. They argue that America's role in the transition to democracy will determine whether these countries choose the model of Eastern Europe and the Baltics or that of the Balkans and the Caucasus. However, we are operating in a post-Cold War international order, where the ever-expanding influence of satellite television, the internet and social media has empowered non-state actors to be increasingly aware of their individual and collective power to determine the fate of nations and regions. Their emergence as key drivers of regime change impedes our ability to see far into the future, which has always been an integral element of American grand strategy. We still believe that big bets are important for strategy, but they now require a caveat: we need to maximize flexibility and course-correction in order to adjust to fragmented polities, conflicting identities, and competing interests. As such, our strategy must be smart and nuanced in order to help the Arab people write their own narrative and ensure that our values and interests are protected now and well into the future.

As a resolutely bipartisan group of national security and foreign policy experts that seek to apply our collective acumen to tackle the most important challenges facing the United States, we chose to convene our 2012 annual Summer Workshop around the topic of the Arab revolutions and American policy. Over the course of four days—enriched by the participation of think tank experts and academics, as well as officials in the Obama administration and members of Congress—we examined and debated the future of American policy in the Middle East, with a special focus on key issues such as: the critical period of transition in Egypt; escalating violence and options of intervention in Syria; the threats associated with a nuclear Iran; the importance of formulating an effective strategy to deal with immediate economic assistance and long-term investment in the region; and the Obama administration's successes and failures during the overall process of transitions.

Our discussions identified several main areas of agreement, including the need to maintain America's strong alliance with Israel, protecting our interests in Egypt by focusing on political, economic and security reform, using social media and other non-military tools of intervention to engage more directly with civil society in Syria, and ensuring that Iran does not emerge a winner in any quest to obtain nuclear weapons. These interlocking strategic goals also highlighted our disagreements on how to tackle them effectively, with some believing that U.S. leadership has been wisely restrained and others arguing that we have lost influence as a result of being too irresolute and reactive in our approach. We also debated the gravity and scope of American influence in the Middle East—and ultimately concluded that the United States has a crucial role to play in shaping the trajectories of these countries during this critical period of transition.

The Aspen Strategy Group, a policy program of the Aspen Institute, was founded more than thirty years ago with an initial focus on the U.S.-Soviet relationship and arms control, but since then has evolved to examine the most critical foreign policy and national security issues confronting the country and the rest of the world. We hope that the frank and open dialogue we had as a group in Aspen is reflected in this book to reveal the complex and delicate task of recalibrating American strategy to shifting geopolitical priorities in the Middle East.

We believe that the Arab revolutions have shown encouraging signs of a region determined to end a decades-long era of arbitary rule, but we must also remain focused on building a comprehensive and flexible strategic framework that will help us navigate the plethora of challenges and opportunities that lie ahead. With the Middle East in turmoil, there could hardly be a more appropriate time for a careful, frank, and bipartisan evaluation of U.S. strategy.

Preface

Nicholas Burns
Director, Aspen Strategy Group
Professor of the Practice of Diplomacy and International Politics
John F. Kennedy School of Government
Harvard University

The Arab revolutions have brought the most significant and historic change to the Middle East in a nearly a century. This book features a compendium of essays on these dramatic events by some of America's most astute observers of Middle East politics and U.S. foreign policy. They were presented in August 2012 at the annual meeting of the Aspen Strategy Group, a nonpartisan organization of former secretaries of state and defense, national security advisors, ambassadors, professors, journalists, and businesspeople.

We spent four days in Aspen, Colorado thinking through American policy toward an Arab world in transition. Most of our members agreed that the revolutions underway in the 22 Arab countries have produced deeply rooted social, economic, and political change. Starting in Tunisia and Egypt, the revolutions swept through North Africa and the Levant and have extended to Yemen and the countries of the Gulf. There is little doubt they will continue and will dominate Arab life and politics in the future. In fact, the Arab peoples may only be witnessing the end of Act I in a five-act drama of revolutions, coups, elections, and struggles for power that may endure for decades to come.

Given their own vital interests in the region, Americans need to reflect carefully on the lessons from the events of the last two years. For more than half a century, Republican and Democratic administrations supported authoritarian Arab leaders. The U.S. achieved many important successes in those years—including the Camp David peace between Egypt and Israel and close security relations with most Arab countries. But it did not press Arab dictators consistently for democratic freedoms and did not often enough take into account the interests and welfare of the Arab peoples themselves. That American policy has been shattered by the revolutions of the last two years. Most at our conference in Aspen agreed there is now a pressing need for a new American strategy that can guide the American government and secure American interests during the inevitable turbulence ahead.

President Obama has begun to chart such a new strategy in responding to the historic changes across the Arab world. He has a difficult challenge in striving to balance competing American interests—our values of freedom and democracy on the one hand and our more concrete interests of energy and stability on the other. In reality, the president has not committed so much to an overarching strategy for the entire region but instead has fashioned individual policies for each of the 22 Arab states. For example, he swung U.S. support to the revolutions in Egypt, Tunisia, and Libya against the established leaders with which it had been friendly. But he has also acted more cautiously in the Gulf, where he has not pressed as openly for conservative governments to reform and where the U.S. must still rely on the continuity of oil and gas exports and the support of the Gulf monarchs against Iran.

Given the breadth of the changes underway, the United States has no choice but to consider major changes to its approach to the Middle East at a time when it is, in some ways, less influential than in the past. America is struggling to find a way to maintain influence with an Egyptian government, the most important in the Arab world, that is now dominated by the Moslem Brotherhood and other Islamist groups. The U.S. administration has worked hard to create an effective working relationship with Egypt's new leaders and to encourage it to maintain the peace with Israel, serve as a buffer with Hamas and other radical groups, and continue to resist Iranian influence in the region. At the same time, the administration has pushed quietly but consistently for a commitment by Cairo's new leaders to greater openness, democracy, and reform.

In Syria, the U.S. has wisely resisted a direct military intervention on the ground in that country's bitter and bloody civil war. But critics also suggest the administration must lead more aggressively to provide faster and more substantial support to the rebel forces that will inevitably overwhelm the Assad government. At stake is whether the U.S. will be able to retain influence with these opposition forces when Assad is gone.

All agreed at our conference that Iran poses a special challenge to the United States. We discussed whether President Obama should now open the first direct talks with Iran in three decades to see if a negotiated solution is possible to stop Iran short of a nuclear weapon. Together with increasingly tough U.S. and European Union sanctions and the threat of force, negotiations will certainly be a principal feature of U.S. policy in 2013. If talks succeed, President Obama will have used diplomacy to stop Iran from advancing its nuclear agenda. But if they fail, many will push for the U.S. to turn to armed force to deny Iran a nuclear future.

There is no question the U.S. will find itself engaged increasingly in the vital Asia-Pacific region in the decades to come, as it will also remain involved in Europe, Africa, and the Americas. However much it may wish to escape the multiple crises of the Middle East—from the Israeli-Palestinian conflict, Iraq, and Iran, to the historic revolutions that are the subject of this volume—it must continue to confront with intelligence, flexibility, and wisdom the many difficult challenges produced by the extraordinary changes across the Arab world.

Part 

The Fourth Annual Ernest May Memorial Lecture

The Old Middle East and the New

Richard N. Haass
President
Council on Foreign Relations

CHAPTER 1

Obama's Strategy for the "Arab Spring" Revolutions:
What Has the Administration Tried to Do—and How Well Has it Succeeded?

David Ignatius
Columnist and Associate Editor
The Washington Post

"The United States needs to think about its interests in the Middle East, their relative importance, and America's ability to affect them at costs that can be afforded and justified."

—RICHARD N. HAASS

The Fourth Annual Ernest May Memorial Lecture

The Old Middle East and the New

Richard N. Haass
President
Council on Foreign Relations

Editor's Note: Richard Haass presented the annual Ernest R. May Memorial Lecture at the Aspen Strategy Group's August 2012 workshop in Aspen, Colorado. The following are his remarks as written for delivery. The Ernest May Memorial Lecture is named for Ernest May, an international relations historian and Harvard John F. Kennedy School of Government professor, who passed away in 2009. ASG developed the lecture series to honor Professor May's celebrated lectures.

I am honored to deliver the 2012 Ernest R. May Memorial Lecture. I was fortunate enough to have been a colleague of Ernie for four years at Harvard's Kennedy School, and even more fortunate to have been a friend for decades. He was truly a gentleman and a scholar.

I want to say a few things about Ernie's scholarship. He chose the conceptual over the quantitative, understanding that just because you could measure something didn't make it significant…and just because you couldn't measure something didn't make it irrelevant.

Ernie also chose the applied over the abstract and the relevant over the remote. In so doing, he did his best to bridge rather than divide the university and the policy world. This was rare, although fortunately he was not alone. Ernie, along with Dick Neustadt, Alex George, Joe Nye, Al Carnesale, Graham Allison, and so many others associated with the Aspen Strategy Group, embodied the sort of work that I have always considered to occupy the sweet spot. It is study that avoids the obsession with theory and numbers that so often characterizes the academy – but it is also real study in that it eschews the embrace of opinions not based upon serious research or analysis that alas is so common to the public space. We would do well to do our best to emulate it.

I was asked to provide some historical perspective on events in the Arab world. This is fitting given that Ernie May's most well-known work was intimately related to looking at history and learning from it, not as an end in itself, but as a guide to policymaking. I will uncharacteristically try to do what I was asked and attempt to place recent events in the Middle East in historical perspective, lay out some conclusions about what we have learned, and then suggest some things about the future.

The Past as Prologue

The sea-changes we are observing in the Middle East are hardly the first dramatic changes in the modern era. To the contrary, we are actually experiencing the fifth era in the region in just over two hundred years, each marked by dramatic, defining events.

The first era of modern Middle East history dates back to the late eighteenth century, a time of European rise and Ottoman decline. It was triggered by Napoleon's surprisingly easy military entry into Egypt in 1798, something that kicked off a debate that continues to this day among Arab and Muslim thinkers about what had gone wrong and why they were so easily defeated by an "inferior" civilization. This first modern era ended with World War I, the demise of the Ottoman Empire, and the division of spoils among the victorious European allies – a division, just to get ahead of ourselves, that one hundred years later is central to events in the region.

The second era was thus a colonial era, one that ended only in the aftermath of the second world war of the twentieth century. What brought the European era in the Middle East to a close was a mix of European exhaustion, the assertion of local nationalism, and the rise of the superpowers. My former professor, the late and wise Albert Hourani, dates the change to 1956 and the Suez crisis, when the United States and the Soviet Union effectively decided that the region was too important and too dangerous to be left to the Europeans to manage or, worse yet, mismanage.

The third era of the modern Middle East lasted for some thirty years and ran parallel to the last three decades of the Cold War. It was heavily influenced by outsiders – again, the United States and the Soviet Union – but not dominated by them. The 1967 and 1973 wars in the region could not be prevented by the superpowers, but they did manage to limit the scope and duration of the conflicts. While this was happening, two other actors of great significance emerged on the scene. The first was OPEC, the global cartel of oil exporters dominated by Arab governments and Iran, that over time would bring enormous wealth and considerable influence to selected states in the region. The second, in 1979, was the birth of revolutionary Iran. It was not just that the United States and the West lost a political-military partner when the Shah was removed, although this was surely important. Rather, the revolution in Iran marked the emergence of political Islam as a powerful force in the region's politics and the rise of a local and often hostile imperial power. A good deal of what dominates the region today can be traced back to then.

A fourth era, one that arrived with the end of the Cold War and the demise of the Soviet Union, was one of American primacy. The highlight was the American-led Desert Storm coalition to which many of the Arab governments contributed and that succeeded in forcing Saddam Hussein and Iraq's army out of Kuwait. This was followed by the convening in Madrid of the first peace conference ever to bring Israel and the Arab governments face-to-face to negotiate peace.

Alas, this era proved to be short-lived, although dating its precise end is highly subjective. The unsuccessful effort by the Clinton Administration to negotiate peace between Israelis and Palestinians underscored the difficulty in translating American advantages in power into influence. Another possible end point would be 9/11 and its manifest demonstration of American vulnerability, as well as the reach of terrorists from the region. Then there was the 2003 Iraq war, which showed clear limits to U.S. power. And, most recently, there were the dramatic political upheavals in important parts of the Arab world. Any or all of these could be cited as evidence that an era of American primacy had come to a close.

Whatever the specific starting date, it is clear that we are now in the fifth era of the modern Middle East. It is a time characterized by political upheavals in a number of Arab countries, growing Shia-Sunni friction, increased regional roles for Iran but also Turkey, continued but somewhat diminished American reliance on the region's oil resources, and an Arab-Israeli conflict that appears to be more distant than ever from resolution.

Take-aways

The recent upheavals were both inevitable and predictable in the strategic sense: Egypt was ripe for change given a widespread sense of decades of poor leadership and no real politics, mostly unimpressive economic performance (the Chinese or Saudi Arabian "model" of placating the public through delivering a higher standard of living was not available), pervasive corruption, and increased public access to information and the means of communication thanks to mobile phones, the Internet, and satellite television. It all combined to create a widespread sense of humiliation, frustration, and possibility. The specific timing and trigger for the upheaval was unpredictable, but if it hadn't been a Tunisian vendor, it would have been something else. Also worth noting is what the upheavals were not caused by or about: Neither al-Qaida nor the Palestinian issue played an observable role.

What else can be said about the events that began in late 2010? Something of a copy-cat effect is at work, as citizens in one country get emboldened by events in another and take to their own streets. Monarchies have proven more resilient than non-monarchies so far – perceived legitimacy matters – but even monarchies are unlikely to enjoy unlimited time and space. The same pressures for change will challenge them sooner or later.

It is much too soon to conclude what the net effect of political change will be; for that reason alone, observers ought to avoid the phrase "Arab spring". There is no reason to assume it will on balance be positive. "Spring" is also a poor choice of words because we are not talking months or even years here but decades. Phrases along the lines of "upheavals" or even "intifadah" are thus preferable.

It has become commonplace to suggest that the United States erred over the years by not doing enough to promote reform and that, as a result, it ended up with partners lacking both stability and democracy. This may well have been true in the case of the Shah's Iran, but in the Arab world, the policy of strategic cooperation with authoritarian governments served a broad range of U.S. interests for decades. Moreover, experience showed it was easier to press for reform than to bring it about. The United States tried with Egypt. U.S. officials made some progress on the economic side, but little on the political. Reform cannot be forced on an unwilling friend; indeed, it is often more difficult to pressure friends and allies than adversaries. Jeane Kirkpatrick's theory of authoritarian regimes being reformable worked well in Asia and Latin America but not in the Middle East. Walking away from an Egypt or Saudi Arabia was not an option given the vital interests at stake, including access to oil, promoting Israeli-Arab peace, and cooperating to meet the challenges posed by terrorism and Iran.

We should have learned that it is tough to oust regimes and even tougher to replace them with something sure to last and sure to be better; Iraq and Afghanistan demonstrate this truth all too well. What is more, neither Iraq nor post-surge (post-2009) Afghanistan is a template for the future. Such large-scale interventions are too costly and do not deliver returns that justify the investment. The limited importance of the U.S. interests at stake only reinforces this point. Such interventions are neither sustainable nor justifiable.

R2P – the Responsibility to Protect – is a doctrine in name only. As Syria shows, no international consensus exists on when it applies and how it is to be implemented. Kofi Annan recently asked, "Is ours an international community that will act in defense of the most vulnerable of our world, and make the necessary sacrifices to help?" The short answer is no: because of differing views of the nature of sovereignty, because of different interests and assessments, and because of a reluctance to commit what would be required in the way of military resources to actually protect those at risk. The reality is the "international community" is not a community.

Consistent with this reality, humanitarian intervention cannot be an all-or-nothing proposition. Policy in this realm must actually be inconsistent, depending on such factors as the certainty or actuality of large-scale human suffering, the projected military difficulty of any intervention given the nature of the society in question and the expected resistance, the prospects for an improved political outcome, the degree of regional and international political and military support for intervening, and the geopolitical context, i.e., the existence of competing interests and claims on resources and attention.

All these criteria will be met only in rare circumstances. Military intervention should not be equated with introducing ground forces, and, more broadly, we should not confuse intervention with direct military intervention. Policy will need to choose from a range of tools, including political and economic sanctions and the threat of war crimes charges against governments, along with the provision of arms, intelligence, financial help, and military advice and training to those being attacked. Real-world policy will likely require an increased willingness to work around the UN Security Council; this is less of a problem than it may seem, as multilateralism and legitimacy are hardly the sole province of this body. Syria is likely to be more of a precedent here than Libya.

Bahrain has the potential to be a big headache. The situation there will often be portrayed as one of interests versus values, but this is an over-simplification. Yes, the United States has important strategic interests in that country, and yes, the government is imperfect, but the opposition to the government cannot be assumed to offer an improvement. Majoritarianism is not the same as democracy. One problem will be in getting the regime to offer real reform given internal divisions and Saudi pressure not to offer too much and set precedents that could come to feed demands for change within Saudi Arabia itself. The other problem will be in getting a majority of the majority to accept any compromise given the pressure coming from internal radicals and from Iran. It would be best for the U.S. government to agree on a course for political reform with the government and stand by it.

And speaking of Saudi Arabia, it is only a matter of time before the combination of population increase, the limits to how much calm can be bought with economic largesse, the impact of examples being set by external events, and the efforts of Iran lead to serious internal challenges there. The alternative to the government is not liberal but more along the lines of the Muslim Brotherhood with the goal of radicalizing Sunnis throughout the region. We had better start preparing for this possibility now.

Change is likely to come much sooner to Jordan given its demographic cleavages, the large influx of refugees from neighboring countries, and economic pressures. Alas, constitutional monarchies of the British vintage do not look to be in the cards for the Middle East.

In all of these cases, outsiders who mean well need to go about it with more than good intentions. It is wrong to confuse elections with democracy, something that must include civil society, constitutions, and checks and balances. There must be a willingness to allow for a level playing field and along with it a willingness to lose and not just stage or win elections. Outsiders also need to give serious thought to the components, pace, and sequence of political and economic reform that they seek to promote.

As these struggles play out, it is probable that secular civilian forces will prove to be weak political actors for the most part. The most critical constituencies are much more likely to be authoritarian (governments and security services) and political Islamists. One question is whether regimes will decide to become more reformist. An even bigger question is how the debates between and among political Islamists will be resolved and what tendencies will emerge. We simply do not know how Islamists will govern. As a result, the U.S. approach to political Islam must be strictly conditional. The United States should neither embrace them nor write them off. The U.S. government should be prepared to extend and withhold aid and criticisms depending on what governments do at home and abroad. The United States should also be willing to be flexible and allow army leaders and the like a political role during transitional periods.

One last prediction: The upheavals will not be good over the near- and mid-term for the Middle East peace process. To begin with, Israel's inclination will be to hold back given all the strategic uncertainty. More fundamentally, the era of making peace with individuals is over. Israel will have to deal with governments who will feel accountable to popular sentiments, something that will make the search for peace far more difficult. Islamic politics will not be friendly to Israel or to making peace with it. There is no clear Palestinian partner. The upheavals will strengthen the hands of Hamas, although this can be partially offset by efforts to increase the capacity of the Palestinian entity on the West Bank. The Iranian nuclear issue is a further distraction. None of this is meant as an argument for ignoring the Israeli-Palestinian issue, but these realities must be taken into account.

Some Final Thoughts

The United States needs to think about its interests in the Middle East, their relative importance, and America's ability to affect them at costs that can be afforded and justified. U.S. interests include promoting a region in which ample oil is produced and exported freely, the proliferation of weapons of mass destruction is frustrated, terrorists cannot operate, Israel is secure, progress is realized toward Israeli-Palestinian peace, and the Arab world becomes more open politically and economically. These interests at times will be in conflict or at least impossible to pursue with equal vigor. Promoting democratic reform is one interest, but it is not the only interest, it is not always doable, and it is certainly not a panacea.

The tension between interests and values is not unique to this part of the world. It applies, too, to U.S. policy toward China and Russia. This tension has constituted the basic fault line of American foreign policy for a century now. The question is how much to focus on a country's nature and how much to focus on its external behavior. The tension is structural and unavoidable unless this country opts for naiveté or pure realpolitik, which it should not and cannot.

Inconsistency is not just unavoidable but necessary, and at times even desirable, given that U.S. interests will vary from country to country, as will the costs and possibility of promoting values and protecting those interests. The notion that inconsistency is a virtue might make the task of carrying out and explaining American foreign policy even more difficult than it already is, but acting in a manner that accepts this notion is certainly preferable to the alternative.

The issues being discussed here are difficult by any yardstick. I am sorry we do not have Ernie May with us to help sort them out, for we could sure use his knowledge and wisdom.

Richard N. Haass is president of the Council on Foreign Relations, the preeminent independent, nonpartisan organization in the United States dedicated to the study of American foreign policy. Until June 2003, Dr. Haass was director of policy planning for the Department of State, where he was a principal adviser to Secretary of State Colin Powell on a broad range of foreign policy concerns. Confirmed by the U.S. Senate to hold the rank of ambassador, Dr. Haass served as U.S. coordinator for policy toward the future of Afghanistan and was the U.S. envoy to the Northern Ireland peace process. He was also special assistant to President George H.W. Bush and senior director for Near East and South Asian affairs on the staff of the National Security Council from 1989 to 1993. Dr. Haass is the author or editor of twelve books on American foreign policy, including *War of Necessity, War of Choice: A Memoir of Two Iraq Wars* (Simon and Schuster, May 2009) and, most recently, the author of *Foreign Policy Begins at Home: The Case for Putting America's House in Order* (Basic Books, 2013). He is also the author of one book on management. Dr. Haass earned a B.A. from Oberlin College and both Master and Doctor of Philosophy degrees from Oxford University, where he was a Rhodes Scholar. He has received honorary degrees from Hamilton College, Franklin & Marshall College, Georgetown University, Oberlin College, Central College, and Miami Dade College. He is a member of the Aspen Strategy Group.

"There is, through this narrative, a continuing tension between U.S. values and interests. Striking that balance wisely is the essence of good foreign policy practice, and although commentators like to demand consistency, it rarely happens that way in reality."

—DAVID IGNATIUS

Obama's Strategy for the "Arab Spring" Revolutions:
What Has the Administration Tried to Do—and How Well Has it Succeeded?

David Ignatius
Columnist and Associate Editor
The Washington Post

Introduction: A Strategic Framework for the Arab Uprisings

The Arab uprisings are a story very much in progress, whose outcome is unknowable. In the hopeful early months, people understandably spoke of these revolutions as being on "the right side of history" and inherently deserving of support, but the past year has illustrated how complicated and uneven the story of revolutionary change can be.

Assessing U.S. strategic decisions requires understanding that policymakers are operating in conditions of extreme uncertainty. Prudence argues against making large bets when the outcome is so unpredictable. Several generations of painful American experience in the Middle East teach us that U.S. power, vast as it is, may not be sufficient to guarantee the desired result.

This paper will summarize some of the ideas that emerged in my course on "Understanding the Arab Spring," taught at Harvard's Kennedy School of Government in the spring semester of 2012. We were fortunate to have off-the-record conversations with Obama administration officials such as Ben Rhodes, Jacob Sullivan, Alec Ross, Robert Ford, and Hagar Hejjar Chemali, as well as visiting Egyptians, Syrians, Saudis, and Tunisians.

The overarching theme of the course, borrowing from Clausewitz's famous metaphor, was that we are experiencing the "fog of revolution" in the Middle East and a corresponding "fog of policy" in Washington. In this setting, it can be impossible to know precisely what's happening on the ground, what effects U.S. actions may have, and whether we are moving closer to or further from achieving our broad policy goals.

The "fog" notion has become so familiar that it is useful to reground it in the relevant passage from Clausewitz's "On War": "The great uncertainty of all data in war is a peculiar difficulty, because all action must, to a certain extent, be planned in a mere twilight, which in addition not infrequently—like the effect of a fog or moonshine—gives to things exaggerated dimensions and an unnatural appearance."

Clausewitz also spoke of a "friction" that makes implementation of policy difficult. He memorably likened it to being underwater: "Activity in war is movement in a resistant medium. Just as a man in water is unable to perform with ease and regularity the most natural and simplest movement, that of walking, so in war, with ordinary powers, one cannot keep even the line of mediocrity. This is the reason that the correct theorist is like a swimming master, who teaches on dry land movements which are required in the water, which must appear grotesque and ludicrous to those who forget about the water."

As a baseline, in the months after the Arab uprisings began in Tunisia in December 2010, policymakers in the Obama administration were working in the shadow of the decade of war that began on September 11, 2001, and stretched through Iraq and Afghanistan. For an administration seeking to "turn the page" on this chapter of American history, there was a wariness about making large new commitments of U.S. forces in the Middle East.

Looking at U.S. policy toward the Arab world over the past eighteen months, it is fair to say that the handbrake was on, even as officials were pressing the accelerator.

There is, through this narrative, a continuing tension between U.S. values and interests. Striking that balance wisely is the essence of good foreign policy practice, and although commentators like to demand consistency, it rarely happens that way in reality. Certainly there was inconsistency in this case: U.S. policy during the Arab uprisings was a zigzag process, like a sailboat tacking to windward—moving this week toward "values" in Cairo, and that week toward "interests" in Bahrain. I would opt for such uneven pragmatism in preference to a rigid application of a policy "rule." But it is worth discussing whether the Obama administration's policy process was more uneven—or to be blunt, more unprincipled—than was necessary or beneficial. America gained flexibility in these months, but at a cost to its stature.

In what follows, I have drawn on dozens of conversations with many U.S. policymakers and foreign officials over the past several years. But these are personal assessments and assertions only, made in the hope of provoking a useful debate.

Egypt

The U.S. policy clock for the Arab Spring didn't really start ticking until January 26, 2011, when the Tahrir Square protests began in Egypt. The uprising that forced Tunisian president Zine El-Abedine Ben Ali into exile on January 15 didn't register sharply in Washington. Tunisia was a traditional French area of expertise and influence, and the French were slow to see the seriousness of the protests. But Egypt was different. Because of its peace treaty with Israel and its close military connection with the U.S., the Egyptian uprising quickly and emphatically engaged Washington, in terms of both interests and values.

Two factors that arose from his own deepest experience shaped President Obama's thinking in the first week of the Egyptian uprising, according to members of his inner circle. First, he concluded that the Egyptian protests against President Hosni Mubarak were just. As a boy in Jakarta, he had watched the corrupting power of President Suharto, an autocratic ruler similar to Mubarak and had seen how this regime of fear had affected his Indonesian stepfather. The demand of Egyptian protesters for justice and dignity also resonated with his experience as an African American, a son of a father raised under British colonialism, and a community organizer.

Second, Obama concluded that in addition to being morally right, the protests could not be stopped, even if America tried to prop up Mubarak. This added a pragmatic counterweight to the pleas from Saudi Arabia and Israel that the U.S. support its longtime ally.

The defining day for U.S. Egyptian policy, for better or worse, was February 1, 2011. That was the day Obama's envoy, Frank Wisner, delivered the message in Cairo that Mubarak must give up power. The Egyptian president probably thought he was meeting Obama's demand when he appeared on television that night and said that neither he nor his son, Gamal, would run for president in September 2011. But Obama wanted immediate change. Going against advice from his secretaries of state and defense, Obama called Mubarak after the speech and told him he must leave office now, not in nine months. A few minutes later, he made the same demand publicly in a White House statement. Mubarak was furious and didn't talk to the president again.

The next day, February 2, the infamous "Day of the Camels," Mubarak's henchmen brutally tried to drive the protestors from the square.

It is interesting to reflect on the choice Obama made on February 1. Had he decided to grant Mubarak a gradual "departure with dignity," along the lines of the Egyptian president's speech, it's possible the Tahrir protests gradually would have ebbed and Egypt would have had a less tumultuous political transition. With American support, the army would probably have sided with Mubarak and, rather than fraternizing with the protestors, would have split the activists and pushed them from Tahrir. But it's also quite possible that the protestors would have dug in and, if troops opened fire, moved to armed opposition. In that case, the U.S. would have owned the bloody outcome, just as Russia is being held responsible for the bloodshed now in Syria.

Obama's closest advisers say he understood from the beginning that Mubarak's fall would inevitably lead to greater political power for the Muslim Brotherhood and other Islamists. Indeed, in my newspaper columns, I have referred to Obama's "cosmic bet" that democratic participation would transform Islamist parties from a violent extremist threat to U.S. interests to a factor for stability and growth.

This bet on Muslim democrats can be traced to Obama's famous June 2009 speech in Cairo. The speech was prepared with the help of intelligence analysts from the National Counterterrorism Center who weighed the impact each passage would have on global jihadists. According to White House officials, two sentences in particular were crafted for the Muslim Brotherhood, and 10 Brotherhood members were invited to sit in the Cairo audience and hear these words: "America respects the right of all peaceful and law-abiding voices to be heard around the world, even if we disagree with them. And we will welcome all elected, peaceful governments—provided they govern with respect for all their people."

This tilt toward the Muslim Brotherhood continued after Mubarak's fall, when the State Department revised its policy on contacts with Brotherhood members in Egypt. In the months before the June 2012 presidential election, the U.S. embassy in Cairo was in regular contact with 6 senior members of the Brotherhood leadership. On the eve of that election, administration officials signaled that for Egypt's economic reconstruction, a victory by the Brotherhood candidate Mohamed Morsi would probably be the best outcome. They cautioned Ahmed Shafiq, the candidate of the old regime, against any broad crackdown on the Brotherhood if he won. A symbolic embrace of Morsi came when Secretary of State Hillary Clinton met with him in Cairo after his inauguration as president.

Obama's cultivation of Turkish Prime Minister Tayyip Recep Erdogan was another instance of his bet that Islamist parties can provide a peaceful exit from the "long war" against Muslim extremism. On his first foreign trip in April 2009, Obama stopped in Ankara and delivered a speech to the Turkish parliament, controlled by Erdogan's AK Party. In the following several years, Obama worked diligently (despite tensions and obstacles) to develop a close personal relationship with Erdogan, cemented during a nearly two-hour meeting during the June 2010 G20 summit in Toronto. Obama continues to talk with Erdogan regularly, and the Turkey relationship has arguably been the most important strategic partnership of the Obama presidency.

Is this "cosmic bet" on the Muslim Brotherhood a wise one? It is too early to say with any confidence. In essence, the question is whether the practical tasks of governing will bend the Brotherhood away from its ideology. Certainly, that hasn't yet happened with Hamas in Gaza, a movement with deep fraternal ties to the Brotherhood, and my own research underlines the depth of the Brotherhood's anti-Western roots. I wrote in a February 15, 2012, column:

> What's clear is that from its inception, the Brotherhood has stressed the importance of liberating Muslims from Western manipulation. This aspiration for dignity and independence is the Brotherhood's strongest appeal, but it may make the organization a difficult partner. The Brotherhood was formed in 1928 by Egyptians who opposed British colonialism. The founder, a schoolteacher named Hassan al-Banna, gathered six friends who worked for the Suez Canal Co. To fend off informers, the group developed elaborate initiation procedures. The movement, at once political, cultural and religious, took off quickly: By one estimate, it grew to 200,000 members by 1938. Banna was assassinated in 1949, after the Brotherhood had attacked the corrupt monarchy of King Farouk.
>
> The anti-Western message was honed by the Brotherhood's other great martyr, Sayyid Qutb. He was a brilliant essayist whose encounter with the United States in the late 1940s proved poisonous. After visiting New York, Washington, Colorado and Los Angeles, he concluded that "the soul has no value to Americans." Qutb's abhorrence of the open sexuality he saw in the United States is clear in this passage quoted in "The Looming Tower" by Lawrence Wright: "A girl looks at you, appearing as if she were an enchanting nymph or an escaped mermaid, but as she approaches, you sense

only the screaming instinct inside her, and you can smell her burning body, not the scent of perfume but flesh, only flesh...."

Olivier Roy, a French expert on the Muslim world, argues that the Brotherhood will learn democracy by doing it: "Democratic culture does not precede democratic institutions; democratic culture is the internalization of these institutions," he says. That, in essence, is the wager Obama has made.

Unlikely testimony that supports Obama's strategy comes from the secret correspondence of Osama bin Laden, taken from his compound in Abbottabad when he was killed on May 2, 2011. By the terrorist leader's own account, Obama out-positioned him in strategic messaging—to the point that bin Laden drafted a letter to his operational deputy, Atiyah Abd al-Rahman, musing that al-Qaeda should find a new name to replace its damaged brand.

Obama had taken the public relations offensive, bin Laden explained, because administration officials "have largely stopped using the phrase 'the war on terror' in the context of not wanting to provoke Muslims," and instead promoted a war against al-Qaeda. Al Qaeda should make a similar rebranding effort, said bin Laden, suggesting a list of 10 alternative names.

Many commentators have endorsed the administration's view that the Arab uprisings signal a turn away from jihadist ideology. But what we are seeing now in Egypt still has a dangerous edge. Take the group Gamaa Islamiya, which under its spiritual leader, Sheikh Omar Abdel Rahman, made the first unsuccessful attempt to destroy the World Trade Center in 1993. In the unfolding drama of the Arab uprisings, the organization formed a Salafist political party with the benign-sounding name "Building and Development Party." This organization, which like al-Qaeda traces its roots to Sayyid Qutb, won thirteen seats in the new Egyptian parliament. Moreover, President Morsi himself has called for the release of the terrorist Sheikh Abdel Rahman.

Pondering what's ahead in Egypt, it is worth recalling the comment made by Albert Hourani in his *History of the Arab Peoples* about the tension between Islam and the modern Western world: "For Muslims, the problem was inescapable: Islam was what was deepest in them. If to live in the modern world demanded changes in their way of organizing society, they must try to make them while remaining true to themselves; and this would be possible only if Islam could be interpreted to make it compatible with survival, strength and progress in the world."

As noted at the outset, this is a cosmic wager. Asked recently for evidence that it was working, an Obama administration official thought for a moment and then cited this statistic: Two years ago, 30 percent of the sermons in Salafi mosques and television programs focused on the evils of the U.S. Today, the number is down to five percent. That doesn't make Muslim democracy a winning bet for the West, but the odds are improving.

Libya

Obama's policy toward Libya displayed the same cautious activism that has characterized his broader strategy toward the Arab uprisings. The White House hates the term "leading from behind," but it has stuck because it accurately characterizes an administration that wants to, as the famous Latin phrase puts it, "make haste slowly." Perhaps the administration would accept the term "strategic reticence."

Like each of the Arab states undergoing change, Libya had some distinct cultural and historical features that shaped its revolution. An East-West divide dating back to Ottoman and even Roman times led to a geographical split in the early days of March 2011; Libya's patchwork of tribal power undermined revolutionary command and post-revolutionary governance; the transition was complicated further by the uniquely bizarre and megalomaniac personality of Colonel Muammar Gaddafi.

In finally deciding to use military force in Libya, the administration evolved what amounts to an Obama doctrine for the Arab uprisings, namely, that in situations where its interests are not directly threatened, the U.S. will use force only when it has regional and international backing. Even then, it will not necessarily take the lead role.

Libya has been a significant success for the Obama administration for several reasons:

First, the administration gathered a coalition that was able, over time, to exercise power in a country that has been as brutally treated by history as any in the Arab world. Libya's experience under Italian colonialism was especially harsh. Lisa Anderson, one of the leading Libya experts, cites an animal census showing that in Cyrenaica, the number of sheep fell from 713,000 in 1910 to 98,000 in 1933; goats fell from 546,000 to 25,000, and camels from 83,000 to 2,600. Measuring loss of human life was harder, but Anderson noted in her book, *The State and Social Transformation in Libya and Tunisia*, that nearly half the population may have died over that period.

Libya's tribal structure was a particular problem for the Italian colonizers. According to Anderson, "Although the Italians made much of their plan to destroy tribal structure and create in its place a society of Libyan Muslim Fascists, they in fact maintained the quarters, fractions and tribes as the only permissible organizational structure…The tribes of the hinterlands had been revived in the face of an administration that has permitted the Libyan population no state and no government."

Gaddafi struggled through his decades of rule with the tribal problem. He declared his "Jamahurriya" state in 1977 as a sort of committee of the whole. In his "Green Book" manifesto, he wrote: "A nation is a tribe that has grown through procreation." Gaddafi tried to break the tribes at first, drawing administrative borders that cut across traditional tribal boundaries, and then by playing tribes off against each other. The military was organized with different units loyal to different tribal leaders; the idea was to prevent any multi-tribal threat to Gaddafi's rule.

Anderson predicted in August 2011, as the end was near for Gaddafi, that "he will leave a legacy of lawlessness and mistrust in Libya that will be very difficult to surmount." That dire picture certainly prevailed for the first six months after Gaddafi's death, an anarchic period in which scores and even hundreds of militias battled for control of the nation and its assets. There were fears, too, that in this chaotic transition jihadist groups would emerge as a dominant force.

The success of secular parties in Libya's July 2012 elections suggests that Islamist rule isn't an inevitable consequence of the Arab Spring. It is worth examining here whether quiet external support for Libyan secular parties and politicians helped steer the outcome in a favorable direction, from the standpoint of Western interests—and whether this is a model for other nations.

Second, Obama managed his limited military intervention well. Here again, as in ousting Mubarak, he decided to take action against the advice of Robert Gates, his seasoned secretary of defense. Obama explained his decision in an important March 28 speech, one of the essential documents for understanding U.S. policy in dealing with the Arab uprisings. Some of the key passages include the following:

> The United States and the world faced a choice. Gaddafi declared he would show "no mercy" to his own people. He compared them to rats, and threatened to go door to door to inflict punishment…. We knew that if we waited—if we waited one more day, Benghazi, a city nearly the size of Charlotte, could suffer a massacre that would have reverberated across the region and stained the conscience of the world. It was not in our national interest to let that happen….

We should not be afraid to act—but the burden of action should not be America's alone. As we have [done] in Libya, our task is instead to mobilize the international community for collective action. Because contrary to the claims of some, American leadership is not simply a matter of going it alone and bearing all of the burden ourselves. Real leadership creates the conditions and coalitions for others to step up as well; to work with allies and partners so that they bear their share of the burden and pay their share of the costs.

Third, Obama kept to the limited policy he had chartered. Wisely, he resisted jittery calls during the summer of 2011, when the war seemed at a stalemate, either to radically escalate U.S. military involvement or to withdraw. He stayed the course, and prevailed with minimal cost to the U.S.—and, it must be said, with limited benefit as well.

Bahrain

If Obama began the Arab Spring on February 1, 2011, by leaning toward a values-based policy, by mid-March of last year he had accepted that, in some situations, U.S. interests will be dominant. That reckoning with realpolitik came in Bahrain. After years of encouraging political reform by Bahrain's ruling Sunni monarchy, and seeking to broker dialogue with the majority Shia population, the U.S. acceded to Saudi Arabia's insistence that the Shia-led uprising be crushed.

The demonstrations began in Manama on February 14, four days after Mubarak's departure in Egypt, and led quickly to a bloody crackdown at the Pearl Roundabout on February 16, which left four dead. With U.S. support, Crown Prince Salman began a dialogue with the opposition Al Wefaq group that culminated in a seven-point plan for reform that, in theory, would have led to a constitutional monarchy. But the compromisers were attacked from both sides: the Iranian-backed Al-Haq movement denounced negotiations as a sell-out; Sunni hard-liners, pressed by Saudi Arabia, insisted on a crackdown. The inflection point came on March 15, when troops from Saudi Arabia and other Gulf Cooperation Council nations surged across the causeway and seized control in Manama.

Watching events in Bahrain unfold was like witnessing a car wreck in slow motion. It had been obvious for years what was coming, yet for all its strenuous diplomatic effort, the U.S. could not avert the collision. What's more, although Obama in the end subordinated his own judgment to that of Saudi Arabia's King Abdullah, the grudging American acceptance of Saudi action, and mildly critical public comment after the invasion, embittered the very Saudis on whose behalf we had pragmatically swallowed our principles.

The Bahrain story is troubling as well for its illustration of the vanishing center during the Arab uprisings. As in Egypt, the young Internet revolutionists couldn't translate a popular movement into organized political power. They were over-zealous at the top of the cycle and paid a severe price. When they failed to cut a deal, more organized and militant groups gained ground.

The baselines in Bahrain are hard military and demographic realities: The U.S. has maintained an important naval base there since 1947 and cultivated relations with the Khalifa monarchy since the country became independent from the British in 1971. The problem of the Shia majority, reckoned at perhaps 70 percent of the population, has been obvious since an Iranian-backed coup attempt in 1981 and a subsequent popular uprising in 1994.

Pressed by the U.S., the Khalifas attempted reform. A February 2001 referendum created a bicameral legislature, but Al Wefaq boycotted elections until 2006, when it won a majority. A similar ambivalence within the Shia movement became a decisive factor in March 2011, when Al Wefaq's moderate leaders were muscled by more militant oppositionists into boycotting the negotiated path offered by Sheikh Salman. The administration had been hopeful enough about a settlement that Jeffrey Feltman, then assistant secretary of state for the Near East, was said to be on his way to Manama when negotiations collapsed.

The very polarization the U.S. feared appears to have deepened. The administration had hoped that a deal between the Khalifa clan and Al Wefaq could marginalize the radicals of Al Haq and their Iranian's patrons. (Al Haq's leader, Hassan Mushaima, was counseled before his return to Manama by members of the Quds force of the Iranian Revolutionary Guards Corps, according to my sources.) The outcome probably left Iran in a stronger position in Bahrain than before the crisis.

Marc Lynch, in his excellent study, *The Arab Uprising*, summed up the Bahrain outcome: "The radicals on each side fed on each other to prevent the achievement of an eminently possible agreement on serious political reforms….[Saudi Arabia] made extremely clear to the Obama administration that it considered Bahrain to be within its sphere of influence. The administration clearly calculated that it had little choice but to defer to the Saudis and accept a fait accompli."

The Saudi-backed crackdown brought sweeping repression: Thirty-five Bahrainis were killed over two months and an estimated 600 people arrested, with security forces targeting even doctors in hospitals. One small positive outcome was that the Bahraini government conducted a fairly honest investigation of the crisis, culminating in a June 2011 report by U.N. legal expert Cherif Bassiouni. This royal commission concluded, among many other findings: "If the Crown Prince's initiative and proposals, at the time, had been accepted, it could have paved the way for significant constitutional, political and socio-economic reforms and precluded the ensuing consequences."

Obama summed up America's frustrating experience in Bahrain when he said in May 2011: "The only way forward is for the government and opposition to engage in dialogue, and you can't have a real dialogue when parts of the peaceful opposition are in jail." The Saudis insist that if they hadn't intervened in March to crush Shia protests in Manama, they would have faced a full-scale Shia uprising by Al-Katif in the eastern province of Saudi Arabia. But as things are turning out, the Al-Katif revolt is gathering momentum anyway.

Bahrain was a painful tilt for Obama toward interests and away from principle (and also from good sense). The best that can be said for this decision is that if the tumult had continued in Bahrain, it would have significantly complicated a still-unfolding confrontation with Iran.

Yemen

Several factors combined to make Yemen a success for Obama administration policy—so much so that policymakers now speak of a "Yemen model" to describe successful transition of power during the Arab uprisings. The departure of President Ali Abdullah Saleh was hardly bloodless, and the country is still far from stable. But there are some reasons (spelled out in more detail in a February 29 column in the *Washington Post*) that explain why things worked out relatively well in Yemen, compared to some of the other Arab cockpits:

--The U.S. could work through a strong regional proxy in the Gulf Cooperation Council. The GCC leaders, Saudi Arabia and the United Arab Emirates, massaged and bankrolled the process, which culminated in an agreement in November 2011 that Saleh would go. In the past, the GCC has often been bootless, but under Abdul Latif al-Zayani, its new Bahraini secretary general, the organization succeeded in organizing Arab cover for the managed transition.

--Counter-terrorism policy provided a strong political-military anchor. Bin Laden regarded Yemen as his best chance for creating a successful "emirate," and the "Al Qaeda in the Arabian Peninsula" affiliate has been aggressive—and has drawn an appropriately tough U.S. response. The counter-terrorism effort, coordinated from the White House by John Brennan, involved U.S. Central Command military personnel (including Joint Special Operations Command), State Department diplomats, and CIA officers. Washington often gives lip service to this sort of "interagency process" but in Yemen it actually worked.

--The U.S. played tribal politics effectively. As with Libya, Iraq, and many Arab countries, Yemen's state structure is loosely overlaid on powerful tribes. U.S. analysts did better exploiting this tribal factor, understanding Saleh's tribal roots as well as those of dissident military officers. The big tribal confederations have been especially important U.S. allies in the fight against Al Qaeda, as bin Laden himself recognized in some of his missives.

--Out of the glare of publicity, the U.S. was able to make a "managed transition" work. To replace Saleh, the U.S. chose Abed Rabbo Mansour Hadi, the longtime vice president. He was installed in February 2012 in a one-man race that gave a veneer of democratic transition. He promised to hold a referendum, within 18 months, on a new constitution.

--U.S. Ambassador Gerald Feierstein and his colleagues in Sanaa succeeded in reaching out early and well to the opposition. Protesters in "Change Square" weren't happy when Saleh's son Ahmed and nephew Yahya were left in charge of two security services, but the U.S. was smart to go for the makable deal when it had one, even at the cost of disappointing some protestors.

Yemen could still blow up, and these positive factors could be undone. But Yemen is an illustration that the U.S. is still able to combine the elements of power—hard and soft, overt and covert, military and diplomatic—and make them work together. It helps if this policy soufflé can be baked at the remote edge of the Arabian Peninsula, far from the gaze of would-be meddlers and critics.

Syria

Syria is the bloodiest of the Arab uprisings and the most frustrating case study in Obama administration policy. Nobody can be happy with the situation as it stands in late July 2012, as I write. But it is possible that, had other courses of action been followed, the outcome could be worse.

Syria policy is conditioned for all the policy players by the experience of Iraq. The Iraqi precedent operates on several different levels. First, there is an understanding that outside military intervention is problematic in a big country with a well-armed military and entrenched *moukhabarat*. Getting "in" isn't easy, with modern air defenses, chemical weapons and other attributes of a modern army. But getting "out" is even harder.

Second, the Iraq example teaches the danger of all-out sectarian warfare in a country bitterly divided between Sunni and Shia (or in the Syrian case, Alawites backed by Iran).

Third, the Syrian resistance (like that in Iraq) includes Al Qaeda-linked Sunni jihadists. Does this argue against arming the opposition (for fear that weapons will leak to the Al Qaeda faction) or for arming pro-Western elements of the opposition (to prevent the jihadists from consolidating their position)? The Obama administration increasingly seems to be blending these two views, probably wisely.

Fourth, the Iraq example is a warning against a sudden political transition that explodes the existing state and military structures, leaving a vacuum that will be filled by sectarian and tribal groups.

The tragedy of Syria is, above all, the shameful story of Bashar Al-Assad, the unlikely successor to his dictator-father. For more than a decade, Bashar was seen as a potential reformer by well-meaning outsiders. Jacques Chirac, the former French president, was his first patron, and Paris sent a series of special advisers in the hope they might lead Bashar toward reform and change. The Israelis were supportive, cautioning President George W. Bush against considering regime change in 2005. Hopeful nods came from American visitors, including Senators John Kerry and Arlen Specter, Representative Howard Berman, and the leaders of some American Jewish groups. Bashar's final enthusiast was Prime Minister Erdogan of Turkey. He and his wife invited the Assads for weekends; he brokered the indirect negotiations with Israel in 2007 that surfaced publicly in April 2008. As late as the summer of 2011, Erdogan was still claiming Bashar would deliver on reform.

By the summer of 2012, Bashar's only remaining friend and protector was Russia, and even Moscow appeared to be pondering how to dispose of this embarrassing ally.

The Assads are a fascinating if horrifying family, marked with blood and vanity like a real-life version of the Corleone family in *The Godfather*. It is easy to cast the parts: Hafez as the old don, Vito; Bashar as his son, Michael, or perhaps better as the weak-chinned Freddo; the hotheaded Sonny played by Bashar's brother Maher (or his late brother-in-law Asef Shawkat); and the murderous Tatatglia family down the street.

Bashar was never supposed to be leader. He was the studious one who married the glamorous British-born Sunni girl, Asma. The successor was meant to be Basil, who was killed in a car accident in 1999. Certainly it was not easy growing up Assad. Consider this haunting passage from his brother Basil, quoted by Patrick Seale in his authoritative book, *Asad of Syria: The Struggle for the Middle East*: "We saw our father at home but he was so busy that three days might pass without our talking to him. We never had breakfast together, or dinner, and I can't remember ever lunching together as a family, or only once or twice, on formal occasions."

My own encounters with Bashar and his entourage have been numerous, and uniformly disappointing. There was a February 2003 interview when he talked animatedly about reform off the record and then woodenly defended his Baathist orthodoxy for quotation. There was a May 2005 encounter, when Bashar's handlers presented themselves as would-be Deng Xiaopings, in advance of a big Baath Party congress the next month that was supposed to deliver reform. But when the congress came, reporters weren't even allowed into the compound, and I wrote instead about watching the Mercedes limousines of the faithful party hacks roar past with their curtains shut to the masses. In other interviews with Assad or his inner circle, in December 2008 and February 2011, there was always the tease of reform, but never the delivery.

It was a testimony to the potency of the Arab uprisings that protest came to Syria, despite its police-state controls and its cloak of anti-Israel steadfastness. In my last visit to Syria in late February 2011, I noted a harbinger of protest: On February 19, a flash mob gathered in Damascus after a policeman beat a driver. Hundreds gathered and began chanting: "We are the people. The people don't want to be humiliated." Cell-phone videos circulated immediately, and police quelled the protest only by arresting the bullying policeman. The big protests in Deraa began two weeks later, in early March, and the local authorities opened fired. The cycle of violence had begun, with Bashar always promising that once he had the situation under control he would implement reform.

Assad counted on regional dynamics to save him. He believed his "rejectionist" credentials and his alliance with Hezbollah and Iran would deter protest. He miscalculated several factors: the rise of Sunni militants, such as the Muslim

Brotherhood; the move away from Syria by Hamas, which voided the Palestinian card; and the increasing isolation of Hezbollah.

But most of all, Assad may have miscalculated the role of the U.S. and its European allies. Perhaps he imagined an ill-considered U.S. or Israeli intervention would allow him to rally Arab nationalist forces. Perhaps he thought the opposition would be deterred by fear of Iran. In all these respects, he misjudged.

Despite the horrors that have unfolded in Syria, my sense is that Obama's decisions have generally been correct. As diplomacy has failed, he has gradually moved toward a limited covert-action policy linked with regional allies—Turkey, Jordan, Saudi Arabia, Qatar, and the U.A.E.—that is helping to shape the opposition and prevent Syria from becoming a magnet for jihadists. It is a cold-blooded, low-visibility policy. In that sense, it is faithful to the guiding insight of the Obama administration, which is that the Arab uprisings allow the United States to step away from the region and let the Arabs write their own history, replete with mistakes that will, at least, be of their own making.

A final question to ponder is how best the U.S. can influence political developments in this region in the years ahead. This story has a long way to run, and its outcome will be crucial for regional and global security. What tools can the United States use to shape political developments? Can this "shaping" be done openly, or is it necessarily something that must be done in secret, to protect the recipients of assistance even more than the donors? Or is the wiser course simply to stand apart, making clear where vital U.S. interests require us to draw red lines, but otherwise watching this history unfold and hoping that it does, indeed, have a "right side?"

David Ignatius is Associate Editor and a twice-weekly columnist for the *Washington Post*, writing on global politics, economics, and international affairs. His column appears on Thursdays and Sundays. He is also creator and co-moderator of Post-Global, an online conversation about international affairs at washingtonpost.com. He joined *The Post* in 1986 as editor of *The Post's* Outlook section, and then served as foreign editor from 1990 to 1992. Prior to becoming a columnist, he was *The Post's* assistant managing editor in charge of business news, a position he assumed in 1993. He continued to write weekly after becoming executive editor of the Paris-based *International Herald Tribune* in 2000, and resumed writing twice a week for the op-ed page in 2003. Before joining *The Post* he worked for ten years as a reporter for *The Wall Street Journal*, covering at various times the steel industry, the Justice Department, the CIA, the U.S. Senate, the Middle East, and the State Department. Mr. Ignatius has written eight novels: *Bloodmoney* (2011); *The Increment* (2009); *Body of Lies* (April 2007), *The Sun King* (1999), *A Firing Offense* (1997), *The Bank of Fear* (1994), *SIRO* (1991), and *Agents of Innocence* (1987). Mr. Ignatius's column won the 2000 Gerald Loeb Award for Commentary, a 2005 Edward Weintal Special Citation, the 1984 Edward Weintal Prize for Diplomatic Reporting, the 2010 Urbino World Press Award, and the 2010 Founders Award from the International Committee for Foreign Journalists. He is a member of the Aspen Strategy Group.

Part 2

CHAPTER 2

Has the Obama Response to the Arab Revolutions Been Effective? Yes, Not Really, and Probably Too Soon to Tell

Peter Feaver
Professor
Duke University

CHAPTER 3

Obama and the Arab Awakenings: U.S. Middle East Strategy in a Time of Turmoil

Martin Indyk
Vice President and Director of the Foreign Policy Program
The Brookings Institution

"To compare it to an earlier revolutionary period—the collapse of the Soviet empire—the Middle East region looks to be headed in the direction of the Balkans or the Caucuses rather than the direction of Eastern Europe or the Baltics. If one grants the administration the more modest long-term goal of a region without new anti-American regimes, an optimistic scoring might allow that goal is still within reach, but by no means guaranteed."

—PETER FEAVER

Has the Obama Response to the Arab Revolutions Been Effective? Yes, Not Really, and Probably Too Soon to Tell

Peter Feaver
Professor
Duke University

Strategy comes in two variants, declaratory and actual/emergent. Declaratory strategy reflects intentions and aspirations. Actual or emergent strategy reflects what happens when administrations struggle to hold on to declaratory strategy after meeting the harsh reality of institutional inertia, political constraints, and the most tyrannical of taskmasters, events, my dear boy, events.[1] Emergent strategy can diverge quite markedly from declaratory strategy, as, for example, when early cold war declaratory nuclear strategy called for a substantial measure of flexibility in nuclear targeting, but the actual nuclear plans were mostly inflexible. The Obama administration's declaratory strategy for the Middle East can be found in the initial premises forged during the 2008 campaign and presented most poetically in the 2009 Cairo speech. The actual strategy the administration has followed emerged from a case-by-case engagement with the revolution.

Measuring the relative effectiveness of a strategy also requires determining the goals the strategy is seeking to achieve. In textbooks, foreign policy strategies are supposed to impose a clear hierarchy of goals, simplifying this measurement problem. In the real world, human actors often stubbornly cling to myriad goals, some of which are logically in tension. Such is the case with the Obama administration's strategic response to the Arab revolutions, where three distinct but interconnected goals are discernible.

The nearest-term goal the administration has pursued is "no more Iraqs (especially before November 6, 2012)," where "Iraq" means a controversial decision for war that yields a bloody conflict that crowds out other national security priorities by committing the lion's share of our defense, diplomacy, and development tools to a venture with uncertain prospects. The administration's response has been effective (so far) at achieving this goal.

The medium-term goal is more ambitious, seizing opportunities to make dramatic progress on longstanding regional *desiderata* such as securing a lasting peace agreement between Palestine and Israel or guaranteeing a nuclear-free Iran or locking in the hard-won-if-overpriced gains of the Iraq war. The administration's response has not really been effective at achieving any of these opportunistic goals.

The long-term goal is hard to specify because the administration has been the most vague on what it hopes ultimately to achieve in the region. One can point to soaring rhetoric that would seem to imply a goal no less ambitious than the one laid out by Obama's predecessor: helping catalyze the region's embrace of modernity by ushering in political systems that are simultaneously representative of and accountable to electorates, yet also protective of individual and minority group rights and built on a sustainable political economic order—in short, that are full democracies.[2] But one can also point to efforts by supporters to lower success's bar to something that seems more achievable: the negative goal of avoiding the establishment of new anti-American regimes in a region where political Islam is here to stay.[3]

The political upheaval of the past three years could prove to be a watershed in overcoming the grip of authoritarian regimes, which has been the most sinister of barriers to achieving the more ambitious version of the long-term goal. Yet toppling a dictator is one thing. Replacing him with a system that yields "human liberty protected by democratic institutions" is quite another and is the work of generations. It is probably too soon to tell how effective the administration's response has been on this score. It is not too soon, however, to note that the optimism of the headiest days of the revolutions has been replaced with something far less hopeful. This was evident even before the terrorist attack that killed the ambassador to Libya and the cascading riots in September 2012 around the anniversary of the 9/11 attacks. As we go to press, the developments look increasingly ominous. To compare it to an earlier revolutionary period—the collapse of the Soviet empire—the Middle East region looks to be headed in the direction of the Balkans or the Caucuses rather than the direction of Eastern Europe or the Baltics. If one grants the administration the more modest long-term goal of a region without new anti-American regimes, an optimistic scoring might allow that goal is still within reach, but by no means guaranteed.

Scope Constraints

In this review, I bracket off Afghanistan, the kinetic global war on terror, and some interesting and instructive cases (Tunisia, Jordan, Bahrain, Yemen, and dogs that have not yet barked). Instead, I will briefly apply my framework of analysis to what I consider to be the five most important cases, not because they are typical but because they engage the most serious U.S. national security interests: Iran, Iraq, Egypt, Libya, and Syria. For the sake of convenience, I will address them in rough chronological order according to when the administration confronted its most pivotal decisions.

Obama's Declaratory Strategy

When the Obama administration spokespeople talk about Middle East strategy, they emphasize the unhappy legacy of Iraq and Afghanistan. Iraq: a war where the security trajectory was improving, but where American political will and public support were not keeping pace. Afghanistan: a war where the security trajectory was worsening, and where there was only a brief political window in which to reverse it. Together, these conflicts imposed serious constraints on Obama's freedom of action in the region.

Less often mentioned, but no less consequential in constraining its freedom of action, was what the Obama team itself brought by way of legacy: one tic and four faulty regional premises.

The tic was a determination to frame every policy in "anything-but-Bush" terms. Every administration has this affliction—the Bush team of 2001 had an acute case— but the Obama administration has had a chronic condition, and its variant is especially noteworthy because it involves zealously bashing the prior administration while simultaneously adopting in substantive form so many of that same administration's policies. The combined effect was to weaken both partisan *and* bipartisan support for the administration's strategy, an effect exacerbated by Obama's decision not to commit as much presidential capital to shoring up public support for national security policies as his predecessors had committed.

The four faulty premises[4] were:

1. A key to progress anywhere in the region was near-term progress on peace negotiations between Israelis and Palestinians.

2. Near-term progress on Israel-Palestine peace was possible because the chief impediment was Israeli intransigence, which itself was due to a failure of the Bush administration to apply sufficient coercive pressure on Israel.

3. Since President Obama was willing to administer such tough love, the Israeli "impediment" could be lifted and progress achieved in the near-term. The key was to boldly and dramatically force the issue by escalating U.S. demands on Israeli settlements policy.

4. President Bush's preoccupation with democracy promotion in the region was ill-timed and thoroughly discredited by the Iraq war. Thus, nothing was likely to happen on that front in the region, perhaps for a generation but for sure not until further progress was achieved on the Israel-Palestine issue.

These were not wildly unreasonable premises. The first is an article of faith of many regional experts and on a superficial level may even be true: many (though not all) other regional problems might be easier to solve if that problem could be solved. Likewise, in 2007, President Bush made a similar bet on the prospects for near-term progress on peace negotiations between Israel and Palestine, as did Clinton-era predecessors eight years earlier.

Counterfactually, had the Obama administration somehow achieved the elusive dream of an Israeli-Palestinian breakthrough in 2009, one could argue that the U.S. hand would have been stronger once the Arab revolutions began. But in fact the exact opposite happened. Instead of progress there was regress on the Israel-Palestine issue. The Obama gambit of forcing the issue on settlement policy was widely recognized as the spanner in the works. And to everyone's surprise, the grass roots did not wait for a resolution of the Palestine question before demanding for themselves what their governments had been demanding for Palestinians for decades: self-rule.[5]

These premises and other strategic judgments received their fullest expression in President Obama's June 2009 speech in Cairo. The Obama team came into office believing the Bush administration had naively and ineffectively pushed democratization in the region. In the Cairo speech, President Obama signaled his commitment to a different approach, one that spoke of human rights aspirations in less ambitious, more self-critical terms. As Obama outlined it, the "problem" was not decades of misrule in the Muslim world but, rather, tension between the United States and Muslims around the world—tension for which both sides shared some blame. Democracy, religious freedom, and women's rights got their mention, but in decidedly less concrete terms than the primary line of concern about anti-Americanism fueled by the unhappy experience in Iraq. Coupled with the administration's clear preference for engaging existing regimes regardless of how tyrannical (cf. Iran below), the implication of the Cairo speech for the democratization agenda in the region was unmistakable: whatever pressure to reform they had felt from Washington under Bush would be relaxed under Obama. Democratization on an accelerated timetable was off the table.

On balance then, the Obama administration initially encountered the serial Arab revolutions after having pursued a declaratory strategy that privileged Israel-Palestine peace, engagement with regimes, and generalized interfaith dialogue ahead of democratization. It was a failing, if not a failed, strategy. The upheavals were so disruptive they might have wrong-footed a team with more forward momentum, but they were nearly paralyzing under the circumstances, especially when the decisive political actors stopped being the regimes and started being the oppressed peoples, which the declaratory strategy had treated as marginal. This may be why the emergent strategy the administration actually followed in each country-case diverged fairly substantially from this declaratory strategy—and why the administration ended up doing less and achieving less (both good and bad) than others scored in earlier revolutionary periods.

Iran

The "Arab Uprising" began in Persian Iran, specifically with the short-lived "Green Revolution" of early summer 2009 in response to a fraudulent presidential election. Experts can disagree about whether the dramatic street protests ever had much chance of culminating in something more significant. The Obama administration, beyond the most tepid of rhetoric (and notwithstanding one appeal to Twitter to delay a software upgrade, an inspired act of interference that almost got the Obama staffer fired), seemed to bet squarely on the side of the status quo ante.

The Obama administration justified their caution on the grounds that if they sided too vigorously with the democracy activists the U.S. embrace would let the Iranian regime delegitimize the movement as a pawn of Western imperialism. Yet a consideration of equal or greater importance seemed to have been the president's commitment to its pre-Green Revolution Iran approach, specifically to the offer to meet unconditionally for bilateral negotiations with President Ahmadinejad.

For a decade, U.S. strategy on Iran has been stuck trying to resolve the same riddle wrapped in a mystery inside an enigma. The riddle was how to slow down Iran's nuclear clock while speeding up Iran's regime-change clock; a different Iranian regime might be more likely to accept a grand bargain that left Iran without nuclear weapons and, failing that, would be less problematic as a nuclear power. The mystery involved increasing the pressure track on Iran, specifically the economic pressure track, when most of the relevant leverage was in the hands of our European allies and other P5 partners who preferred to play good cop to our bad cop. The enigma involved sequencing negotiations and sanctions without exacerbating the other challenges; our partners would be reluctant to increase pressure once negotiations started for fear of being blamed for causing the diplomacy to fail; endless fruitless negotiations would simply allow Iran to run out the clock; painful sanctions might hurt the Iranian people more than the regime and thereby weaken the Iranian public's otherwise surprisingly strong sympathy for the United States; and the closer the clock ticked down to zero, the more difficult it would be to restrain Israel from launching a preventive kinetic strike.

The key to all of this was establishing sufficient pressure on Iran in advance of negotiations, to maintain them throughout the negotiations process, and, if possible, to have the nuclear clock stopped or slowed while negotiations unfolded. The Bush administration attempted to secure this in 2006 by offering indefinite high-level negotiations with Iran, provided that Iran suspended enrichment during the talks; and by securing the agreement of our European allies to ramp up pressure on Iran substantially if Iran rejected this offer. Iran did, and our European partners did, and by the end of 2008, Iran was under more severe sanctions than ever before. Iran, however, inched closer to a nuclear capacity, albeit on a slower-than-expected track because of other activities that were frustrating Iran's nuclear progress.

The incoming Obama administration could have picked up right where the Bush administration left off, using the already demonstrated Iranian intransigence and leveraging Obama's sky-high popularity to push for even greater economic sanctions, but it believed that first it had to demonstrate the additional futility of direct, unconditional talks.[6] Thus, for the first year or so, the administration avoided confrontation with Iran so as to preserve the possibility of such talks but otherwise did little in the way of increasing the prospects of success for those talks by ramping up economic pressure on Iran in advance. This avoidance of confrontation dominated the administration response to the escalating street protests in Tehran. It even shaped the way the administration played the public announcement that Iran had a second, secret enrichment facility at Fordow; rather than using the global shock to rapidly push through new rounds of sanctions, the administration responded cautiously, trying to reinvigorate negotiations with a new proposal to off-shore the enrichment program. Not until June 2010, a year after the Green Revolution and nine months after the smoking gun of the Fordow revelations, did the Obama administration's efforts succeed in getting the U.N. to impose a fourth round of tough sanctions. The United States followed up with additional rounds of tough sanctions in January 2012, and the European Union followed suit with still more economic pressure in July 2012. But during this period, the Obama administration fought hard against efforts by the U.S. Congress to stiffen Iranian sanctions more decisively, and at key junctures it was our European partners who pushed harder on the pressure track than did the United States—a dramatic role-reversal from the prevailing pattern of the previous decade.

So how to score the Iranian case? The Obama administration has unambiguously (as of press time) avoided a kinetic war with Iran, which was the single most likely candidate to become an "Iraq." According to reports, the administration may have engaged in other acts tantamount to war, but it has resolutely avoided something on the scale of Iraq circa 2003, thus meeting an important strategic goal.

The score is less favorable for the intermediate goal of seizing opportunities to secure other key policy objectives. The administration failed to leverage the Green Revolution, which was the best chance in decades of splintering the regime; to salvage any case here, the administration has to claim that the revolution was doomed to fizzle from the start. The administration did leverage Iranian nuclear misbehavior into the kind of severe sanctions the strategy long required yet lacked, but took eighteen months to do so, squandering what seemed like excellent opportunities for more vigorous action earlier. Other delays in the Iranian program compensated somewhat for the costs of this delay, but Iran has crossed multiple redlines and is closer than ever to having a break-out capacity that is immune even to conventional attack.

Scoring against the longest-term perspective, the trajectory toward full democracy or toward any new regime in Iran that is not anti-American is not promising, but it is too soon to tell. The Obama administration can rightfully claim that insofar as nudging Iran along the democratization and pro-American path goes, it accomplished no less than what Reagan, Bush 41, Clinton, and Bush 43 accomplished in their first term. But it accomplished no more, either, and the United States is in greater danger of losing the short and intermediate goals—either through slipping into outright war with Iran or through Iran slipping across the nuclear threshold—than at any other time in a prior presidential tenure. Iran does not constitute a great foreign policy success.

Iraq

The Obama administration's Iraq strategy seems to have been established some time around October 2002, when then-State Senator Obama gave his fiery denunciation of the venture. Ensuing events only hardened his view. Obama never wavered from his proposal to abandon the Iraq war on the fastest possible schedule (deemed to be about 16 months hence from whatever was the then-current date), and he strenuously opposed both the surge and any post-surge policy that attempted more of a gains-maximization approach in Iraq. On the contrary, Obama's strategy involved cutting future possible losses (and foregoing future possible gains), which paradoxically meant locking in current losses, albeit with a twist: the administration embraced the theory that the way to elicit more cooperative behavior from Iraqis was to credibly threaten to leave, thus convincing Iraqis they needed to step up and end their dependency on the United States. This theory made a virtue out of Obama's preferred policy of leaving Iraq. Not only would this end U.S. involvement, but it would hasten the achievement of the goals involvement was seeking to accomplish. The Iraqis might not be likely to cooperate anyway (hence we should cut our losses), but the best way to get them to cooperate was to leave (hence the additional virtue of leaving).

The leave-Iraq-as-fast-as-possible strategy, which might have been catastrophic if implemented when first proposed by presidential candidate Obama, was more viable when adopted by President Obama in 2009 because of the hard-won gains of the 2007 surge.[7] The great strategic achievement of the surge was to enable Bush's successor to finish the Iraq war on terms of his own choosing, rather than have the enemy impose its terms on us. The surge gave Obama a broader menu of choices than he would have had if his own anti-surge advice had been heeded. Obama chose the option closest to his longstanding view that it was not worth expending any additional resources on Iraq.

The Obama administration tweaked its campaign position ever so slightly to conform it to a timeline laid out in the Bush-negotiated 2008 Status of Forces Agreement with Iraq. There was even a chance the Obama administration would revise it still further, since the president authorized the negotiations anticipated by the 2008 agreement for a follow-on Status of Forces Agreement that would provide for a sizable stay-behind force in Iraq (similar to, albeit much smaller than, what was done in Japan, Germany, and Korea).

The negotiations ended in failure, however. Obama defenders would claim they were doomed from the start. They were unpopular in Iraq, and there appeared no overlap between the irreducible demands of both parties. Obama critics would point to a variety of missteps that hobbled the negotiations, the most important of which included:

- President Obama invested minimal personal capital, abandoning the leader-to-leader-cultivated relationship the Bush administration prioritized.

- The administration lead was Vice-President Biden, a person of considerable stature, but who had to overcome an especially high hurdle before he could win the trust of the Iraqis because of his earlier proposal to divide up Iraq.

- Obama's initial country team in Iraq never achieved the unity of effort of the Petraeus-Crocker team.

- Once a competent negotiating team was assembled, the administration appeared to undercut it with leaks about the likely failure of negotiations.

- The theory that convincing Iraqis we would leave would elicit cooperative behavior proved flawed. Prime Minister Maliki was even less cooperative with the Obama administration than he had been with Bush.

- The State Department never adequately resourced nor planned for the daunting post-war mission its own strategy required.

- The administration talked only of ending the Iraq war and made little effort to mobilize political support at home or abroad for any follow-on policy.

- Finally, some would argue the president did not really want to leave meaningful numbers of troops in Iraq and so the administration never seriously pursued a Status of Forces Agreement, only going through the motions.

The score? Obama unambiguously achieved the short-term goal, in this case rephrased to be "no more Iraq by November 6, 2012."

The intermediate goal of seizing opportunities beyond the opportunity to get out of Iraq has not really been achieved. On the one hand, the American phase of the war is over and Americans are not fighting and dying in Iraq; the security trajectory is eroding, but not (yet?) catastrophically, and Iraqi security is still better than it was at the darkest days of the war; Iraq has not (yet?) moved irrevocably off of the path to full democracy and still has brighter prospects in that regard than two next-door-neighbors, Syria or Iran. On the other hand, American interests in Iraq are not securely guaranteed; progress in Iraq on the political, security, and economic fronts has largely plateaued and probably eroded; American leverage inside Iraq is less than it has been in a decade, perhaps even eclipsed (or at least in danger of being eclipsed) by that of Iran; and there is no stay-behind force to serve as an internal hedge, a regional make-weight, or a point of leverage over Iran. Increasingly, ours must be a strategy based on hope rather than influence. The kindest spin one can offer is to claim that no greater opportunities were achievable. If true, that would make all of the Obama missteps and shortfalls irrelevant. Perhaps this is why, on this one policy issue, the Obama team has been quick to claim an exaggerated equivalency between their Iraq policy and the one they inherited from Bush.

It is too soon to judge the longer-term goal of an Iraq achieving full democracy, or at least an Iraq that stays friendly to the United States. This remains a tantalizing possibility. But it is by no means a foregone conclusion, especially when Prime Minister Maliki increasingly looks like a dictator. Our capacity to nudge Iraq in a positive direction recedes by the day. Historians may look back on the last several years as an interval of missed opportunities.

Egypt

Egypt may be the hardest case to assess. The Obama administration's strategy oscillated the most rapidly on Egypt; any spot on the widest range of outcomes (from successful counter-revolution to benign full democracy) still seems possible; and the stakes may be the highest, if the old cliché "as Egypt goes, so goes the region" is correct.

The Obama administration's earliest action on Egypt involved a retreat on the democratization front, slashing democracy funding and giving the Mubarak government something of a veto over which groups could receive the remaining widow's mite. Once the Tahrir Square protests proved the assumption that Egypt was not ripe for political revolution was mistaken, Obama visibly struggled to answer the question: is the devil we know better than the devil we fear? Initially, Obama answered yes, and he stuck with that answer despite being whipsawed by leaks indicating that the administration might be leaning one way and then perhaps another, sometimes within the same 24-hour news cycle. Strategically, the choice was whether to lead, or at least seek to catalyze events, or whether simply to be led by events—to bide one's time until it was clear on which side history would come down, and then to try to get onside as quickly as possible. The administration never completely chose between alternative strategies, thus defaulting to the last option, leading from behind events. The confusion was personified in the mission to send former Ambassador Frank Wisner to encourage Mubarak to accelerate a graceful step-down from power; the desired optics of a deft display of American influence was marred within days when the White House was forced to walk back from Wisner's comment that "President Mubarak's continued leadership is critical…"

To be sure, by the timelines of Middle East history, the administration switched its policy on Mubarak fairly rapidly, and the Department of Defense seemed especially effective at leveraging our longstanding military-to-military partnership in talking the Egyptian military down from using force against the protestors. But the administration agonized over its stance long enough to convince all parties they had been betrayed by the United States. The democracy activists believed, not without merit, that an earlier embrace would have catalyzed a more rapid and more graceful departure, perhaps even a departure while the revolution was most visibly led by secular liberals, thus positioning them best for influence in the new political order. Mubarak and other leaders in the region believed, not without merit, that the administration ultimately abrogated a decades-long implicit guarantee that U.S. pressure to reform would never be strong enough actually to force the regime from power. All regional watchers, therefore, believed that American ambivalence validated their own preferred approach not to count on the United States when it really matters, which may be why Saudi Arabia, Bahrain, and several other Gulf Cooperation Council states believed they could act with impunity to suppress Tahrir-Square-like protests in Manama. Perhaps most consequentially, it is still an open question whether the United States has an Egypt strategy that shapes rather than simply reacts to events.

The score? Obama's approach readily avoided "another Iraq" and, indeed, of all the cases reviewed here, achieved the most optimistic near-term outcome: a relatively peaceful departure of the dictator in which agency is unmistakably in the hands of Egyptians (although whether the greater agency is with the Egyptian people, Egyptian military, the Muslim Brotherhood, or other power centers cannot be determined).

On intermediate goals, some opportunities were lost. A more proactive American role might have been able to serve other *desiderata*: modeling more graceful exits for dictators, which would have been useful in Syria; setting more enforceable red lines, which would have been useful in Bahrain; and securing stronger commitments on Israel while empowering liberal blocs and forging institutional guarantees for religious freedom, which would be useful everywhere. But they may have been out of reach even if the administration had managed a maestro performance. The fundamental clash of interests could not be finessed. Mubarak had to be replaced by a political system that answered to an electorate more sympathetic to Islamism than the United States would wish. Mubarak dealt himself and us this unhappy hand, and the failure of the Bush administration to make greater progress in its own strategy pushing for political reform in Egypt set the table for the limited success of the Obama administration.

In the long term, Egypt should prove the decisive test of whether political Islam can come to terms with modernity, full democracy, and the United States. The disastrous events on the eleventh anniversary of the 9/11 attacks, when the Muslim Brotherhood-led government was slow to stop a mob, ostensibly protesting a religiously offensive video, from breaching the perimeter of the U.S. embassy in Cairo and replacing its flag with a black Islamic flag showed just how much President Mohammed Morsi is struggling to pass that test. The United States will not determine whether there will be a happy ending, but no political actor outside Egypt will likely feature more consequentially.

Libya

The pattern of a scramble to catch up with rapidly unfolding events was repeated in spades in Libya. Initially, the administration followed a clear strategy of publicly lamenting the looming humanitarian disaster, admonishing Qaddafi to address the grievances peacefully, but resolutely avoiding any military intervention—in sum, monitoring the situation closely but, above all, avoiding any American commitment to an intervention directed at alleviating the humanitarian crisis, let alone achieving regime change. Importantly, the administration kept its foot on the brakes even while NATO allies were seeking to press on the accelerator. The administration stuck with this strategy longer than many of its supporters did, and a psychological turning point was the spectacle of Obama's recent policy planning director issuing a strongly worded *demarche* to the president on the pages of the *New York Times*.[8] The chasm between a reluctant United States and a forward-leaning NATO was finally bridged when Obama joined David Cameron and Nicolas Sarkozy to support a U.N. Security Council resolution authorizing a no-fly zone.

The sequence gave rise to the most famous articulation of the Obama doctrine, "leading from behind," a phrase attributed to an anonymous White House staffer that will likely be to this administration what "bring it on" or "old Europe" was to the last. President Obama did not embrace the label, but he made it clear that he saw the U.S. commitment to the Libya operation as a limited liability, one in which our allies and partners would do the vast bulk of the heavy lifting and the United States would make a few, narrowly circumscribed contributions, primarily at the outset. Without using this analogy, the administration framed the mission as if it were a case of the United States loaning our pick-up truck to a bunch of friends hoping to move a piano up to a third-floor apartment. We would give them the keys to the truck, but nothing more; if they got stuck, that was not our problem.

In fact, the U.S. role expanded well beyond that. Metaphorically, we ended up having to drive the truck, help pay for the gas, supply the truck insurance, secure the dolly, and help push the piano around some tight corners. The strategy got very wobbly as the months dragged on, and the Obama administration had to honor "lead from behind" more in the breach than in the observance, but they resolutely avoided an expensive ground commitment. Along the way, they may have also put to rest the Pottery Barn rule, for having participated in the breaking of Libya they nevertheless managed not to buy it. But the administration successfully resisted more expensive forms of mission creep. The administration could (and did) boast about the comparative low cost of toppling Qaddafi versus toppling Hussein, making Libya its exemplar of how it hoped to wield American power.

The Libyan cost-benefit calculation looked somewhat promising until the terrorist group attacked the U.S. consulate in Benghazi and killed Ambassador Christopher Stevens and three other aides on September 11, 2012. Libya was by no means on an irreversible path toward stable democratization, but it seemed in better shape nine months after the death of Qaddafi than Iraq was at a similar stage. Tribal/sectarian violence was moderate. One worrying uncertainty was and still is the fate of a vast surface-to-air-missile arsenal; if some of those reappear in a terrorist attack, the net assessment would change dramatically. Until the killing of the ambassador, the most direct negative consequence had been the spread of instability from Libya to Mali, the collapse of which must surely count on the counter-revolution side of the tote board. Until quite recently, Mali was one of the more hopeful African success stories, but the government has long struggled with separatist movements fueled by religious extremism. The fall of the Qaddafi regime unleashed a flood of weapons and an exodus of radical Islamists that has already toppled the democratic government of Mali and threatens to turn parts of the country into a safe haven for networks of terrorists inspired by militant Islamism.

The terrorist attacks, which the Obama administration originally tried to dismiss as merely mob violence in response to a religiously offensive video, have raised far more troubling questions about Libya's trajectory. Moreover, the full reckoning turns on how one tabulates other hard-to-quantify costs, especially those that extend beyond Libya. The Libyan operation dealt one more body blow to an already weakened nonproliferation diplomatic framework, for it was lost on no one, certainly no one in Tehran or Pyongyang, that Qaddafi was toppled *after* agreeing to give up his WMD in a grand bargain. The Libyan venture likewise undermined Russian and Chinese support for an interventionist United Nations Security Council in much the same way the Iraq venture did, and for the same reasons. The Russians complained, not without cause, that the UNSC authorized only a no-fly zone, and that the United States and its allies twisted the UNSC resolution into something authorizing regime change. The Russian response: fooled by Bush in this way, shame on the United States; fooled by Obama in the same way, shame on Russia if they ever cooperate again.

The score? Odds-defying success on the near term goal of "no more Iraqs." Libya also merits a mixed but arguably positive-tilting score on the intermediate goal of seizing opportunities to advance U.S. interests. On January 1, 2011, no one would have put toppling Qaddafi as a Top 10 goal for U.S. national security, but the world may well be a better place without him. The damage to nonproliferation and to the effectiveness of the U.N. is not trivial, but neither institution was in strong shape already, so the damage at worst is moderate. Arguably, the wobbly nature of the U.S. commitment also contributed to a decline in Arab, EU, and Israeli confidence that the Obama administration could be counted on if the going got really tough; such doubts, however, probably preceded the Libyan operation, so the additional damage was moderate. Only the knock-on effects in sub-Saharan Africa (which could grow quite large) and the nagging fear that Libya's arsenal will reach the hands of terrorists are potentially large enough to shift the reckoning.

As for the long-term goal of moving the region away from anti-Americanism and toward full democracy, it is too soon to say. Perhaps the attacks were an anomaly. Certainly the newly elected Libyan government responded more quickly and encouragingly than did the Morsi government next door in Egypt. Perhaps this will come to be seen as just a particularly tragic detour on a path to the restoration of stability. If so, the Libyan operation may yet earn a positive score on Obama's balance sheet.

Yet the strongest critique of the Libyan operation may be it was a Pyrrhic success that set an unreasonable standard for international legitimacy and catalyzed Russian and Chinese obstructionism, leading to the deaths of tens of thousands who wait in vain for Western assistance, which brings us to…

Syria

As of press time, the Obama administration's strategic response to the civil war in Syria has not strayed far from the first page of the Libyan playbook: publicly lamenting the humanitarian disaster, exhorting the regime to yield power, but resolutely refusing to commit American power to intervene decisively.

Reasonable people can debate whether Obama is breaking with the Libyan model or perhaps just following it too closely. On the one hand, Obama retreated from his non-interventionist stance on Libya at the *possibility* of tens of thousands of victims, whereas he has not budged at the *reality* of that very death toll in Syria. Likewise, he did not shrink from using U.S. military power to topple the Libyan dictator who had mostly come clean on his WMD programs and largely stopped sponsoring terrorist groups, whereas Obama has not escalated the confrontation with the Syrian dictator who has not acknowledged his nuclear program, maintains one of the world's largest arsenals of chemical and biological weapons, and actively supports some of the most lethal terrorist groups active today. And, most importantly, Syria matters for U.S. interests in a way that Libya does not; a breakthrough in Syria might well have been on many Top 10 lists for 2011 national security goals. Even a sympathetic Obama supporter might concede that the administration zeroed in on the capillary and veered off of the jugular. A critic might be harsher: leading from behind became following from behind.

On the other hand, while the justificatory predicates for U.S. intervention are present, the enablers are not. Russia and China are actively blocking U.N. Security Council action on the fool-me-twice principle referenced above. Our NATO allies, perhaps chastened by their near-death experience in Libya (and certainly lacking the imminent interest of waves of refugees washing up on their shores), have reverted back to their traditional proclivities and are slow-walking through the crisis. Unlike in Kosovo (or, arguably, in Libya), they are not willing to act under the cover of the penumbra of a U.N. Security Council resolution; they are demanding what they know the Russians and Chinese will not give them: explicit authorization. Even Turkey, who is the most affected by the crisis, left unexploited the opportunity to invoke Article V of the NATO Charter, which would have made the Gulf of Iskenderun as infamous as the Gulf of Tonkin.

If the Libyan model created an Obama doctrine of "the United States will only join when others lead and are willing to pay the lion's share," then Obama is following it precisely. Despite all the concessions inherent in the Russian reset, the administration has so far been unable to elicit the requisite Russian support to secure U.N. authorization. Without U.N. cover and without other states seizing the leadership initiative, the Obama administration has been very slow to act. According to David Ignatius, the administration did not even authorize non-lethal intelligence cooperation with the Syrian opposition until very recently, and according to other reports, the administration's intelligence efforts have thus far been both tardy and ineffective.[9]

The scoring is grim. The Obama strategy has thus far secured the short-term goal of no more Iraqs, defined narrowly in this instance as "U.S. ground troops intervening in a bloody sectarian civil war in the region." But a year's worth of ineffectual global action, some of which must be credited to the Obama ledger, has resulted in another "Iraq" of sorts, i.e., "a bloody sectarian civil war in the region." If the United States does end up intervening, there is now a higher likelihood that it will enter a boiling conflict zone akin to Iraq, summer of 2006, rather than a simmering one akin to Iraq, summer of 2003. And, ironically, the failure to act decisively earlier may have contributed to the rapidity with which the civil war is spinning out of control, thus increasing the likelihood that the Obama administration will be unable to avoid costly action after the election. The absence of vigorous U.S. leadership has also worried Arab and European leaders; their doubts about U.S. resolve may circumscribe the risks they are willing to run and the commitments they are willing to shoulder. President Obama could be looking at his worst-case scenario: a costly commitment that requires a disproportionate U.S. role to have any chance at success.

The myriad opportunities presented by the Syrian crisis have all gone unexploited: the chance to set back Iran's regional ambitions; the chance to tilt the balance of power in Lebanon back to one more favorable to our interests; the chance to neutralize Syrian WMD; the chance to cripple a major supporter of Hezbollah and Hamas. Yet all of the risks that the Obama administration rightly seeks to avoid remain real and pressing: most obviously, that even without U.S. intervention, the Syrian civil war is slowly spiraling toward a regional sectarian war, with Sunni and Shia regimes actively arming the belligerents. If the Syrian civil war does not end with a clear winner and a rapid post-conflict reconciliation, the stakes will rise for all parties, who are amply armed and well-positioned to escalate the conflict by exacerbating sectarian fissures throughout the region.

As for the long-term prospects for full democracy in the region, the Syrian case (thus far) seems destined to show up on the negative side of the ledger. Even if it ends up as a place where human liberty flourishes protected by democratic institutions, it is likely to have first passed through the crucible of sectarian civil-war. The more modest long-term goal of a new regime that is more sympathetic to U.S. interests might be achievable, but it is unlikely the new Syrian political order will start out with a meaningful debt of gratitude toward the United States. Thus far, the Syrian case is teaching all of the wrong lessons: dictators need to be more vigorous and more ruthless to hold onto power; great-power autocrats will protect protégés more effectively than the international community will oppose them; active alliances with terrorists and terrorist-sponsoring states buys regime protection; better to have WMD arsenals than to give them up; and the United States is not the staunchest of fox-hole allies.

Concluding Caveats

The Obama administration's emergent strategy in response to the Arab revolutions has been unevenly effective. The administration has achieved what evidently is its highest priority near-term goal: avoiding another Iraq. The administration has made little progress, however, toward achieving other intermediate objectives and, aside from the Libyan case, the United States has not been nimble in exploiting opportunities. Of course, the final reckoning depends on whether the region emerges with an arc of stable, full democracies, thus reconciling itself at last with modernity—and, in the process, not becoming bastions of anti-American sentiment and policy. It is too soon to say, but the tragic disruptions following the anniversary of the 9/11 attacks and continuing on through September 2012 mean that only the most sanguine supporter could be optimistic.

I have evaluated the Obama strategy primarily on its own terms, against its own stated or implicit goals. One could use other metrics: is the United States more respected, feared, and influential in the region today than it was four years ago? Such a scorecard would be no more favorable to the administration. The soft-power asset bubble that President Obama's extraordinary popularity generated at the outset has largely popped, and the American position in virtually every corner of the region (except perhaps Afghanistan) is more equivocal than it was a few years ago. The exaggerated emphasis on the "pivot" to Asia, which in the region was interpreted as a desire by the Obama administration to downgrade U.S. involvement in the Middle East, has perhaps exacerbated this loss of influence.

I have resisted one predictable line of defense: that the United States is too weak to have any influence on events in this region, so President Obama should not be blamed for anything (or credited with anything, though I have rarely heard an administration defender admit that part of the syllogism). Of course, the United States is not strong enough to dictate terms and guarantee favorable outcomes. The United States has never been *that* strong, but we have been and are strong enough to count. There has been a noticeable relative decline in U.S. influence in recent years, but we are still the external actor with the greatest leverage over events. The Obama administration should not be criticized for events unfolding in an unfavorable direction, but it is not a captious cavil to note when it appears the administration has failed to wield American influence in a very effective way.

I have also resisted two predictable lines of critique. The first is that the Obama administration's approach has been driven by domestic political considerations and public opinion and is thus not sufficiently "strategic" in the sense of grounded in a careful and coherent delineation of American regional interests. According to this critique, Obama pursued engagement with rogue regimes because that was (allegedly) not what Bush did; did not pursue democratization because that is what Bush did; pursued the exit from Iraq because Iraq was unpopular; and accelerated the push for a Palestinian state because that *was* popular. Another variant of this critique emphasizes the disconnect between the public messaging of the administration's strategically oriented area experts and the tight-knit circle of political advisors closest to the president. There is something to this critique, but it may be unfair to the president who, I would argue, sincerely believes that his own political interest in avoiding an expensive and uncertain intervention in the Middle East in the near-term also is squarely in harmony with the overall American interest. Moreover, trading across domestic and foreign policy priorities is a quintessentially strategic thing to do. It can yield unsuccessful foreign policies, but it may yield more successful national policies. It may be a wrong-headed or even disastrous strategy, but it is a strategy.

I have also resisted the charge that the Obama administration's explicit rejection of a region-wide strategy in favor of an emergent, country-by-country approach has produced only ad hoc inconsistency. I am not above making such a charge myself, particularly in the heat of a campaign, but it is hyperbolic because every strategy, even one that poses as a sweeping and principled doctrine, will of necessity require a case-by-case implementation in which reasonable cost-benefit calculations may introduce inconsistencies. This does not mean principles are useless or that strategy is merely responding to events. It means principles are guides and measuring sticks, and sometimes effective strategies don't measure up.

Besides, as I see it, a region-wide pattern does emerge from a country-by-country analysis. The Obama administration has pursued a lead-from-behind strategy, sometimes following other actors more willing to shoulder the burdens of intervention and other times following events to see in which direction they are culminating. It is a strategy that minimizes errors of commission at the risk of more errors of omission. It is better at achieving negative goals, like avoiding another Iraq, and not as good at achieving positive goals, like helping push the Arab revolutions toward full democracy.

Peter D. Feaver is a Professor of Political Science and Public Policy at Duke University, Director of the Triangle Institute for Security Studies and Director of the Duke Program in American Grand Strategy. From June 2005 to July 2007, Dr. Feaver was on leave from Duke University to be Special Advisor for Strategic Planning and Institutional Reform on the National Security Council Staff at the White House where his responsibilities included the national security strategy, regional strategy reviews, and other political-military issues. From 1993 to 1994, Dr. Feaver served as Director for Defense Policy and Arms Control on the National Security Council at the White House where he was responsible for the national security strategy review, counter proliferation policy, regional nuclear arms control, and other defense policy issues. Dr. Feaver is author of *Armed Servants* (Harvard Press, 2003) and *Guarding the Guardians* (Cornell, 1992). He is co-author, with Christopher Gelpi and Jason Reifler, of *Paying the Human Costs of War* (Princeton, 2009); with Susan Wasiolek and Anne Crossman, of *Getting the Most Out of College* (Ten Speed, 2012, 2nd ed.); and with Christopher Gelpi, of *Choosing Your Battles* (Princeton, 2004). Dr. Feaver is co-editor, with Richard H. Kohn, of *Soldiers and Civilians* (MIT, 2001). He has published numerous other monographs, scholarly articles, book chapters, and policy pieces on American foreign policy, public opinion, nuclear proliferation, civil-military relations, information warfare, and U.S. national security. He co-moderates [with Will Inboden] Shadow Government, a group blog at ForeignPolicy.com. He is a member of the Aspen Strategy Group.

[1] On emergent strategy, see Ionut Popescu, "Design and Emergence in the Making of American Grand Strategy." Ph.D. dissertation, Duke University.

[2] In his March 28, 2011 speech explaining the Libyan intervention, President Obama phrased it thus: "I believe that this movement of change cannot be turned back, and that we must stand alongside those who believe in the same core principles that have guided us through many storms: our opposition to violence directed at one's own people; our support for a set of universal rights, including the freedom for people to express themselves and choose their leaders; our support for governments that are ultimately responsive to the aspirations of the people. Born, as we are, out of a revolution by those who longed to be free, we welcome the fact that history is on the move in the Middle East and North Africa, and that young people are leading the way. Because wherever people long to be free, they will find a friend in the United States. Ultimately, it is that faith—those ideals—that are the true measure of American leadership."

[3] This is the metric proposed in a recent Center for a New American Security (CNAS) report, Bruce W. Jentleson, Andrew M. Exum, Melissa G. Dalton, and J. Dana Stuster, *Strategic Adaptation: Toward a New U.S. Strategy in the Middle East*, CNAS, June 2012, http://www.cnas.org/files/documents/publications/CNAS_StrategicAdaptation_JentlesonExum_0.pdf.

⁴ This is adapted from Peter Feaver, "Egypt's unrest reveals Obama's Middle East strategy is all wrong," *Foreign Policy*, January 29, 2011.

⁵ Nor did they focus on the Israel-Palestine conflict in their demands for an end to authoritarian rule.

⁶ A common yet bogus critique of the Bush "suspend-for-suspend" offer misconstrued it as requiring the Iranians to unilaterally concede everything before negotiations started. This was false. The condition was that Iran had to suspend while negotiations were ongoing, not that they had to agree up front to suspend permanently. In exchange, the United States and the P5 (plus Germany) offered to suspend their sanctions for the life of the negotiations. It was a generous suspension for a suspension offer. But the idea that Bush's demands had been unreasonable became Obama policy after the candidate responded to an Iran question in a primary debate. Obama claimed he would sit down for unconditional, direct talks with Ahmadinejad at the outset of negotiations. After Senator Clinton pounced on what she considered a gaffe, the Obama campaign refused to back down and, instead, elevated unconditional bilateral summitry into a principled policy.

⁷ There is a misguided critique that claims the surge actually accomplished nothing of consequence in changing the Iraqi security trajectory. The critique mostly hinges on straw-manning the surge—properly understood, the surge involved both an increase in resources *and* a change in ways and means. The anti-surge arguments are debunked in Peter D. Feaver, "The Right to Be Right: Civil-Military Relations and the Iraq Surge Decision," *International Security* 35: 87-125; and Stephen Biddle, Jeffrey A. Friedman, and Jacob N. Shapiro, "Testing the Surge: Why Did Violence Decline in Iraq in 2007?" *International Security* 37: 7-40.

⁸ Anne-Marie Slaughter, "Fiddling While Libya Burns," *New York Times*, March 13, 2011.

⁹ David Ignatius, "Looking for a Syrian Endgame," *Washington Post,* July 18, 2012; Greg Miller and Joby Warrick, "In Syria Conflict, U.S. Struggles to Fill Intelligence Gaps," *Washington Post*, July 23, 2012.

"Perhaps Obama was just lucky; perhaps the worst is yet to come. But something else is afoot which makes it possible for the United States to confront its worst Middle Eastern nightmares with greater equanimity."

—MARTIN INDYK

Obama and the Arab Awakenings:
U.S. Middle East Strategy in a Time of Turmoil[1]

Martin Indyk
Vice President and Director of the Foreign Policy Program
The Brookings Institution

The Historical Context

U.S. strategy in the Middle East has been fairly consistent for the last six decades, regardless of which party held the presidency. It has been inspired by a straightforward, bipartisan, and uncontroversial assessment that the national interest lies in securing the free flow of oil from the Gulf at reasonable prices and preserving the security and well-being of Israel. The former required befriending the Arabs, the latter required supporting Israel. As the United States, therefore, became more involved in securing its interests in the Middle East, it also developed a derived—lately it is described as "vital"—national interest in settling the conflict between them.

To protect and promote these interests in such a volatile region, successive American presidents sought stability and developed a variety of strategies for achieving that elusive goal. They looked for pillars of steadfastness first in Iran, then in Egypt, Saudi Arabia, and even Syria (Henry Kissinger brokered Syria's intervention in Lebanon to end the civil war there). In the process, they allied the United States with authoritarian leaders in the region based on the sole criterion of whether those leaders would help preserve stability. This became known as "Middle East exceptionalism," a deliberate policy of overlooking the leaders' denial of freedom and human rights for their own people in return for securing their cooperation in preserving American interests. When the Shah of Iran was overthrown, Ronald Reagan turned to Saddam's Iraq to balance the ayatollahs; when Saddam belied his interest in stability by invading Kuwait, George H.W. Bush turned to Egypt and Saudi Arabia to counter him. Along the way, as American diplomacy succeeded in brokering Israel-Egypt peace, American military power succeeded in evicting Saddam's army from Kuwait, the Soviet Union collapsed, and the United States emerged as the dominant power in the region, manifested in

Bush 41's convening of the October 1992 Madrid Middle East peace conference. Bill Clinton then tried to reach beyond preserving stability to fashion a Pax Americana. He sought to resolve the Israeli-Palestinian conflict, bring Syria and the Gulf Arabs into the American-led peace camp, and use that coalition to isolate and contain the destabilizing impulses of Baghdad and Tehran. The strategy depended on working with the authoritarian leaders of Egypt, Saudi Arabia, and Jordan.

By the end of the Clinton administration, that strategy was in trouble. Containment of Saddam was collapsing; comprehensive peace proved to be a mirage; and the ayatollahs were launching their own bid to dominate the Sunni Arab world via Hezbollah, Hamas, and a nuclear weapons program. After 9/11, George W. Bush upended the strategy. Instead of containment of Iraq, he decided on regime change; instead of resolving the Israeli-Palestinian conflict, he decided to ignore it (for seven out of his eight years); and instead of embracing America's authoritarian Arab allies, he pressed them to democratize. As his secretary of state, Condoleezza Rice, famously argued in her own Cairo speech in 2005: "For 60 years, my country, the United States, pursued stability at the expense of democracy in this region, here in the Middle East, and we achieved neither. Throughout the Middle East the fear of free choices can no longer justify the denial of liberty."[2] That didn't work out so well either: with Hamas winning democratic elections in Palestine and al Qaeda insurgents and pro-Iranian Shiites vying for control in Baghdad, Bush backed off his "freedom agenda."

Obama's Middle East Strategy

Thus, when Barack Obama entered the Oval Office, he could hardly be blamed for returning to most of the elements of the default strategy: he vowed to end the war in Iraq, engage with Iran, and resolve the Israeli-Palestinian conflict. As for America's authoritarian Arab allies, Obama made it clear he would not promote democracy in the Middle East—at least not the way Bush did. He portrayed himself as a realist in the Eisenhower-Kennedy-Reagan-Bush 41 tradition rather than an idealist in the Bush 43 mold. His visionary rhetoric rarely included the word "democracy." In his June 2009 Cairo speech, for example, he distanced himself from George W. Bush by declaring that "no system of government can or should be imposed by one nation on any other." His national security strategy white paper, issued in May 2010, buried the section on promoting democracy and human rights abroad on page 38 of a 52-page document.[3] The approach he described there of "principled engagement with non-democratic regimes" was typically progressive but pragmatic, working with the pharaohs and sheikhs rather than supporting those who would overthrow them. When it came to reconciling the tension between America's democratic values and its strategic interests in the Middle East, Obama would follow the time-honored tradition of favoring core national interests.

The White House published the white paper nine months after the Iranian regime had brutally suppressed widespread demonstrations provoked by its hijacking of the presidential elections. At the time, Obama had hesitated to criticize the regime's bloody crackdown of this "Green Revolution" partly because of his desire to keep the hope of engagement with the Supreme Leader alive, and partly because he did not want to risk validating charges that the demonstrators were "American agents." Whatever the justification, he had reinforced the impression, created by decades of American support for authoritarian regimes in the region, that the United States could not be relied upon to support the people if they rose up against their leaders.

That credibility problem was compounded by Obama's failure to resolve the Israeli-Palestinian problem or close Guantanamo Bay—the two hot-button issues he had promised the Arabs he would deal with in his 2009 Cairo speech. In responding to the revolutions that swept across the Arab world in January 2011, Obama was also constrained by his determination to end America's decade-long involvement in wars in the greater Middle East, not start new ones. That meant he would be reluctant to bless military intervention. Moreover, the Great Recession at home and America's anemic recovery from it meant he had limited economic resources to deploy in support of democratic transitions.

Finally, Obama was taken by surprise. It's not as if his administration was oblivious to the stresses in the system. There had been a White House review of the stability of our Arab allies, and Secretary of State Hillary Clinton had bluntly warned all the Gulf rulers a few weeks before the Arab awakenings broke out that they risked "sinking into the sand" of unrest and extremism unless they liberalized their political systems.[4] But nobody inside the U.S. government (nor outside, for that matter) predicted the self-immolation of a fruit seller in Tunisia would provide the spark for the revolutionary impulses that would sweep across the Arab world.

Thus, Obama was poorly positioned to cope with such a profound challenge to the Arab regimes on which the United States had based its strategy for so many decades. From this position of weakness he had to adapt quickly to events that the United States could not hope to control and forge a new balance between its interests in prolonging a stable order that was quickly collapsing and America's democratic values, which were now being trumpeted in the streets and squares of the Arab world. He was bound to make mistakes as he struggled to find his footing on a constantly shifting deck.

It is too early to make a definitive judgment about his success or failure, since the Arab awakenings will likely play themselves out over the next decade, and only when the dust finally settles will it be clear whether the United States is better or worse off as a consequence of the strategy Obama deployed in the vortex of history. Nevertheless, we can make an interim assessment based on the way he is dealing with the multiple challenges to U.S. interests.

Obama's Arab Awakenings Strategy

On close observation, Obama's strategy can be defined by the following characteristics:

1. Variable geometry: Events quickly convinced Obama and his advisers they were dealing with manifold challenges to U.S. interests, and it made no sense to try to react to different situations in different parts of the Arab world with the same approach. It was an "anti-doctrine," summed up as "no one size fits all."

2. Stand on the "right side of history": Perhaps because he sees himself as an historic figure, Obama was quick to grasp that the millions of protestors in Tahrir Square represented an historic development, that Mubarak's time was up, and that any American attempt to help stem the tide would be counterproductive. Given how much the United States had invested in Egypt as the cornerstone of its position in the region and the foundation stone for resolution of the Arab-Israeli conflict, this was a decision with potentially profound strategic consequences. As time passes and the consequences of Mubarak's overthrow become clearer, second-guessing the wisdom of this approach is inevitable. But it's not as if there was a better option at the time. Mubarak's regime was tired and dysfunctional; the army would have been reluctant to crack down on the multitudes in the Cairo streets regardless of American preferences; and the bloody conflict that would have inevitably ensued would have destabilized the most important country in the Arab world far more than an Islamist government dependent on American aid. Obama's

choice was not between a relatively benign status quo and a revolution; it was, rather, between a relatively peaceful revolution and a horribly violent one. In those circumstances, I believe he made the right choice.

3. Avoid disruption to the free flow of oil: With one-third of the people of Bahrain protesting in Pearl Circle, Obama might have been expected to get on the right side of history there, too. Trouble in North Africa and Yemen had already caused the price of a barrel of oil to rise into the $90 range, and strife in Libya would soon remove its supply of sweet crude from the market, which would drive the price beyond $100. Turmoil in Bahrain that spread to Saudi Arabia's eastern province and threatened Saudi oil exports could cause a panic in the market. With the U.S. economic recovery already sluggish and Obama's reelection prospects hinging on growth that could generate jobs, he simply could not countenance instability in Saudi Arabia. Here was a case in which interests trumped values, regardless of whether Obama's soul cried out for freedom. That realist judgment led Obama to stand quietly on the sidelines when Saudi-led Gulf Cooperation Council (GCC) forces entered Bahrain to help the king suppress the demonstrators.

4. Avoid U.S. involvement in a new Middle East war: The onset of U.S. presidential elections heightened Obama's consciousness of the war-weariness of the American people and their lack of interest in a new Middle East adventure. He was determined to avoid military intervention in Libya, but when the leaders of France and Britain, backed by the Arab League, insisted on preventing what looked like an inevitable massacre in Benghazi, Obama agreed to provide the necessary military support as long as others took the lead and the U.S. role remained secondary after the initial destruction of Qaddafi's air defenses. Unintentionally branded by the White House as "leading from behind," the language nevertheless accurately captured this characteristic of Obama's strategy. It explains his refusal to respond to calls for military intervention in Syria even though doing so might staunch the humanitarian disaster and sectarian war unfolding there and would strike a strategic blow to Iran's pretensions to dominate the region (in other words, it is the one Arab awakening where values and interests coincide).

5. Shore up the non-proliferation regime: With every rule, however, there is an exception. In Obama's case, he harbors an overriding concern to prevent the proliferation, or use, of weapons of mass destruction because that would

challenge a fundamental pillar of the emerging global order he is attempting to shape. If Syrian President Bashar al-Assad deployed his chemical weapons against his own people, transferred them to Hezbollah, or allowed Al Qaeda types to get hold of them, that could generate U.S. military intervention in Syria.[5] That same concern has already led Obama, in dealing with Iran's nuclear ambitions, to take containment off the table and place the military option firmly on the table.

6. Preserve the U.S.-sponsored Israel-Egypt and Israel-Jordan peace treaties: Obama's understanding of the critical role these two agreements play in preserving U.S. interests in regional stability and the security of Israel led him to successfully deter the Egyptian military from intervening against its people so that its role could be preserved, not only as the supposed midwife of an orderly democratic transition (that didn't work out so well), but also as the protector of the peace treaty with Israel (which so far has worked quite well). In Jordan's case, Obama understands he must do what he can to help King Abdullah navigate treacherous waters as the king tries to respond to the demands of his people for democratic reforms against steadfast opposition from his East Bank establishment (backed by Saudi Arabia), a deteriorating economy, and turmoil on his border with Syria. This concern for preserving the peace, however, does not yet extend to resolving the Israeli-Palestinian conflict. Having tried and failed before the onset of the Arab awakenings, Obama is opposed to reengagement, partly because it is bad politics in an election year, but also because, unlike their Arab brothers, the Palestinians are for the moment relatively quiescent, and their Gulf Arab patrons are preoccupied with other concerns (Iran's nuclear program, "Persians" in Baghdad and Bahrain, turmoil in Syria and Egypt). The Palestinian leadership is also split and lacks a coherent strategy. Meanwhile, Israelis see no point in tearing themselves apart at a time when the basic "land for peace" bargain looks increasingly questionable to them. That could change now that Obama has won a second term, in part because he may want to remove the stigma of failure on this issue from his legacy, but more importantly because a more successful effort to promote the two-state solution might help shore up Israel's peace treaties with Egypt and Jordan and facilitate Arab and European support if preventive action against Iran's nuclear facilities becomes necessary.

7. In the Arab republics, where transformations are already underway, try to shape them in the direction of democracy, economic recovery, and respect for human rights: This means actively engaging with those who have won free and fair elections even if they espouse an antithetical ideology "to help build sustainable democracies that will deliver real results for the people who deserve them,"[6] as Obama's secretary of state has articulated the objective. The most visible and critical element of this effort is the engagement with the Muslim Brotherhood in Egypt. This represents a revolution in U.S. policy toward the movement that spawned Islamic extremism. Obama is placing a big bet that, rather than attempting to impose Sharia law and customs on a quarter of the Arab world's population, the Muslim Brotherhood's need to generate tangible results for those who voted for it will lead it to prefer the stability that comes from cooperating with the United States and preserving the peace treaty with Israel. Obama made a judgment that it would be less damaging to U.S. interests to try to shape this dramatic development than to support its suppression by military means. His administration is certainly engaged in a determined effort, from pressing the Egyptian military to respect the Muslim Brotherhood's victory in the presidential elections to providing economic assistance that can help President Mohamed Morsi succeed in righting the Egyptian economy and meeting the needs of the people. But it is a gamble. Standing on the right side of history now means accepting that the cornerstone of America's strategic position in the Arab world will likely be in the hands of a democratically elected Islamist religious party that is at its core anti-Western, anti-secular, and anti-Israel.

8. In the Arab monarchies, where transformations have yet to take place, encourage them to undertake meaningful political reform: This is easier said than done. Obama and Secretary of State Clinton have outlined their new policy of support for human rights in the Arab world, specifically calling on the King of Bahrain to engage in a meaningful dialogue with his opposition. They have urged the kings and sheikhs to embrace reform, open their political systems, diversify their economies, and respect the rights of all their citizens, including women and minorities. But because Obama is dependent on Saudi Arabia to help keep the price of oil in reasonable bounds, especially when the United States is promoting an embargo on oil imports from Iran, he has avoided pressing his case, leaving the Sunni Arab monarchs—especially in oil-poor Jordan and Shia-rich Bahrain—vulnerable to the next wave of Arab awakenings.

An Interim Assessment

All these characteristics lumped together make for a strategy that often looks reactive and improvised, but that is not necessarily a weakness. In the face of rapidly moving events that are beyond U.S. control, a flexible approach that protects America's core interests while doing whatever possible to shape the events in directions that will promote America's core values is probably the best that can be done under the circumstances.

Obama certainly helped promote popular demands for freedom and democracy across the Arab world, protected civilians in Libya, and assisted in toppling unpopular dictators in Egypt, Libya, and Yemen, while doing his best to protect American interests in stability in the Gulf. There were tactical missteps:

- The unnecessary humiliation of Mubarak which led Saudi Arabia's King Abdullah to distrust Obama's efforts in Bahrain, and Obama's related failure to push effectively for meaningful reforms in Bahrain;

- Obama's repeated call for Qaddafi's overthrow even though United Nations Security Council Resolution 1973 only authorized the protection of the Libyan people, thereby providing the excuse for Russia and China to block Security Council action on Syria; and

- Obama's consequent tardiness in pushing for Assad's ouster, which has cost the United States a greater ability to prevent the descent into chaos and sectarianism in Syria.

But overall Obama's innate pragmatism has served the United States quite well in the face of the upending of America's decades-long embrace of Arab authoritarian regimes that have now suddenly disappeared.

It is, however, too soon to assess the strategic consequences for the United States in the Middle East. In Egypt—the most important strategic test—Obama's dependence on the Egyptian military to serve as the midwife of democracy and the Muslim Brotherhood to uphold the Israel-Egypt peace treaty underscores what a risky business the United States is now engaged in. The inherent populism of the Arab revolutions combines with a latent enmity toward the United States for its backing of Israel and the *anciens regimes* and the institutional weakness of newly elected Arab governments to leave the U.S. position in the Arab world vulnerable to untoward events. This vulnerability was underscored by the way an obscure video defaming the Prophet Muhammad could spark anti-American demonstrations that threatened a fundamental pillar of Obama's new strategy: the U.S. ability to work with post-revolutionary Arab governments.

Moreover, Obama's unwillingness to organize and promote an orderly transition to a post-Assad Syria risks leaving the United States as a bystander while a Sunni-Shia/Alawi sectarian war spreads from Syria to Iraq and Lebanon. Should it also spread to Bahrain (where a Sunni minority is busy suppressing the political aspirations of a Shia majority), it could jeopardize the stability of neighboring Saudi Arabia (whose Shia minority is already in the early stages of revolt) and thereby threaten a core U.S. strategic interest. Along the way, it could also threaten the stability of Jordan, another core U.S.—and Israeli—strategic interest.

President Obama will therefore need to undertake an urgent review of the U.S. approach to the revolution in Syria. This is the arena where America's values in preventing a deepening humanitarian crisis that has already claimed the lives of almost 30,000 Syrians and America's strategic interest in dealing a blow to Iran's efforts to dominate the Middle East heartland coincide. Engaging President Putin in an attempt to secure Russian cooperation in the transition to a post-Assad Syria will be crucial, since that would allow for more active U.N.-blessed intervention and a greater ability to convince Assad to quit while guaranteeing more credibly the security of the Alawite and Christian communities once he does. But if Russian cooperation proves unachievable, then arming the opposition in concert with Turkey and the Gulf Arabs in an effort to gain greater influence over events on the ground will likely be the best way to reconcile the strategic need to intervene with the American people's reluctance to be involved in yet another conflict in the Arab world.

Cutting the Syrian conduit for Iran's meddling in the Levant would provide a strategic windfall for the United States and its Arab and Israeli allies. That shift in the regional balance of power, if sustained, could open up an opportunity to advance American interests in resolving the Israeli-Palestinian conflict. Hamas has already evacuated its external headquarters in Damascus. In doing so it has departed the Iranian-led "rejectionist" camp, whose declared objective is the destruction of Israel, and joined the Muslim Brotherhood-led camp, whose declared commitment is to uphold Egypt's peace treaty with Israel. That has already helped to produce a prisoner-swap deal with Israel, a de facto ceasefire policed by Hamas, and its acceptance (though not yet implementation) of a reconciliation deal with Fatah. If U.S. engagement with the Egyptian Muslim Brotherhood could help produce a unified Palestinian partner to peace negotiations with Israel, prospects for progress on the Israeli-Palestinian front might actually improve, and that could also relieve pressure on the Israel-Egypt peace treaty as President Morsi became a partner to a U.S.-led effort to resolve the Palestinian problem.

At the same time, President Obama will need to negotiate a new compact with the Saudi leadership that secures its support for meaningful political reform in Bahrain and Jordan as an integral step in buffering these small, vulnerable monarchies from the fallout of sectarian conflict in Syria. The Saudi king's distrust of American intentions, generated by George W. Bush's enthroning of a Shia government in Iraq and Obama's humiliating insistence that Hosni Mubarak depart the scene in Egypt, will not easily be overcome. It is compounded now by Obama's embrace of the Muslim Brotherhood in Egypt which the Saudis see as a rival to their leadership of the Islamic world. Moreover, the Saudi royal family is likely to face its own succession crisis in the next four years as the gerontocracy gives way to the next generation of rivals within the various family branches.

Riding the waves of instability generated by the Arab awakenings will become a lot more difficult for President Obama if the revolutionary impulses spread to the Gulf. A looming confrontation with Iran over its nuclear program will compound the pressure in this vital region, and the potential for Iran to play payback for the blow it might be dealt in Syria at the hands of its Gulf Sunni rivals by stirring Shia revolts in Bahrain and Kuwait can cause even greater complications. It is therefore critical for President Obama to try to get ahead of the game by forging new understandings with the Saudi and GCC leaderships.

Living with Middle East Instability

The Arab awakenings have demonstrated that the United States can actually live with a degree of turmoil in the Middle East without its core interests necessarily being disrupted. A revolution took place in strategically vital Egypt, and yet oil continued to flow from the Gulf at reasonable prices and an Arab-Israeli conflict was not ignited. Perhaps Obama was just lucky; perhaps the worst is yet to come. But something else is afoot which makes it possible for the United States to confront its worst Middle Eastern nightmares with greater equanimity.

The natural gas and shale oil revolution in the United States and Canada is rendering the United States far less dependent on Middle Eastern oil for its own energy needs at the same time as the major rising powers are becoming far more dependent (50 percent of China's and 65 percent of India's energy imports originate in the Gulf). By the end of this decade, the United States is likely to be a net energy exporter, while China and India will become almost completely dependent on the Gulf for the rising energy imports needed to fuel their dramatic growth. To be sure, the strategic interest in the free flow of oil and gas from the Gulf to America's allies and major trading partners will continue, and oil will remain a globally traded commodity whose price will impact the well-being of the global economy in which the United States has a large stake. Nevertheless, with America's own energy supplies secure, it can afford to be less alarmed about threats to Middle Eastern oil. To the extent that makes the United States less concerned about maintaining stability in the Middle East, it should also make President Obama in his second term more willing to press for meaningful political reform among America's Arab allies, and thereby more willing to put an end to the policy of Middle East exceptionalism. If President Obama does that, he will have developed a new balance between American values and interests in the Middle East that will better protect and promote both.

Martin Indyk is Vice President and Director of the Foreign Policy Program at Brookings. Previously, he was founding Director of the Saban Center for Middle East Policy at Brookings. Ambassador Indyk served in the Clinton Administration as Special Assistant to the President and Senior Director for Near East and South Asia in the National Security Council, twice as U.S. Ambassador to Israel (1995-1997, 2000-2001), and as Assistant Secretary of State for Near East Affairs. Prior to government service he was the founding executive director of the Washington Institute for Near East Policy. He is the author of two books: *Innocent Abroad: An Intimate Account of U.S. Peacemaking Diplomacy in the Middle East* (Simon & Schuster 2009) and *Bending History: Barack Obama's Foreign Policy* (Brookings Press 2012) with Kenneth Lieberthal and Michael O'Hanlon. He is also a regular contributor to *Foreign Affairs* and other foreign policy journals. He serves on the boards of the Lowy Institute for International Policy, the Institute for National Security Studies, and a number of NGOs including the New Israel Fund, the Israel Democracy Institute, and America Abroad Media. Ambassador Indyk was educated in Australia where he received a B.Econ (hon.) from the University of Sydney, and a Ph.D. in International Relations from the Australian National University.

[1] This article is based on his chapter on the Arab awakenings in *Bending History: Barack Obama's Foreign Policy*, Brookings Institution Press, 2012 (coauthored with Michael O'Hanlon and Kenneth Lieberthal).

[2] Secretary of State Condoleezza Rice, Remarks at American University in Cairo, June 20, 2005, www.offnews.info/downloads/Document-458.pdf.

[3] As the National Security Strategy document explains, Obama's strategy would be to work with nondemocratic regimes on counterterrorism, nonproliferation, and economic ties but also "to create permissive conditions for civil society to operate and for more extensive people-to-people exchanges." If rebuffed, "we must lead the international community in using public and private diplomacy, and drawing on incentives and disincentives, in an effort to change repressive behavior." See White House National Security Strategy, May 2010, www.whitehouse.gov/sites/default/files/rss_viewer/national_security_strategy.pdf.

[4] Mark Landler, "Clinton Bluntly Presses Arab Leaders on Reform," *The New York Times*, January 13, 2011.

⁵ In an impromptu press conference on August 19, 2012, Obama signaled this intention in the clearest terms: "We have been very clear to the Assad regime, but also to other players on the ground, that a red line for us is if we start seeing a whole bunch of chemical weapons moving around or being utilized. That would change my calculus." See James Ball, "Obama Issues Syria a 'Red Line' Warning on Chemical Weapons," *The Washington Post*, August 20, 2012.

⁶ See remarks by Secretary of State Hillary Clinton to the gala dinner celebrating the U.S.-Islamic World Forum, April 12, 2011, www.state.gov/secretary/rm/2011/04/160642.htm.

Part 3

"…the situation in Egypt today is not as straightforward as it was when a grim cartel of generals ran the country, and it is genuinely more difficult for the Obama administration to find Morsi in violation of the conditions for U.S. assistance. Democratic legitimacy is a powerful talisman against international opprobrium."

—TAREK MASOUD

Losing Egypt

Tarek Masoud
Associate Professor of Public Policy
Harvard University

For decades, American policymakers have fretted that an Islamist takeover in Egypt would wrench that country out of its comfortable slot in the U.S. orbit. After all, the Muslim Brotherhood, Egypt's leading Islamist movement (which in January 2012 won a plurality of parliamentary seats and in June 2012 won the country's presidency), has long declared its antipathy toward both American hegemony in the region and the state of Israel. For example, in 2004, with the U.S. invasion of Iraq still fresh, Mahdi Akif, the movement's newly-installed General Guide (he resigned in 2010), wrote:

> The Arab and Islamic worlds today are witnessing relentless and ongoing attempts to impose change upon it from the outside, sometimes with force, at other times through intense pressure. And it is a certainty that these external attempts do not really aim to achieve true reform for the sake of the peoples of the region, but rather aim in the first and last instance to preserve America's hegemony and its control over the riches and resources of the region, the supremacy of the rapacious Zionist entity in the land of Palestine, and to prop up governments that will be more compliant with its general strategy.[1]

In April of that same year, Egypt's current president, Mohamed Morsi—then a member of the People's Assembly from the Nile Delta governorate of al-Sharqiya— took to the floor of parliament to mourn Israel's assassination of Hamas co-founder Abd al-Aziz Rantisi and to demand that then-President Hosni Mubarak expel the Israeli ambassador, cut all ties with the Jewish state, and support Hamas "financially and, if possible, militarily."[2]

Akif's and Morsi's fulminations against the United States and its closest ally were not just their individual opinions, but rather reflected a core Brotherhood belief in the necessity of resistance to western dominance. In Article 2 of the movement's general bylaws, the Brotherhood aims to "liberate the Islamic nation in all of its parts from every non-Islamic power, to help Muslim minorities everywhere, and to strive to unite the Muslims until they become one community."[3]

Thus, when Mohamed Morsi kicked off his presidency with a fiery speech in which he promised to secure freedom for Omar Abdel Rahman, the notorious "blind sheikh" who was sentenced to life imprisonment in 1996 for plotting to blow up New York City landmarks, observers had reason to believe that a new era of confrontation between Egypt and the United States was upon us. And when Israel launched Operation Pillar of Cloud against Hamas in November 2012, one could have been forgiven for thinking that Morsi would do what he had asked Mubarak to do eight years previously and put Egypt's (admittedly modest) muscle behind the Palestinian radicals.

Alas, none of this came to pass. Though a brief flash of Morsi's anti-American streak showed itself in his reluctance to condemn acts of vandalism at the U.S. embassy in September 2012, on foreign policy the Egyptian president has otherwise behaved in ways Washington would consider responsible. Instead of arming Hamas during the Israeli assault, he worked with the Obama administration to bring about a cessation of hostilities, earning praise from the American president for his pragmatism and "engineer's precision."[4] Morsi remains a critic of America's hegemony abroad and its way of life at home. He apparently still believes, as he told a CNN interviewer in 2005, that the official narrative of what happened on September 11, 2001, is a fiction.[5] But in all the ways that are important to American foreign policymakers, he has pursued an international course for Egypt that so far has appeared to deviate little from that of his overthrown predecessor.

In a narrow sense, then, what journalist David Ignatius has called the Obama administration's "cosmic wager" on the Muslim Brotherhood's "peaceful intentions" seems to have succeeded.[6] Morsi has demonstrated that an Islamist government by the Nile represents little threat to U.S. interests and can even be a useful partner. Consequently, according to Ignatius, the Obama administration has become the Brotherhood's "main enabler," promising $1 billion in debt relief for Morsi's government (on top of the $1.5 billion in aid Egypt already receives), and backing Egypt's bid for a $4.8 billion loan from the International Monetary Fund (IMF), and a $2 billion package from the World Bank.[7] The Obama administration probably believes this economic assistance is one way to bind Morsi (and the Brotherhood) to American interests.

It is worth asking, however, if this policy is likely to succeed in the long term. Critics point to the Brotherhood's inherent anti-Americanism and long record of anti-Semitism, and conclude that any accommodation the group makes to American interests or to Israel's existence is at best a temporary expedient. In this telling, we should expect a Muslim Brotherhood-led Egypt one day to take its place alongside Iran and North Korea, once it has pocketed all that America has to give and weaned itself off of its dependence.

But even if one accepted this dim view of the Brotherhood, it is not clear that Egypt—a country of 85 million people, a third of whom are illiterate, and whose total gross domestic product is less than half that of Belgium (with only 10 million people)—would ever be in a position to forego the military, economic, and diplomatic benefits of alliance with the United States. Moreover, when one examines U.S. interests in Egypt, it is clear they are Egyptian interests as well, and thus likely to be preserved even without American patronage and largesse.

What are those interests? Given the frequent mentions of U.S. national interests in Egypt, it is remarkable how seldom they are spelled out. Often, it seems that good relations with Egypt are viewed as a national interest in and of themselves. For example, when former U.S. ambassador to Egypt Daniel Kurtzer was asked if the $70 billion in aid that Egypt has received over the last 60 years was a good investment, his first response was to note that it had bought "30 years of very strong relations with the most important country in the Middle East."[8]

Robert Satloff attempts to lay out a clearer set of interests in the form of five conditions for continued friendship between the United States and Egypt. Some of the conditions Satloff enumerates—an Egyptian government that respects freedom of speech, upholds the rule of law, and fights corruption—are not really American interests at all.[9] They may be valuable to Egyptians, and they might make core U.S. interests easier to obtain or maintain, but on their own they are not essential to American power or prosperity.

Satloff, however, identifies five areas that could be viewed as U.S. interests: freedom of navigation through the Suez Canal, peace with Israel, assistance in the fight against terrorism, recognizing South Sudan, and respecting "all other treaty obligations and duties incumbent upon a peace-loving member of the United Nations" (by which one assumes the author means the Nuclear Non-Proliferation Treaty).[10] Though one might question Satloff's elevation of South Sudan to a core U.S. interest, what is remarkable about all of the items on his list is that they are equally Egyptian interests, too. The Suez Canal is a major source of hard currency for the Egyptian government at a time when it needs every dollar it can get. Peace with Israel may offend Egyptian citizens eager for redress of the wrongs done to their Palestinian brothers, but Israel's military might and the fragility of Egypt's economy make the prospect of hostilities with the Jewish state too frightening to contemplate.[11] Many of the terrorists that strike at the United States emerged from Egypt and represent as much of a threat to the safety and stability of that country as they do to the safety and stability of the United States. South Sudan sits astride the Nile, Egypt's sole source of water. Good relations with Juba are thus essential if Cairo is to have any hope of getting the South Sudanese to refrain from diverting the river or extracting a greater share of its waters. And, finally, Egypt's dependence on western trade and aid render it exceedingly unlikely that the country would risk becoming a pariah by thumbing its nose at international obligations like the Nuclear Non-Proliferation Treaty.

Thus, practically all of the core U.S. interests in Egypt are ones the Egyptians have as much reason to wish to pursue and maintain as the U.S. does. Even in the absence of U.S. aid, Mohamed Morsi would neither wage war on Israel nor shut down the Suez Canal nor embark on a quixotic quest to reunify the Sudan. The break between the U.S. and the Egyptians, if it comes, will not come because the Egyptians threaten a key American interest. Rather, the greater threat to the U.S.-Egyptian relationship is that domestic events in Egypt render it politically impossible for the United States government to maintain the partnership on its present terms. In the remainder of this essay, I discuss two possible sources of a potential rupture between the U.S. and Egypt, assess their likelihood, and explore measures the United States can take to avoid them. The conclusion of this analysis is that the United States is better off investing its resources in promoting pluralism in Egypt rather than deepening its relationship with the Muslim Brotherhood. Though a more pluralistic Egypt will be more unruly in the short term and may not be as cooperative on foreign policy or economic issues as one controlled by the disciplined, conservative, and rational Muslim Brotherhood, it is also less likely in the long term to produce deep disruptions to the U.S.-Egypt relationship.

Potential Disruptions

Two sets of developments have the potential to force a break between the U.S. and Egypt. The first is the stalling of Egypt's transition to democracy. If Mohamed Morsi, who currently faces a profound—and, it seems, popular—challenge to his rule falls back on Mubarak-era tactics such as stifling the press, imprisoning regime opponents, and abusing protesters, it will be difficult for the United States to remain indifferent. The second—and in this author's view, more serious—source of a potential cleavage rests in the fate of Egypt's Christian minority. If that community, which has been the subject of abuses in the past, experiences a diminution of its rights or (more likely) its physical security, it will be next to impossible for the Obama administration (or its successors) to resist calls to halt aid to Egypt or even impose harsher penalties against Cairo.

Democratic Reversals

Though Mohamed Morsi was elected to office in part with the help of liberals eager to prevent Mubarak protégé Ahmed Shafiq from taking power and reversing the gains of the revolution, the new president and his party have done little to return the favor. Early in his tenure Morsi made pro-forma efforts to reach across ideological lines, such as appointing liberals, women, and Christians to advisory posts, but in all the ways that matter, the president has promoted his party and its Islamic agenda. Most egregious, from the standpoint of Morsi's opponents, was the manner in which the Muslim Brotherhood and its Salafi allies dominated the 100-member committee tasked with writing the constitution. The representatives of secular, liberal parties made up a small minority of the committee—in proportion to their paltry vote shares in the November 2011-January 2012 parliamentary election—and they chafed under their marginal role. The draft charter seemed set to deepen the Islamization of Egyptian law and society, to retain outsized powers for the president, and to preserve Egypt's long and unfortunate tradition of exempting the military from meaningful civilian oversight. As a result, several liberal members of the assembly resigned in late 2012, as did the entire four-person delegation representing Egypt's three Christian churches. Liberal politicians appealed to the Supreme Court to halt the constituent assembly's work—as a previous court had done in April 2012—on the grounds that the committee was unrepresentative of all Egyptians.

Instead of attempting to repair the widening breach between himself and his erstwhile allies, Morsi went on the offensive. On November 22, fresh from his success negotiating the ceasefire between Hamas and Israel, he issued a unilateral amendment to Egypt's interim constitution, in which he declared his decisions above judicial review and empowered himself to take "the necessary actions and measures to protect the country and the goals of the revolution."[12] The ostensible aim of this radical move was to protect the constituent assembly from dissolution by the Supreme Constitutional

Court, which Morsi painted as a cabal of counter-revolutionary Mubarak holdovers. But the effect was to heighten fears of an impending Islamist dictatorship, even among those who had previously been untroubled by the constitutional tussles being played out in the country's newspapers. Opponents of the president organized mass protests in Tahrir Square in Cairo and throughout Egypt. At least two people were killed, and several Muslim Brotherhood offices were vandalized and burned.

Morsi's opponents had by now united behind former International Atomic Energy Association chairman Mohamed ElBaradei in a grandly-named National Salvation Front, and they called on the president to rescind his decree. Instead, Morsi escalated the crisis, calling for a snap referendum on the draft constitution. Since the conservative, religious character of that document was a principal grievance of the president's opponents, it was unsurprising that this move was met with more demonstrations. Protesters camped out in front of the presidential palace, and a clash with Muslim Brotherhood supporters resulted in several deaths (mainly, according to press reports, from the Brotherhood's side). The opposition alleges that Muslim Brotherhood vigilantes captured and tortured some of the protesters in order to extract confessions that they had been paid by members of Mubarak's old National Democratic Party.

So far, the Obama administration's response to the crisis touched off by Morsi's maneuverings has been muted, and many in Egypt's non-Islamist political class view this as evidence of the fact that the United States is indifferent to how Egypt is governed, as long as the country cooperates with the United States geostrategically. Of course, this view is exaggerated. The U.S. Congress in particular has repeatedly signaled an intense interest in the progress of democracy in Egypt. In December 2011, when Egypt was still governed by the Supreme Council of the Armed Forces (SCAF), which had just executed a raid on NGOs in Egypt, including the National Democratic Institute and the National Republican Institute, Congress instituted a provision stipulating that the secretary of state must certify that "the Government of Egypt is supporting the transition to civilian government including holding free and fair elections; implementing policies to protect freedom of expression, association, and religion, and due process of law" before Egypt can receive its annual appropriation of $1.3 billion in military aid.[13] As Senator Patrick Leahy of Vermont, the author of the provision, declared, "We want to send a clear message to the Egyptian military that the days of blank checks are over."[14]

But the Obama administration has generally been more reluctant than the Congress to condemn or punish the Egyptians. For example, in May 2012, Secretary of State Hillary Rodham Clinton took advantage of a loophole in the Leahy provisions that allowed her to release the aid to Egypt without certifying its democratic progress. Part of this difference between the administration and Congress is standard, executive-branch resistance to congressional meddling in foreign policy. But part of it—at least since Morsi's election in June 2012—is a function of the fact that the current government in Egypt has a compelling claim to democratic legitimacy. After all, Morsi and his party have been democratically legitimated at the polls at least three times since Mubarak's overthrow (in the November 2011-January 2012 parliamentary elections, the June 2012 presidential elections, and the December 2012 constitutional referendum). Thus, Morsi is not unjustified in painting his opponents as anti-democrats who reject the expressed will of the majority. And the wave of arsons of Muslim Brotherhood offices throughout Egypt during the protests against the president's November decree enables him to claim that his opponents are not above using terror to overturn a legitimate, democratic order. Therefore, the situation in Egypt today is not as straightforward as it was when a grim cartel of generals ran the country, and it is genuinely more difficult for the Obama administration to find Morsi in violation of the conditions for U.S. assistance. Democratic legitimacy is a powerful talisman against international opprobrium.

As of this writing, it is not known whether Morsi will take even more draconian measures, such as shutting down independent media outlets or arresting key opposition figures. Such actions will undoubtedly make it more difficult for the Obama administration to maintain its equanimity with regard to the current crisis. This is an area, however, where the U.S. can have influence. Morsi understands that the $4.8 billion IMF loan package, the promise of $1 billion in U.S. debt relief, as well as assistance from the World Bank and the European Union, have been stalled due to the protests, and he is eager to secure these funds to stave off a foreign currency shortage that, among other things, would prevent Egypt from being able to purchase wheat for its massive bread subsidies program.[15] Though Morsi may be tempted to settle scores against political opponents, economic constraints may prevent him from doing so.

Abuses against Religious Minorities

If the Obama administration can exert influence over Morsi to prevent a full-blown democratic reversal, U.S. pressure is less likely to achieve results in the area of minority rights. This is because the most egregious abuses against Egypt's Coptic Christians are not the result of active state policy or formal discrimination (although these doubtless exist), but rather emerge from local disputes—such as commercial disagreements and personal feuds between families and clans. In previous years, the Egyptian state (and, in particular, its heavy-handed police force) had been able to limit the eruption of these disputes into wider spasms of bloodshed, but the retrenchment of the security apparatus in the wake of Mubarak's overthrow has diminished its ability to keep the peace. Past patterns of episodic anti-Christian violence can be expected to continue or intensify, but now they will be perceived, particularly in Congress, not as functions of Egypt's chronically weak state institutions, but rather as the direct outcome of the extreme religious ideology of the president and his party.

Christians make up anywhere between 5 and 15 percent of the Egyptian population. The indeterminacy of their number is a function of the old regime's skittishness with respect to sectarian issues. As the Egyptian leftist politician, Rif'at al-Sa'id, put it to Fouad Ajami, "We count everything in Egypt: cups, shoes, books. The only thing we don't count are the Copts."[16] The last national census to explicitly enumerate the country's Christians was conducted in 1986 (two national censuses have been conducted since then). Unlike many Christian communities in other Arab countries, which can trace their origins to Greek or Armenian diasporas, the Coptic community is indigenous to Egypt. When Arab armies conquered Egypt in the seventh century, the country they found was almost entirely Christian, and it remained so for several hundred years until mass conversions to Islam took place in the fourteenth century.[17] As several writers have pointed out, the words "Copt" and "Egypt" share the same etymological root.

Coptic politicians, activists, and intellectuals have long complained of official government discrimination against their community, particularly in the onerous, Ottoman-era regulations placed on building (or even repairing) Christian churches.[18] But many of these restrictions had been eased during the Mubarak years, and the new Egyptian constitution promises to guarantee equal treatment to Christians, Muslims, and Jews in the building of their houses of worship. A more significant cause of concern for Egyptian Copts has been the violence to which their community has been periodically subjected, particularly in southern Egypt, a hotbed of Islamic militancy that also contains the country's greatest concentrations of Christians.[19]

Though U.S. policymakers have not been blind to anti-Christian violence in the past—for example, abuses against Copts are always mentioned in the State Department's annual report on international religious freedom—neither has it been a first-order issue in Egyptian-American relations. Consequently, Coptic human rights groups in the United States—such as the U.S. Copts Association, Coptic Solidarity, the Coptic Assembly of America, as well as the fringe National American Coptic Assembly—have long struggled to remedy Washington's inattention to the plight of their co-religionists in Egypt.

During the Mubarak era, the task of these Coptic human rights groups was complicated by the fact that the U.S. tended to view the Egyptian government as the well-meaning, if beleaguered protector of the country's Christians against a rising tide of Islamist violence. Thus, when, in September 2000, former Florida Senator Connie Mack, a Republican, introduced a resolution calling on the Egyptian government to investigate violence against Coptic Christians in the southern Egyptian village of al-Kosheh, the resolution died uncontroversially in committee.[20] Similarly, after the January 1, 2011, bombing of a church in the coastal city of Alexandria, which killed 21 people and injured another 79, the U.S. response was not to condemn Mubarak for presiding over the massacre of Christians, but rather to "offer any necessary assistance to the Government of Egypt" in dealing with the attack.[21]

After Mubarak's overthrow in February 2011, the benefit of the doubt that his regime had received regarding Egypt's Christians was extended to the interim military government of the Supreme Council of Armed Forces. But as the collapse of the Egyptian police led to an increase in anti-Christian violence, including church burnings in the poor neighborhood of Imbaba in May 2011, U.S. expressions of unease grew louder. That year's State Department report on religious freedom "raised strong U.S. concerns about religious violence and discrimination" in Egypt (previous years' reports had omitted the word "strong").[22] The United States Commission on International Religious Freedom recommended that the secretary of state designate Egypt a "country of particular concern," along with such repeat offenders as Burma, Iran, Turkmenistan, and Vietnam.[23]

The traditional narrative of the Egyptian state as the guardian of the country's Christians was further strained when 24 Christian protesters were killed by military police on October 9, 2011. It is worth noting that Senator Leahy marshaled support for his bid to render Egyptian aid conditional on democratic progress by showing his colleagues in Congress a photograph of an Egyptian armored vehicle crushing a Coptic protester during the October 2011 clashes. "The Egyptian military was literally running over [him]. The assumption was that he died. [...] I said, 'Do you really want to vote for a blank check, and then see a picture like that the day after the vote, and have to explain it?'"[24]

If it was increasingly difficult for the U.S. administration to remain silent during abuses of Christians under an ostensibly secular military regime, it will be impossible for it to do so when those abuses occur in an Egypt governed by the Muslim Brotherhood. Though movement leaders have in recent years attempted to overcome their reputation for religious bigotry, fears remain. Islamists point to their new constitution's explicit recognition of the Christian right to worship freely and to govern itself according to its own religious laws, and they note the document declares that all Egyptians are possessed of equal opportunities to compete for and hold public offices. Christian writers complain, however, that the constitution's elevation of shari'ah and its empowerment of a Muslim institution, al-Azhar, to weigh in on lawmaking, are clear evidence of a Muslim-supremacist agenda.

For their part, the Muslim Brotherhood's leaders appear to view the status of the Copts as a strictly internal issue, and they chafe at suggestions that the government of Egypt needs to do more to protect them. When, in September 2011, during the period of the SCAF's sole administration of the country, Egypt had been named a "country of particular concern" by the U.S. Committee on Religious Freedom, the vice president of the Brotherhood's political party rejected the report and labeled it a U.S. attempt "to jeopardize the relationship between the Muslims and the Copts."[25]

A further source of worry is the tendency of supporters of Morsi to single out Christians as the main antagonists in the struggle between the president and his opponents. At a pro-Morsi rally in December 2012, Islamic preacher Safwat al-Higazi delivered what he called "a message to the Egyptian Church and to all the symbols of the Church." Amid shouts of "God is Great," he warned the Church, "Don't you dare ally with the remnants of the old regime against the legitimate elected representatives of the people."[26] Muhammad al-Biltagi, secretary general of the Cairo branch of the Muslim Brotherhood's Freedom and Justice Party, said in a radio interview that 60 percent of the protesters in front of the presidential palace were Christians angry at the ascent of Islam in Egypt.[27]

During the first phase of voting in Egypt's December constitutional referendum, the Muslim Brotherhood published an incendiary article on its website claiming that Christians in the southern governorate of Suhag were being sent text messages from an anonymous source urging them to vote against the constitution. "Say no to an Islamic state," the text messages allegedly read, "we want a Coptic state."[28]

Thus, what we confront in Egypt today is a combustible combination of a weak state unable to control communal violence and a political crisis that is increasingly taking on sectarian overtones. Though it may be possible for Morsi to reign in members of his party, he cannot undo what has already been said. More importantly, the more systemic problem of an insufficient police presence—particularly in those parts of southern Egypt with the greatest proportion of Christians—suggests that another episode of anti-Coptic violence is practically inevitable. Given Congress's increased activism on this matter, and the increased effectiveness of advocacy organizations in the United States in putting the Coptic issue on the public agenda in this country, it is difficult to see how such an episode would not trigger a major crisis in relations with the Islamist government of Mohamed Morsi.

Beyond the Brotherhood

Readers could be forgiven for interpreting the foregoing as a counsel of despair. If anti-Christian violence is all but inevitable, equally inevitable (some would say) is the continued electoral success of the Muslim Brotherhood. After all, the movement is repeatedly lauded as the most organized and popular political force in Egypt, and observers have been predicting its political ascent for the better part of 30 years. Thus, if abuses against Copts take on greater urgency when the Muslim Brotherhood is in charge, and if the Muslim Brotherhood is always going to be in charge, there is almost nothing the United States can do to forestall the eventual rupture in relations. Either the U. S. Congress would have to turn a blind eye to grievous violations against Christians under an Islamist government, or it would have to intervene in Egyptian politics in a manner akin to the CIA-sponsored coup against Iranian Prime Minister Mohammad Mossadegh in 1953, neither of which is plausible or morally acceptable.

The Muslim Brotherhood's dominance, however, is more contingent than is commonly realized. Though the Brotherhood captured approximately 40 percent of the seats in the November 2011-January 2012 parliamentary elections, its electoral performance since then has been increasingly lackluster. For example, in the first round of the presidential election in May 2012, Mohamed Morsi only won 25 percent of the vote, with former Air Force general Ahmed Shafik close behind with 24 percent.[29] If we include the vote share of Abd al-Mun'im Abu al-Futuh, a former Brotherhood member turned critic and self-styled liberal, Islamists captured no more than 43 percent of the vote.

There are several reasons for the Brotherhood's modest performance in the first round of the presidential election: increasing popular dissatisfaction with the movement's performance in parliament, the personal charisma and appeal of some of

Morsi's opponents, and Morsi's own deficiencies as a candidate. What is remarkable about that election is not just Morsi's modest performance, but the strong showing of the old regime, embodied in Ahmed Shafiq, and of the revolutionary left, embodied in Hamdin Sabahi, a leftist and now a leading member of ElBaradei's National Salvation Front who came in third with 23 percent of the vote. If the 11 percent of the vote captured by former Mubarak foreign minister and Arab League secretary general Amre Moussa is added in, then non-Islamists or secularists captured a clear majority of the vote (58 percent). The first election's results suggest strongly that the Muslim Brotherhood can be beaten.

The rise of Sabahi is particularly worth investigating. A member of parliament from 2000 to 2010, Sabahi is the founder of a well-regarded but small leftist, nationalist party called the Dignity Party, which, though established in 1996, was only officially licensed after Mubarak's overthrow. In the 2011 parliamentary election, Dignity won 6 seats, but this was only in coalition with the Muslim Brotherhood's Freedom and Justice Party.

How was Sabahi able to go from being the head of a fringe party to come within striking distance of the 84-year-old Muslim Brotherhood in the country's first free presidential election? In part, the answer lies in Sabahi's personal appeal. Handsome, eloquent, with a common touch and an easy religiosity, Sabahi is someone to whom many Egyptians can relate. Presidential elections in Egypt, as in the United States, are largely contests between personalities. The Muslim Brotherhood may have the most extensive grassroots operation, but the media coverage provided to presidential candidates is a great equalizer, enabling them to compensate for their organizational deficits and get out the vote with their charisma and personality.

Sabahi's relative electoral success is also indicative of the emergence of a new political force that could prove to be a genuine contender for political power in post-Mubarak Egypt—the Egyptian left. With his repeated affirmations of the rights of workers and the poor, Sabahi was the beneficiary of a powerful desire in Egyptian political life for a political alternative that is unabashedly redistributive. The Muslim Brotherhood, long thought to be the party of the poor, is actually ambivalent at best, and hostile at worst, to the kind of state intervention in the economy that most Egyptians support. For example, though the religious provisions of Egypt's new constitution got the most attention, the document also articulates a neoliberal vision for the economy, including "linking wages to productivity" (Article 14), limiting the number of trade unions to "one per profession" (Article 53), and reducing the state's responsibility to provide to free health care for all to one where health care is free only for those "who are unable to pay" (Article 62).

Public opinion surveys provide evidence for the proposition that Egyptians favor "leftist" economic policies. For example, when Egyptians are asked to place themselves on a ten-point scale from "left" to "right," a large proportion place themselves firmly on the left. This is represented in Figure 1, which is a kind of histogram of the ideological self-placement of a random sample of 3,000 Egyptians interviewed by the World Values Survey in 2005. The horizontal shape represents the proportion of respondents who placed themselves at each point along the continuum. The shape bulges at "6," which suggests that the plurality of Egyptians put themselves slightly center-right. But what is striking is how the shape also bulges on the far left, reflecting how many Egyptians self-identify as leftist.[30]

FIGURE 1: A significant proportion of Egyptians place themselves on the "left" politically.
(Source: World Values Survey, Egypt, 2005)

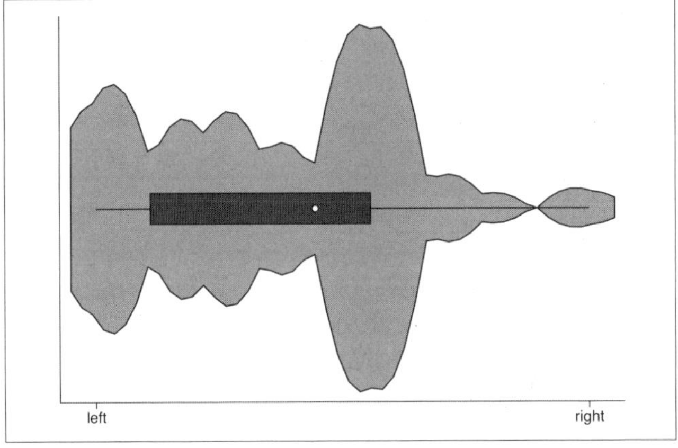

One might argue that asking Egyptians to assign labels like "left" and "right" to themselves is unlikely to capture their preferences or provide us with an accurate picture of the kinds of policies they want. In order to rectify this shortcoming, colleagues and I conducted a nationally representative survey of 1,675 Egyptians in November 2011. Citizens were asked several detailed questions about their policy preferences. In each question, voters were presented with two contrasting policy ideals and asked to indicate which one was closer to their own views. For example, we presented each respondent with a ten-point scale representing, we said, the entire range of views regarding the role of government and individual welfare. At one end, we said, are those who believe that "government should be responsible for seeing to citizen welfare." At the opposite end, we said, are those who believe that "individuals should be responsible for their own welfare." Some people, we said, place themselves somewhere in the middle between these two extremes. We then asked respondents to place themselves along the continuum, choosing 0 or 10 if they were at one of the extreme positions, or 1, 2, 3, 4, 5, 6, 7, 8, or 9 if they believed themselves to be somewhere between the extremes. The results are shown in Figure 2. As can be seen by the large "bulge" at the left of the figure, the vast majority of Egyptians polled believe that welfare is government's responsibility.

FIGURE 2: Most Egyptians believe that the government, as opposed to the individual, is responsible for citizens' well-being (November 2011).

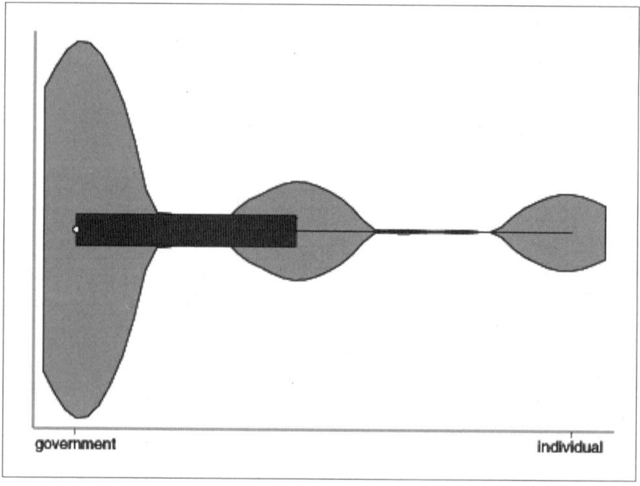

We repeated the exercise by asking respondents to tell us where they stand on redistribution. Specifically, they were presented with two views: at one pole was the view that "government should raise taxes on the rich to spend on the poor," and at the opposite pole was the view that "government should focus on economic growth, not redistribution." Figure 3 shows how respondents placed themselves on that continuum, with the vast majority favoring greater redistribution.

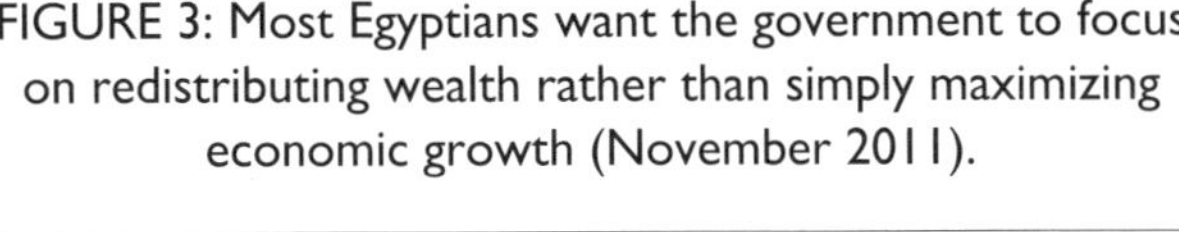

FIGURE 3: Most Egyptians want the government to focus on redistributing wealth rather than simply maximizing economic growth (November 2011).

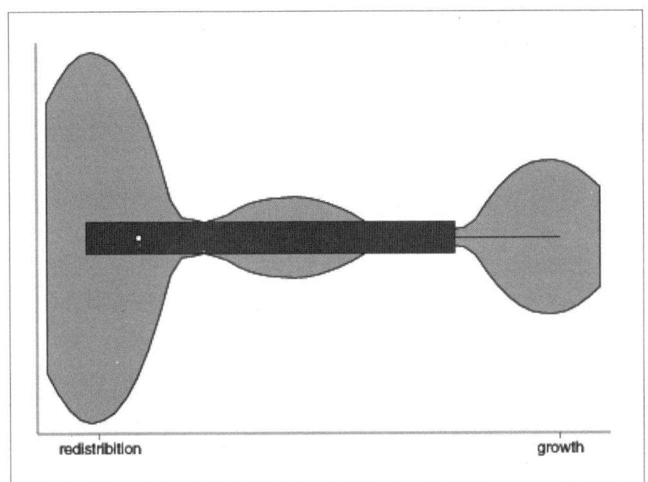

These public opinion analyses indicate that politicians who can tap into latent preferences for redistribution and government provision of welfare have the potential to be electorally successful, especially as the Muslim Brotherhood reveals itself to be less committed to these kinds of policies. In November, Morsi courted middle-class rage when he lifted the subsidy on 95-octane gasoline, and in December he met with even greater opposition when he issued a raft of tax hikes on everything from alcohol and cigarettes to cooking oil and cement (which were then hastily postponed). Such policies cannot but help to buoy leftist fortunes.

A further source of potential leftist strength is the country's increasingly vibrant labor movement. As historian Joel Beinin has argued, workers were a critical component of the protests that brought down Mubarak and "deserve more credit for his ouster than they typically receive."[31] Before the revolution, one of the main reasons no genuine leftist alternative emerged was because the Mubarak regime suppressed labor activism. Though there is evidence that the Muslim Brotherhood would also like to limit the power of organized labor, this will be more difficult than it was in the past. If leftist politicians like Sabahi can link with this newly assertive labor movement, there is every reason to expect the result to be a powerful electoral coalition.

Of course, one should have no illusions that the secular left is made up of ready friends of the United States. For example, a year before Egypt's revolution, Sabahi told an Egyptian newspaper: "People are unhappy. They want better living conditions. They want to say 'no' to the U.S. and Israel."[32] Abdel Halim Qandil, another member of the anti-Morsi coalition and one of the leaders of the Egyptian Movement for Change (also called "Kifaya" or "enough"), once declared, "Egypt falls under American hegemony and Israeli occupation and the regime is loyal to them. Therefore, opposition toward Israel and America is a cornerstone of Kifaya's program."[33]

What does this all of this suggest for U.S. policy? At the very least, it suggests that the U.S. investment in the Brotherhood as the only credible force that can govern Egypt after the collapse of the old regime is misplaced. It further suggests that the United States should weigh its desire to help Morsi's government deal with Egypt's economic crisis against its interest in seeing genuine alternatives to the one-party state in Egypt (be this the Muslim Brotherhood or, as was the case prior to February 11, 2011, the National Democratic Party). And it suggests that, when evaluating potential partners in Egypt, the pliancy of a group's foreign policy views, or its level of hospitality to free enterprise and open markets, is not its most important characteristic.

Conclusion

In a 1994 interview with the journalist Mary Anne Weaver, Hosni Mubarak—then beginning the third of what would be five terms in office—leveled this accusation at his ostensible patrons in the U.S. administration:

> Your government is in contact with these terrorists from the Muslim Brotherhood. This has all been done very secretly, without our knowledge at first. You think you can correct the mistakes that you made in Iran, where you had no contact with the Ayatollah Khomeini and his fanatic groups before they seized power. But I can assure you, these groups will never take over this country; and they will never be on good terms with the United States. These contacts will never be of any benefit to you or to any other country which supports these groups.[34]

History has shown that Mubarak was wrong about a great number of things. For example, in that interview, he was clearly wrong about the impossibility of the Brotherhood being on "good terms" with the United States. But he was correct in intuiting that Egypt's superpower patron had reason to be nervous about placing all of its eggs in his ruling party's basket. Though the United States eventually froze contacts with the Brotherhood—in part to placate the Egyptian president—it would do well to learn from that past mistake. That means not only compensating for years of non-communication with the political party that now dominates Egypt, but also stepping up relationships with those that are in opposition to it.

Pivoting from the Brotherhood to pluralism will not be easy. Egypt's liberals are a fractious bunch, and several Egyptian writers have suggested the United States is hardwired to prefer to deal with a single actor when it comes to Egypt—be it Mubarak, the SCAF, or the Muslim Brotherhood.

It is impossible to know whether this last charge is true. But what is true is that as long as the U.S. focuses its attentions on the Brotherhood to the exclusion of its opponents, it may win over the Islamists, but it will almost certainly lose Egypt.

Tarek Masoud is an associate professor of public policy at Harvard University's John F. Kennedy School of Government. He is the co-editor of *Problems and Methods in the Study of Politics* (Cambridge University Press, 2004) and *Order, Conflict, and Violence* (Cambridge 2008), and his writings on Egypt and political Islam have appeared in the *Journal of Democracy, Middle Eastern Law and Governance*, the *Washington Quarterly*, the *Wall Street Journal*, and the *New York Times*, among others. He was named a Carnegie Scholar in 2009, and is a term member of the Council on Foreign Relations. He holds an AB from Brown and a Ph.D. in political science from Yale.

[1] Mahdi Akif, *Mubadarat al-Ikhwan al-Muslimun hawl mabadi' al-islah fi misr (The initiative of the Muslim Brothers on the principles of reform in Egypt)*, (Cairo: Dar al-Manara, 2004), p. 3.

[2] Tarek Masoud, "Provocateur-in-Chief," *Slate*, July 2, 2012.

[3] See Tarek Masoud, "The Muslim Brotherhood," in John Esposito and Emad Shahin, eds., *Oxford Handbook of Islam and Politics*, (Oxford: Oxford University Press, 2013).

[4] Peter Baker and David D. Kirkpatrick, "Egyptian President and Obama Forge Link in Gaza Deal," *The New York Times*, November 21, 2012.

[5] In an interview with CNN's Jonathan Mann in 2005, Morsi apparently said, when asked about the events of September 11, 2001: "I cannot understand what happened in September 11th, this is not convincing, and an airplane or a craft just going through it like a knife in butter. I don't see that. Explain it to me. They didn't do it, make a fair trial, they didn't do it. What's going on? There is something fishy." See "Egypt: A test case for democracy," "CNN Presents," November 20, 2005, http://transcripts.cnn.com/TRANSCRIPTS/0511/20/cp.01.html.

[6] David Ignatius, "A 'cosmic wager' on the Muslim Brotherhood," *The Washington Post*, February 15, 2012.

[7] David Ignatius, "Our Man in Cairo," *The Washington Post*, December 7, 2012.

[8] Tom Curry, "What the United States has at stake in Egypt," MSNBC.com, January 28, 2011, http://www.msnbc.msn.com/id/41317259/ns/politics/t/what-united-states-has-stake-egypt/#.UM6J_HPjlCc.

[9] Robert Satloff, "U.S. Interests in Egypt: A Proposed Statement of U.S. Policy," Washington Institute of Near East Policy, January 31, 2011, http://www.washingtoninstitute.org/policy-analysis/view/u.s.-interests-in-egypt-a-proposed-statement-of-u.s.-policy.

[10] Ibid.

[11] The question of whether Israeli security is a core *American* national interest is a controversial one. Walt and Mearsheimer argue that it is not, and declare that the only case that can be made for an American security guarantee for Israel is a moral (or, to put it less charitably, a sentimental) one. They tell us that, "in the event Israel was conquered, neither America's territorial integrity, its military power, its economic prosperity, nor its core political values would be jeopardized." Though I would argue that American "core political values" are not as detached from the question of Israel's survival and flourishing, as the authors contend, there are also genuine material interests at stake. For example, to take the authors' own far-fetched scenario, were Israel "conquered," the fate of its (unacknowledged) nuclear arsenal would be of critical concern to the United States. After all, those weapons would not simply disappear, but rather would fall into *someone's* hands. Given that the authors believe "inhibiting the spread of WMD in the region," and preventing "groups like al Qaeda from gaining access to any form of WMD" are core strategic interests, it stands to reason that, if only for non-proliferation reasons, the authors should view Israel's security as more than just a moral issue. See John J. Mearsheimer and Stephen Walt, *The Israel Lobby and U.S Foreign Policy*, (New York: Farrar, Straus, and Giroux, 2007).

[12] What Morsi did precisely was to issue an amendment to the country's interim constitution (which had been put in place by the generals in March 2011). Morsi was empowered to do this because at the time he constituted both the executive authority (as president) and the legislature (since the Supreme Court dissolved parliament in June 2012).

[13] Consolidated Appropriations Act of 2012, Section 7041, a, 1.

[14] Statement of Senator Patrick Leahy, Congressional Record, Friday, February 3, 2012, Available at: http://www.leahy.senate.gov/press/leahy-ties-eyptian-governments-ngo-raids-to-us-aid.

[15] Isobel Coleman, "Egypt, Investment, and the IMF," Democracy in Development Blog, Council on Foreign Relations, August 27, 2012, http://blogs.cfr.org/coleman/2012/08/27/egypt-investment-and-the-imf/.

[16] Fouad Ajami, "The Sorrows of Egypt," *Foreign Affairs*, 74, 1995.

[17] Tamer el-Leithy, *Coptic Culture and Conversion in Medieval Cairo, 1293–1524*, Ph.D. dissertation, Princeton University, 2004.

[18] Mohamed Maarouf, "Egypt Government Caves to Church Demands on Places of Worship Law," *Egypt Independent*, October 19, 2011, http://www.egyptindependent.com/news/egypt-govt-caves-church-demands-places-worship-law.

[19] Such violence is by no means restricted to the South. See Moheb Zaki, "Egypt's Persecuted Christians," *The Wall Street Journal*, May 18, 2010.

[20] Senate Resolution 367, 106th Congress, 2nd Session. September 22, 2000, http://thomas.loc.gov/cgi-bin/query/z?c106:S.RES.367:

[21] Bourzou Daragahi and Amro Hassan, "Coptic church bombing in Egypt is latest assault on Mideast Christians," *Los Angeles Times*, January 1, 2011. Text of the president's statement is available here: http://www.gpo.gov/fdsys/pkg/DCPD-201100002/html/DCPD-201100002.htm.

²² United States Department of State, Bureau of Democracy, Human Rights, and Labor, International Religious Freedom Report for 2011, http://www.state.gov/j/drl/rls/irf/religiousfreedom/index.htm#wrapper.

²³ Annual Report of the United States Commission on International Religious Freedom (covering April 1, 2011 to February 29, 2012), March 2012.

²⁴ Sara Sorcher, "Congress: Threat to Withhold Egypt Aid Could Bolster U.S. Credibility," *National Journal*, February 8, 2012. Though the article does explicitly mention that the photograph that so moved Leahy was taken during the military's October 9 crackdown on Coptic protesters, the description of the photograph and the timeframe leave little doubt. See, for example, Rym Momtaz, "Egyptian Army Vehicles Crush Christian Protestors," ABC News, October 25, 2011, http://abcnews.go.com/Blotter/egyptian-army-vehicles-crush-christian-protestors/story?id=14809888#.UNOBWI5Avd4.

²⁵ "Coptic Intellectuals in Egypt Reject US Religious Freedom Report," Ikhwanweb.com, September 16, 2011, http://www.ikhwanweb.com/article.php?id=29037.

²⁶ Video available at http://new.elfagr.org/Detail.aspx?nwsId=242959&secid=1&vid=2#.UNOF5o5Avd4.

²⁷ Essam el-Ibaidi, "Christians angry after Biltagi and Higazi declare that Copts are fighting the Islamic project," *al-Wafd*, December 14, 2012.

²⁸ Hussam Abd al-Raziq, "Christians send SMS messages to voters in Suhag instructing them to vote against the constitution," Ikhwanonline, December 15, 2012, http://www.ikhwanonline.com/new/Article.aspx?ArtID=131916&SecID=230.

²⁹ Egyptian presidential elections, unlike American ones, require the winner to have won an outright majority of votes, instead of just a plurality. If no one earns a majority, a runoff is held between the top two vote getters. This is what happened in Egypt. In the first round of the election, Morsi and Shafiq emerged as the two most successful candidates. The two men then faced each other in a runoff in June 2012, in which Morsi edged out his opponent with 52 percent of the vote.

³⁰ To be more precise, I should say that this represents how many Egyptians self-identify as leftists when they are asked to choose between left and right. Many who select "left" in this exercise might not think of themselves primarily as leftists at all, but rather as Islamists, environmentalists, musicians, southerners, etc.

³¹ Joel Beinin, "The Rise of Egypt's Workers," Carnegie Endowment for International Peace, June 2012, http://carnegieendowment.org/2012/06/28/rise-of-egypt-s-workers/coh8.

³² Mahmoud Mosalem, "Q&A: Hamdin Sabahy on the Constitution, the presidency," al-Masry al-Yawm, January 19, 2010

³³ Quoted in Tarek Masoud, "U.S. must back democracy in Egypt, regardless," *Los Angeles Times*, February 9, 2011.

³⁴ Mary Anne Weaver, *A Portrait of Egypt: A Journey Through the World of Militant Islam*, (New York: Farrar, Straus and Giroux, 1999), p. 165.

"The U.S. objective should be not just to spread its message of good will but also to communicate what the United States does and does not stand for and to better understand the Egyptian public's mindsets in order to inform U.S. policy."

—MICHÈLE FLOURNOY & MELISSA DALTON

Egypt: How Should the U.S. Respond?
Dilemmas and Recommendations for U.S. Policy

Michèle Flournoy
Senior Advisor
Boston Consulting Group

Melissa Dalton
Visiting Fellow
Center for a New American Security

Introduction

As Egypt navigates its political transition, its trajectory has significant implications for the United States.

Home to 90 million people, Egypt has been an historical bellwether and a natural political and cultural center for the Middle East region. The revolution that swept aside the Mubarak regime in 2011 did more than transform Egypt; it sent shock waves across the region, inspiring similar uprisings across the Arab world.

But the future of Egypt remains uncertain. In some senses, its progress over the last 19 months has been remarkable. Egypt held competitive legislative and presidential elections for the first time in its long history. Formerly outlawed Muslim Brotherhood and Islamist parties gained a majority of parliamentary seats and the presidency. Power struggles between entrenched Egyptian institutions and emerging powerbrokers, however, challenge Egypt's political transition. For example, although President Mohamed Morsi's dismissal of top Supreme Council of the Armed Forces (SCAF) leadership mitigated Egyptian and international concerns that the SCAF might seek to monopolize power, the Council may still resist necessary economic reform initiatives that could threaten its interests. While President Morsi's policies thus far are rightly focused on fixing Egypt's economy, concerns remain about the Muslim Brotherhood's ability to govern responsibly over the long term.

In the midst of these tumultuous events, and despite the strong relationship between the U.S. and Egyptian militaries, the United States has found that it has only limited leverage with the new president, SCAF, and other Egyptian actors. Going forward, the United States must revitalize its policy approach to create opportunities for additional leverage. The window to do so will not remain open for long. Currently, the Egyptian public has high expectations that the United States and the international community will help safeguard the democratic transition and assist in the reform and recovery of the Egyptian economy.[1] At the same time, elements of the Egyptian population harbor a deep-seated anti-Americanism that occasionally flares into protests or even violence, as occurred recently after the posting of a highly offensive anti-Islamic video on YouTube.

Nevertheless, the United States has a rare opportunity to recalibrate its relationship with a new Egypt. It must find a way to engage all parties while backing the process of political transition, not a particular camp. Meanwhile, the rest of the Middle East is watching; what the United States does in Egypt, and the ultimate trajectory of Egypt, matter greatly for the rest of the region.

U.S. Interests in Egypt

The United States has longstanding interests in Egypt. Its primary interest centers on preserving the 1979 Egypt-Israel Peace Treaty as a critical pillar of regional peace and stability. Although newly elected President Morsi is a member of the Muslim Brotherhood, he has indicated that he is committed to upholding Egypt's international obligations, including the peace treaty.[2] Tensions between Israelis and Egyptians in the Sinai, however, could precipitate a conflict that could undermine the greater peace. In the past, Egypt has also served as a mediator in defusing tensions between Israelis and Palestinians and in negotiating prisoner exchanges.[3] It is unclear whether the new Egyptian government will continue to play this role. But even if a cold peace remains in the short term, the United States has a deep interest in preserving the treaty to protect Israeli security, regional stability, and the sanctity of international legal commitments. Over the long-term, if a democratic Egypt in which Islamist parties play a prominent role is nevertheless able to sustain the treaty, it could actually deepen the peace to be a more enduring one.

The United States has other strong interests in Egypt, including:

- Enabling Egypt's transition and stabilization through political, economic, and security reform, which could have demonstrative effects for the rest of the region;

- Maintaining U.S. and international access to the Suez Canal (although Egypt also has an interest in permitting access in order to obtain substantial transit revenues);[4]

- Securing over-flight rights (particularly in the event of regional military contingencies);[5]

- Partnering in counterterrorism initiatives; and

- Encouraging Egypt to play a stabilizing role with its African neighbors, especially Sudan.

Recommendations for U.S. Policy

To secure its interests, the United States should work with the international community to help Egypt establish a five-to-ten year plan to address core political, economic, and security objectives. Priority should be given to completing the current political transition to a full-fledged democracy, reforming and revitalizing the Egyptian economy, and maintaining internal stability and peace with Egypt's neighbors.

The essence of the U.S. policy approach should be to use its economic and security assistance to Egypt—and its ability to shape the assistance provided by other countries and key international institutions such as the International Monetary Fund—to press Egypt's civilian and military leaders to continue the democratic transition process and to embrace economic reforms critical to Egypt's long-term prosperity and stability. This approach will require the United States to continue its intensive diplomatic outreach to new Egyptian interlocutors, including pursuing the more differentiated approach to political Islam that has been seen in recent months.

Supporting Egypt's Democratic Transition

The first pillar of U.S. policy should be to provide unwavering support for the process of democratic reform and political transition in Egypt. For starters, the United States should continue to leverage its relationships with the SCAF as well as current and former officials to encourage the emergence of a new political order in Egypt. This should include pressing adoption of political, economic, and security reforms and openness to a more inclusive democratic process with competing power institutions.

Specifically, the United States should undertake a multidimensional diplomatic engagement strategy aimed at encouraging President Morsi and the SCAF to publish a timeline for the political transition process, including dates for specific electoral, legislative, and constitution-drafting milestones. Among the political reforms Egypt's new government should consider as the political transition progresses is the establishment of a national security council comprised of both civilian and military leaders.[6] This new body could not only oversee the development of national security policy but also reinforce civilian control over the military.

At the same time, the United States must also remain cognizant of the limits of U.S. leverage with the SCAF and new power brokers (the Muslim Brotherhood and others) and ensure that its diplomatic outreach includes actors across the Egyptian political spectrum. To this end, the United States should continue to pursue a differentiated approach to political Islam.

Political Islam is not monolithic, nor should U.S. policy be.[7] The United States should engage all actors across the spectrum, including Salafists, but should stand firm on its red lines for U.S. assistance, including Israeli security, the protection of the U.S. diplomatic mission in Egypt, human and minority rights, and commitments to nonviolence. The initial U.S. engagement with the Muslim Brotherhood in early 2012 is a good start. The United States should be willing to work with all pragmatists who have common interests in Egypt's progress.

A second element of U.S. diplomatic outreach should focus on providing support to the development of Egyptian civil society, political parties, and democratic institutions, including the non-Islamist revolutionary forces that led the Tahrir Square protests in early 2011 but have yet to organize effectively. The challenge is doing so in ways that do not elicit a backlash of nationalist sentiment or hostile actions from existing political stakeholders. Even with a coalition of international supporters, however, Egyptian leaders may resist foreign assistance as impinging on national sovereignty, particularly as emerging Egyptian leaders seek to burnish their nationalist credentials and gain popular support. The crisis involving U.S. NGOs in early 2012 illustrates how even well-established U.S. institutions and programs could be at risk as Egypt navigates its transition.[8] To help mitigate that risk, the United States should be even more transparent about the purposes of its political, economic, and security assistance, publishing the details of its programs online and explicitly noting the objectives of assistance projects in all forms of diplomatic outreach.

A third component should entail structuring diplomatic initiatives so they engage the Egyptian public, not just the regime; as the events of early 2010 demonstrated, the

"Arab street" matters much more on a strategic level than the United States previously assessed.[9] Public engagement could include social media, "e-diplomacy," town hall meetings, and civil society outreach, which the U.S. government has initiated but should strengthen. At the same time, given deep skepticism among Egyptians about American motivations, the United States should be realistic about the degree to which it can engage the Egyptian public. It should enhance public-private partnerships and encourage direct engagement between private actors. It should also acknowledge that domestic events in the United States may reverberate more profoundly in Egypt now[10] as the Egyptian public becomes more politically assertive, and simply as a consequence of an increasingly interconnected world. The U.S. objective should be not just to spread its message of good will but also to communicate what the United States does and does not stand for and to better understand the Egyptian public's mindsets in order to inform U.S. policy.[11]

Finally, the United States should promote Track 2 diplomatic efforts to engage Egyptian actors outside of government who may become future leaders or are otherwise in a position to influence Egypt's trajectory. The United States should adopt this multipronged diplomatic approach to enhance its credibility and to ensure that it is making inroads with emerging power brokers.

Reforming and Revitalizing Egypt's Economy

No matter who wields power in Egypt, the economy will top the list of Egyptian priorities. Egypt's dire economic situation has worsened over the past year and a half. Its economy has contracted by 0.8 percent, resulting in the loss of one million jobs. Foreign investment fell from $6.4 billion in 2010 to $500 million in 2011. Egypt's budget deficit is now 10 percent of GDP, the largest in the Arab world.[12] The economic conditions that preceded the Egyptian revolution, which included soaring costs of living, would be exacerbated in the event of an Egyptian default or currency devaluation. Indeed, Egypt's economy may be approaching a tipping point.

The United States and the international community should focus their near-term policy efforts on working with Egypt to create an economic strategy to address immediate needs. With the international community, the United States should help Egypt create a vision for its economic future, provide debt relief on an urgent basis,[13] accelerate targeted economic assistance packages to critical development areas, and encourage European Union and Gulf partners to do the same. In so doing, the United

States and its international partners can also enhance their leverage with Egyptian interlocutors to press for economic and political reform and to uphold its international obligations, particularly the Camp David Accords.

Revitalizing the Egyptian economy will be no small task. Egypt has yet to define a unifying vision to address its fundamental economic problems. The SCAF will likely remain resistant to relinquishing its influence and interests in the economy.[14] The Muslim Brotherhood recognizes the need to engage the West and build a robust, international business community, but will place special emphasis on providing a social safety net.[15] President Morsi raised public sector wages, but has not yet defined how to offset the impact on Egypt's already significant budget deficit.[16] Furthermore, putting the Egyptian economy on a solid footing for the future will undoubtedly require fundamental structural reforms that will be deeply unpopular.

While supporting free market reforms, the United States should be open to supporting economic models that may not be wholly free market. It should lead the international community in advising and assisting Egypt as it addresses short-term problems and adopts deeper reforms over the next ten years. No economic policy in Egypt will succeed, however, in the absence of sufficient political stability for investors to risk their capital and for tourists to begin visiting again.

The IMF made this clear by linking its $3.2 billion assistance package under consideration to political stability.[17] The United States should encourage President Morsi and his emerging government to renew negotiations on the IMF package.[18] It should partner with the EU to provide debt relief. Drawn-out appropriation and planning processes will make it difficult to respond quickly, however, and all Egyptians may not receive the benefits of new initiatives. Washington should press to obtain the required authorities for the Middle East and North Africa Incentive Fund to create a relatively more nimble mechanism to aid Egypt and other transitioning countries. The United States and the EU should also partner with Arab Gulf countries to direct investment in accordance with Egypt's eventual strategy, not just groups that support Gulf interests. The United States, however, will be challenged by the tension of partnering with the Gulf on reform in North Africa while being perceived as ignoring reform calls in the Gulf countries themselves.[19]

Absorption capacity in Egypt will also remain a challenge. Institutions and technical expertise may not be in place, and economic benefits may not be shared widely and deeply. The United States should thus combine its financial assistance with training and advisors to enable Egypt to enhance this capacity.

Lastly, the United States and the IMF should seek to persuade the SCAF to publish its military budget, with the understanding that a classified annex may be necessary to protect certain sensitive activities. In doing so, Egyptians and the international community would have more visibility into how entrenched the SCAF is in the Egyptian economy.[20] Publishing the SCAF's military budget could, in the short term, help inform steps to disentangle the SCAF over the next 10 years, as part of a broader Egyptian transition strategy. While members of the SCAF may be resistant to doing so, they could be persuaded by the fact that if they do not take this step, other forces within Egypt may do it for them, or could take more drastic measures sooner than the SCAF would like.

Security Assistance and Reform

One of the most important policy questions for the United States is whether and how to condition the $1.3 billion of security assistance it provides to Egypt each year. In weighing this issue, U.S. decision makers should be realistic about the necessity, but also the potential limitations, of conditioning security assistance and tying it to political reform or other milestones. On one hand, the United States should consider the demonstrative effects of not conditioning aid.[21] Regimes in Bahrain, Libya, Yemen, and throughout the region are undoubtedly observing the U.S. response to the Egyptian government's actions as an indication of how far U.S. tolerance may stretch. On the other hand, threats to cut off aid unless specific democratic benchmarks are achieved could produce a nationalist backlash among Egyptian leaders and sour the very relations with the Egyptian military that provide Washington a modicum of access and influence. In addition, once aid is conditioned, it may become a less effective point of leverage down the road. Washington has utilized the aid-cutoff lever many times, for example, with Pakistan, with remarkably poor results. Pakistani military leaders largely ignored U.S. demands and often found other sources of funding and arms.[22]

Alternatively, the United States could leverage its robust security assistance to Egypt in a different way. It should encourage Egypt to play a constructive role in reviving the peace process between Israel and the Palestinians, pressing Hamas to eschew its anti-Israel stance and reconcile with the Palestinian Authority. For its part, the United States should make clear that as long as Egypt continues to abide by its obligations under the Camp David Accords, it will be favorably disposed to continue to provide steady levels of security assistance. In the event that Egypt missteps, rather than reacting to the latest news cycle, U.S. leaders should step back and assess whether an infraction by the Egyptian government in the political transition process or in fully implementing the peace treaty truly undermines U.S. interests before considering whether and how to condition aid. There may come a point at which Egypt crosses the threshold and the effects of its transgression may undermine the U.S. interest in supporting transitions throughout the region. But the United States should make this judgment carefully.

Beyond recalibrating its security assistance to Egypt, the United States should encourage Egypt to focus more on threats emanating from the Sinai and to take steps to defuse a potential escalation of conflict with Israel. Several recent incidents in the Sinai have heightened Egyptian and Israeli security concerns. Following an April 2012 rocket attack launched by militants into the Israeli resort city of Eilat, Israelis increasingly worry about their southern border, magnified by overall Israeli concern about the products of Arab uprisings.[23] A few weeks before the riot at the Israeli embassy in Cairo, Israeli soldiers killed several Egyptian border guards after an attack in Israel by Palestinian militants who had crossed Israel's southern border.[24] Egyptians were predictably enraged. More recently, an August 2012 militant attack killed 16 Sinai-based Egyptian border guards and prompted a significant Egyptian security sweep across the Sinai, reportedly with cautious approval from Israel.[25]

In light of this increasing threat, it is possible to imagine a scenario in which Israel could conduct military operations in the Sinai against militants.[26] The United States should recognize that the Egyptian government has little control over the Sinai, with its complex networks of Bedouin, smugglers, and an unknown number of militants.[27] It should, nonetheless, press Egypt to do more to counter smuggling and lawlessness in the area. The United States should also work with both Egypt and Israel to highlight the risks of conflict, and press each state to put in place more robust crisis management mechanisms to prevent tactical skirmishes from escalating. Specifically, the United States should be clear with Egypt that U.S. assistance and advocacy depend on Egypt's maintaining its peace with Israel. It should be clear with Israel that the strategic ill effects of a unilateral, uncoordinated Israeli military incursion into the Sinai would almost certainly outweigh whatever tactical successes it may achieve.

The United States should also encourage the SCAF to change the biennial joint BRIGHT STAR exercise to focus more on the capabilities needed to enhance Sinai security. These capabilities could include counter-smuggling, intelligence, surveillance and reconnaissance (ISR), and counter-terrorism.[28] U.S. and Egyptian law enforcement personnel should also participate. Because the 1979 Israel-Egypt peace treaty requires Egyptian demilitarization of the Sinai Peninsula, Egyptian internal security personnel will likely constitute any new Sinai security force in practice.[29] Indeed, the Egyptian security sweep in the Sinai following the August 2012 attack on Egyptian border guards included joint Egyptian army and police patrols.[30] The United States should also encourage the SCAF to use its $1.3 billion in U.S. foreign military financing to purchase arms and platforms for Sinai security. The SCAF may resist refocusing BRIGHT STAR and its arms purchases, but the United States and its partners might illustrate linkages between militants crossing the Sinai and threats to Egypt's core economic interests, including the Suez Canal and its tourism industry.[31]

Conclusion

The stakes for the United States and the international community in Egypt's transition are high and the outcomes still uncertain. In order to help Egypt develop a coherent vision for its future and implement the necessary political, economic, and security reforms, the United States must do everything in its power to help Egypt's leaders chart and navigate a responsible, transparent, inclusive, and sustainable transition path. In so doing, the United States will have to wrestle with several vexing policy dilemmas, including how best to support the development of Egypt's civil society, political parties, and democratic institutions without provoking a nationalist backlash; working with the IMF to determine how best to incentivize painful and unpopular economic reforms in the face of entrenched political interests, without creating instability that could stall political reform; and how best to condition U.S. security and economic assistance on political reform and Egypt's adherence to its international obligations, particularly the Camp David Accords.

The United States must be realistic about the limits of its leverage with Egypt, as the Egyptian people have the pen in writing the next chapter of their history. That said, U.S. leadership still matters in this critical region, and the United States must also seek every opportunity to increase and use what leverage it has wisely. The coming months are critical for Egypt's democratic transition, for its economy, for the U.S. relationship with a new Egypt, and ultimately for the stability and future of the broader Middle East.

Michèle Flournoy recently joined the Boston Consulting Group as a Senior Advisor. From 2009 to 2012, she served as Under Secretary of Defense for Policy, the principal adviser to the Secretary of Defense on national security and defense policy, oversight of military plans and operations, and in National Security Council deliberations. Ms. Flournoy also co-led President Obama's transition team at DoD. In January 2007, Ms. Flournoy co-founded the Center for a New American Security (CNAS), a non-partisan think tank dedicated to developing strong, pragmatic and principled national security policies, and served as CNAS' President. Previously, she was senior adviser at the Center for Strategic and International Studies and a distinguished research professor at the Institute for National Strategic Studies at the National Defense University (NDU). In the mid-1990s, she was Principal Deputy Assistant Secretary of Defense for Strategy and Threat Reduction. She received the DoD Medal for Distinguished Public Service in 1998, 2011, and 2012, the CJCS Joint Distinguished Civilian Service Award in 2000 and 2012, and the Secretary of Defense Medal for Outstanding Public Service in 1996. Ms. Flournoy serves on the Defense Policy Board, the DCIA's External Advisory Board, and the Board of Directors of CNAS and the Atlantic Council. She is also a Senior Fellow at Harvard's Belfer Center and a member of the Aspen Strategy Group and the Council on Foreign Relations. She earned a B.A. from Harvard University and an M.Litt. in International Relations from Balliol College, Oxford University.

Melissa Dalton is a Visiting Fellow at the Center for a New American Security. Ms. Dalton's research focuses on U.S. strategy in an evolving Middle East region. Ms. Dalton is a Foreign Affairs Specialist in the Office of the Secretary of Defense (OSD). She has served in several positions in OSD-Policy, including as the Lebanon and Syria Country Director from 2007-2010, as a policy advisor to the Commander, International Security Assistance Force in Kabul, Afghanistan in 2010, and as the Special Assistant to the Under Secretary of Defense for Policy from 2010-2012. Prior to her work in OSD-Policy, Ms. Dalton was a Middle East analyst at the Defense Intelligence Agency from 2003-2005. She studied Arabic and taught English in Damascus, Syria in 2006. Ms. Dalton holds a M.A. in International Relations from the Johns Hopkins University School of Advanced International Studies. She earned a B.A. in Foreign Affairs from the University of Virginia.

[1] Matt Bradley, "Egyptians Shift Views of the U.S.," *The Wall Street Journal*, June 29, 2012.

[2] Pamela Falk, "Egypt Will Stand by Its Pacts with Israel," CBS News, July 9, 2012, http://www.cbsnews.com/8301-503543_162-57469086-503543/egypt-will-stand-by-its-pacts-with-israel-says-new-u.n-ambassador/.

[3] Jeremy M. Sharp, "Egypt: Transition under Military Rule," Congressional Research Service, June 21,2012.

[4] Jeremy M. Sharp, "Egypt-United States Relations," Congressional Research Service Issue Brief for Congress, June 15, 2005, 4.

[5] Ibid.

[6] "Lost in Transition: The World According to Egypt's SCAF," Middle East/North Africa Report No 121, (International Crisis Group, April 24, 2012), http://www.crisisgroup.org/en/regions/middle-east-north-africa/egypt-syria-lebanon/egypt/121-lost-in-transition-the-world-according-to-egypts-scaf.aspx.

[7] Bruce Jentleson, Andrew Exum, Melissa Dalton, and J. Dana Stuster, "Strategic Adaptation: Toward a New U.S. Policy in the Middle East," Center for a New American Security, June 2012, http://www.cnas.org/strategicadaptation.

[8] Ahmed Morsy, "Egypt's NGO Crisis: Political Theater Preventing Democratic Progress," The Atlantic Council, March 8, 2012, http://www.acus.org/egyptsource/egypt%E2%80%99s-ngo-crisis-political-theater-preventing-democratic-progress.

[9] Jentleson et al, "Strategic Adaptation."

[10] An amateur film, made in the United States and posted on the Internet, depicted the Prophet Muhammad in a negative light and prompted Egyptian protesters to storm the U.S. Embassy in Cairo on September 11, 2012. See Tamim Elyan and Omar al-Mosmari, "U.S. Cairo, Libya Missions Attacked, U.S. Official Reported Dead," Reuters, September 12, 2012, http://uk.reuters.com/article/2012/09/12/uk-egypt-usa-protest-idUKBRE88A12V20120912.

[11] Jentleson et al, "Strategic Adaptation."

[12] Sinan Ülgen, "Supporting Arab Economies in Transition," *International Economic Bulletin*, Carnegie Endowment for International Peace, July 5, 2012, http://carnegieendowment.org/2012/07/05/supporting-arab-economies-in-transition/ck6p.

[13] The United States is reportedly finalizing agreement on $1 billion in debt relief for Egypt. See Matt Spetalnik, "U.S. Nears Deal for $1 Billion in Debt Relief," Reuters, September 4, 2012, http://www.reuters.com/article/2012/09/04/us-egypt-usa-idUSBRE88301A20120904.

[14] Zeinab Abul-Magd, "The Egyptian Republic of Retired Generals," Middle East Channel, ForeignPolicy.com, May 8, 2012, http://mideast.foreignpolicy.com/posts/2012/05/08/the_egyptian_republic_of_retired_generals and Ahmed Morsy, "Is Egypt Turning Islamist?" Atlantic Council Egypt Source, December 7, 2011, http://www.acus.org/egyptsource/egypt-turning-islamist.

[15] Nathan J. Brown, "When Victory Becomes an Option: Egypt's Muslim Brotherhood Confronts Success," Carnegie Endowment for International Peace, January 2012. http://carnegieendowment.org/2012/01/10/when-victory-becomes-option-egypt-s-muslim-brotherhood-confronts-success/8y4l. The Brotherhood's Freedom and Justice Party's platform listed on their English Web site places a strong emphasis on privatization, with preference given to Egyptian investors over foreign investors; creating a more law-abiding business environment that is more inviting to foreign investment; reassessments of tax, social security and subsidy policies; and the elimination of usury in line with Islamic financial practice. "FJP 2011 Program on Economic Development," Freedom & Justice Party, December 4, 2011, http://www.fjponline.com/article.php?id=188.

[16] "Morsi Raises Government Salaries," *Daily News Egypt*, July 3, 2012, http://thedailynewsegypt.com/2012/07/03/morsi-raises-government-salaries/.

[17] Adam Schreck, "IMF Still Waiting on Egyptian Economic Plan," Associated Press, May 2, 2012, http://finance.yahoo.com/news/imf-still-waiting-egyptian-economic-094741727.html.

[18] President Morsi's government is reportedly appealing to Egypt's Parliament to approve a $4.8 billion loan from the IMF to stave off a balance of payments crisis. See Carina Kamel, "Egypt Finance Minister Appeals to Parliament Members to Accept IMF Loan," *Al-Arabiya News*, September 4, 2012, http://english.alarabiya.net/articles/2012/09/04/235934.html.

[19] Danya Greenfeld and Rosa Balfour, "Arab Awakening: Are the US and EU Missing the Challenge?" Atlantic Council, June 2012, http://www.acus.org/publication/arab-awakening-are-us-and-eu-missing-challenge.

[20] The SCAF is entrenched in Egypt's "deep state." The practice of retired generals passing into high-level civilian jobs in government or industry began with Nasser and has fluctuated over time. Since Mubarak's ouster, the practice has accelerated. Particularly concentrated pockets of retired officers in civilian jobs include areas necessary to tourism and trade (Alexandria, Suez, commercial shipping ventures) and the oil and gas industries. Retired officers also serve prominently in government oversight bodies from the

head of the Supreme Presidential Elections Commission to the Supreme Constitutional Court. The same Supreme Constitutional Court is locked in a back and forth power jockeying with President Morsi over who has the authority to convene parliament. The Court is popularly perceived as an arm of or at least ally of the SCAF in its efforts to limit the Muslim Brotherhood's role in the new Parliament. See Zeinab Abul-Magd, "The Egyptian Republic of Retired Generals," Middle East Channel, ForeignPolicy.com, May 8, 2012, http://mideast.foreignpolicy.com/posts/2012/05/08/the_egyptian_republic_of_retired_generals.

[21] Shadi Hamid, "The Real Reason the U.S. Should Consider Cutting Military Aid to Egypt," *The Atlantic*, July 2, 2012, http://www.theatlantic.com/international/archive/2012/07/the-real-reason-the-us-should-consider-cutting-military-aid-to-egypt/259302/.

[22] Bruce Riedel, "Don't Leverage Egypt's Aid," *The National Interest*, June 21, 2012, http://nationalinterest.org/commentary/dont-leverage-egypts-aid-7100.

[23] "Egypt's Sinai Turning into a Wild West," *Jerusalem Post*, April 24, 2012, www.jpost.com/MiddleEast/Article.aspx?id=267358.

[24] Phoebe Greenwood, "Egyptian Border Guards Killed during Israeli Raid on Militants," *The Telegraph*, August 19, 2011, http://www.telegraph.co.uk/news/worldnews/middleeast/israel/8710372/Egyptian-border-guards-killed-during-Israeli-raid-on-militants.html.

[25] Reuters, "Egypt Identifies Suspects in Sinai Killings," September 6, 2012, http://www.reuters.com/article/2012/09/06/us-egypt-sinai-suspects-idUSBRE8850KG20120906.

[26] Steven A. Cook, "The Wages of the Sinai," From the Potomac to the Euphrates blog on CFR.org, May 3, 2012, http://blogs.cfr.org/cook/2012/05/03/the-wages-of-the-sinai/.

[27] "Egypt's Sinai Question," Middle East/North Africa Report No. 61 (International Crisis Group, January 30, 2007), http://www.crisisgroup.org/en/regions/middle-east-north-africa/egypt-syria-lebanon/egypt/061-egypts-sinai-question.aspx.

[28] The last BRIGHT STAR exercise was held in October 2009. The 2011 exercise was postponed due to Egypt's tumultuous internal situation. "Exercise BRIGHT STAR 09/10, U.S. Central Command, http://www.centcom.mil/brightstar/. AFP, "Egypt, U.S. Delay 'BRIGHT STAR' Exercise," Defense News, August 17, 2011, http://www.defensenews.com/article/20110817/DEFSECT04/108170301/Egypt-U-S-Delay-Bright-Star-Exercise.

[29] Due to the January 2011 uprising in Egypt, Israel agreed to Egypt's deployment of 800 troops to the Sinai as an internal security measure in early 2011. Associated Press, "Israel Allows Egypt Troops in Sinai for First Time Since 1979 Peace Treaty," *Haaretz*, January 31, 2011, http://www.haaretz.com/news/diplomacy-defense/israel-allows-egypt-troops-in-sinai-for-first-time-since-1979-peace-treaty-1.340405.

[30] Reuters, "Egypt Identifies Suspects in Sinai Killings."

[31] Tamim Elyan, "In Sinai Militant Islam Flourishes - Quietly," Reuters, April 1, 2012, http://www.reuters.com/article/2012/04/01/us-egypt-sinai-idUSBRE83006120120401.

Part 4

"Many people have argued that before making this fateful decision [on Iraq], U.S. policymakers should have stepped back and conducted one last searching examination of possible alternative courses of action. If that is the case, then it is now time—and perhaps almost past time—to make such an effort with respect to Iran..."

—STEPHEN J. HADLEY

Iran Options Outline

Stephen J. Hadley
Principal
RiceHadleyGates LLC

The purpose of this outline is to set out the range of the most plausible approaches to the confrontation between the international community and the current Iranian regime over its nuclear program, a program that virtually the entire international community believes is a vehicle for achieving an advanced nuclear weapon capability, if not a nuclear bomb itself.

Why Conduct a Review of Iran Options Now?

A review of Iran options is necessary because of the American experience in Iraq. U.S. military action there was not, as many suggest, either a war of choice or a war of preemption. It was, rather, a war of last resort. After 12 years of diplomacy, 17 UN Security Council resolutions, increasingly targeted economic sanctions, multiple international inspection efforts, no-fly zones over both northern and southern Iraq, the selective use of U.S. military force in 1998, and Saddam Hussein's rejection of a final opportunity to leave Iraq and avoid war, the United States and the international community were out of options. The choice was either to capitulate to Saddam Hussein's defiance of the demands of the international community or to make good on the "serious consequences" promised for such defiance. The United States and its international partners on Iraq chose the latter course.

Many people have argued that before making this fateful decision, U.S. policymakers should have stepped back and conducted one last searching examination of possible alternative courses of action. If that is the case, then it is now time—and perhaps almost past time—to make such an effort with respect to Iran, for there is a better than even chance that sometime in 2013 the United States and its international partners will find themselves similarly out of options and face the choice of either military action against Iran or accepting an Iran with a clear path to a nuclear weapon. If there are alternatives to these two grim choices, now is the time to find them and to think through carefully the military options available.

Problems Posed by the Iranian Regime

The international community in general, and the United States in particular, have a broad set of grievances and concerns about the behavior of the Iranian regime. They would like to see an Iran that:

(1)   Does not pursue weapons of mass destruction of any kind;

(2)   Does not support terrorists;

(3)   Does not intervene in the internal affairs of its neighbors;

(4)   Respects rather than infringes upon the freedom and human rights of the Iranian people; and

(5)   Respects the right of the Iranian people to chart their own future through democratic means.

The United States needs a comprehensive strategy for seeking to advance these objectives. This paper, however, will focus primarily on options (described below) for dealing with the immediate confrontation over the Iranian regime's nuclear program. I say "primarily" for two reasons. First, because among the considerations in evaluating each of the options described below will be the extent to which it could contribute to or detract from the achievement of these broader objectives. Second, because there are measures the United States and the international community are to some extent already taking—and could significantly expand—that would both enhance the prospects of resolving successfully the confrontation over the nuclear issue and, at the same time, make progress on these other issues more likely.

These measures include:

(1)   Strengthening our diplomatic, economic, security, and military ties with friends and allies in the region;

(2)   Accelerating the fall and departure of the Assad regime and its replacement with a cross-sectarian regime that can both unify Syria and be less friendly with and beholden to the Iranian regime;

(3)   Weakening, to the extent we can, the ties between the Iranian regime and China and Russia;

(4)   Pushing back hard against any Iranian attempts to expand its influence in the Gulf, Afghanistan, or Iraq and its support of international terror and terrorists;

(5) Continuing sanctions that have set back the Iranian economy and government revenues; and

(6) Making clear to the Iranian people that the United States and the international community have no quarrel with them, that their current economic hardships and international isolation are the result of the policies of the Iranian regime, that a change in those policies will bring dramatic benefits, and should that occur, the whole world will welcome Iran with open arms as a respected member of the international community.

Options for Dealing with the Iranian Nuclear Program

The choices below should properly be viewed as a set of "nested" options that could lead sequentially from one to another. For this reason, they should be seen not in two dimensions, with the task being to pick one of the options from among the list, but in three dimensions as a family of options through which the policy of the United States and the international community could move over time, depending on the success or failure of prior options. These will, in turn, depend heavily on the choices made by the Iranian regime.

Option 1: Seek an Interim "Stop the Clock" Agreement

The United States and the international community would seek to negotiate with the Iranian regime an interim agreement that would seek to prevent further Iranian progress toward a nuclear weapon capability (and to freeze at current levels the risk of a covert "breakout" to a nuclear weapon) in order to buy time for the longer negotiation that would be required to reach a permanent settlement of the nuclear issue. Neither side would be asked to concede its current position on the core of the nuclear issue (i.e. uranium enrichment). Iranian enrichment at the 3.5 percent level would continue (and Iran would retain its stockpile of this low enriched uranium), and the existing sanctions regime would remain in place. Because of these unresolved issues, both sides would have an incentive to continue negotiations to reach a more permanent agreement.

The basic bargain underlying the interim agreement could look something like this:

(1) Iran would agree under intrusive International Atomic Energy Agency (IAEA) inspection and verification procedures to (a) cease any enrichment beyond 3.5

percent (i.e. cease its 20 percent enrichment and ship its 20 percent stockpile out of the country), and cease further expansion of operations at its deep underground Fordow enrichment plant (whether by increasing the number or upgrading the quality of the centrifuges), and (b) commit that during the period of the interim agreement it would not take any further steps toward developing a nuclear weapon capability, so long as the United States and the international community continued to abide by the agreement.

(2)   The United States and the international community would agree to provide (a) fuel for the Iranian medical research reactor (the Tehran Research Reactor or "TRR"), medical isotopes, and civilian aircraft spare parts, and (b) commit not to impose any additional sanctions (although they would be free to continue implementation and enforcement of existing sanctions) during the period of the interim agreement so long as Iran continued to abide by its terms (including that the Iranian regime would not take any further steps towards developing a nuclear weapon capability).

According to press reports, the Obama administration has already proposed something along these lines that the Iranian regime has so far flatly rejected. While willing to suspend enrichment at the 20 percent level (and perhaps ship its current 20 percent enriched inventory out of the country), the regime's negotiators flatly rejected anything having to do with Fordow and insisted on Iran's right to enrich at the 3.5 percent level. In return, the Iranian negotiators wanted a complete lifting of sanctions and a long list of other demands.

While the Iranian negotiators may come around, especially as additional U.S. sanctions on the Iranian Central Bank and the EU Iranian oil embargo/insurance ban that became effective July 1 begin to bite, the outlook is not bright.

Potential Benefits of Option 1:

- Would freeze in place on an interim basis the most obvious avenues for enhancing Iranian nuclear weapon capability and entering the "zone of immunity" of concern to Israeli officials (i.e. where Israel's ability to stop the program by military means becomes in doubt);

- Is nonetheless a fairly minimalist agreement of a confidence-building nature intended to build trust and lead to a negotiated resolution of the overall confrontation over the nuclear issue; and

- Buys time for sanctions and other pressure measures to have effect, giving the Iranian regime an incentive to move beyond an interim "stop the clock" agreement to negotiate a permanent resolution.

Potential Costs of Option 1:

- The "minimalism" that is its primary attraction is also its limitation. It leaves centrifuges in operation at both Natanz and Fordow, which arguably allows the Iranian regime to continue to develop a nuclear weapon capability (i.e. by improving centrifuge operations and by developing more advanced centrifuge designs). It also provides time for Iran to strengthen the defenses around its nuclear infrastructure and make it more immune to military action (e.g. by moving underground).

- This option is contingent upon Iranian authorities allowing—and the IAEA imposing—intrusive inspection and verification measures to ensure Iranian compliance with the interim agreement.

- Israel could view the interim agreement as insufficient in meeting its security interests, potentially leading to an Israeli military strike that dissolves the unity of the international sanctions effort and moves Iran to an explicit decision to develop a nuclear weapon.

Option 2: Seek an Interim "Medium for Medium" or "More for More" Agreement

This option could be attractive in itself or as a place to move in the event that the more minimalist "Stop the Clock" option (Option 1 above) does not succeed, especially if U.S. officials conclude that Option 1 simply does not offer the Iranian regime enough to make that option attractive. Under Option 2, the United States and the international community would seek to negotiate an interim agreement that requires greater concessions from both sides but still stops short of a final agreement, and still does not force either side to concede on the core issue of Iran's right to enrich.

The basic bargain could look something like this:

(1) In addition to providing a) fuel for the Iranian medical research reactor (TRR), medical isotopes, and civilian aircraft spare parts, and b) committing not to impose any additional sanctions, the United States and the international community would agree to alleviate some of the existing sanctions as Iran comes into compliance with its obligations under the interim agreement (e.g. a renewable 90 day / 180 day suspension of the EU Iranian oil embargo / insurance ban).

(2) In addition to agreeing under intrusive IAEA inspection and verification procedures to cease enrichment beyond 3.5 percent (i.e., ceasing its 20 percent enrichment and shipping its 20 percent stockpile out of the country) and to cease further expansion of operations at its Fordow enrichment plant (whether by increasing the number or upgrading the quality of the centrifuges), Iran would be required to ship its 3.5 percent enriched stockpile out of the country (maintaining a stockpile in the country of no more than approximately 800 kg of 3.5 percent enriched uranium, arguably less than that required to make a nuclear weapon if further enriched to the 90 percent plus level), although Iran's enrichment at the 3.5 percent level could continue.

If additional elements were required to get an agreement on a "more for more" basis, they could be drawn from the list of elements – from both sides contained in the description of the Final Agreement option (Option 3) below.

Potential Benefits of Option 2:

- Would freeze in place on an interim basis the most obvious avenues for enhancing Iran's nuclear weapon capability and for entering the "zone of immunity" of concern to Israeli officials (i.e. where Israel's ability to stop the program by military means becomes in doubt);

- Would reduce Iran's stockpile of 3.5 percent enriched uranium to low levels and increase the presence of international inspectors, making it more difficult for Iran covertly to break out and pursue a nuclear weapon; and

- Could build trust and confidence while still leaving enough unresolved issues to give the two sides an incentive to seek a permanent negotiated resolution to the confrontation over the nuclear issue.

Potential Costs of Option 2:

- Leaves centrifuges in operation at both Natanz and Fordow, which arguably allows the Iranian regime to continue to develop its nuclear weapon capability (i.e., by improving centrifuge operations and by developing more advanced centrifuge designs) and provides time for Iran to strengthen the defenses around its nuclear infrastructure and make it more immune to military action (e.g., by moving underground);

- May take too long to negotiate (leaving Iran free in the interim to move forward with its nuclear program) and would in any event be contingent upon Iranian authorities allowing—and the IAEA imposing—intrusive inspection and verification measures to ensure Iranian compliance with the interim agreement; and

- Could make it much harder for the United States and the International community to increase the pressure or to shift to one of the other options described below, if the Iranian negotiators were to stall on moving beyond an interim agreement.

If an interim agreement is reached, a deadline for finalizing a permanent agreement or an expiration date might be included in the interim agreement to try to force negotiations to a conclusion, but such devices are difficult to enforce in the face of pressure to continue negotiations. To have any chance of having its intended effect, the United States and the international community would have to commit in advance to imposing new sanctions if the deadline is missed, recognizing that this would risk being used by the Iranian regime as a pretext for further movement toward a nuclear weapon capability.

Option 3: Seek a Final Agreement that Resolves the Nuclear Issue

Achievement of an interim agreement under Option 1 or 2 buys time for an effort to achieve a broader, final agreement that resolves the nuclear issue. Alternatively, the effort to achieve either interim agreement described above may fail for reasons that do not necessarily discredit seeking a negotiated resolution, for example, because neither interim agreement offers enough benefit to either side to be worth the effort. In that event, U.S. and international negotiators might move to a "big for big" type of approach and seek an agreed final resolution of the nuclear issue in a single negotiating step. The problem, of course, is that a final agreement is likely to take substantial time to negotiate, and without an interim agreement in place, the Iranian regime would be free to move forward with its nuclear program during the period of negotiations.

If a final agreement could be achieved, there would be enormous pressure from substantial parts of the international community to "declare victory," unwind the sanctions and other elements of the existing "pressure" effort, and resume normal relations with the Iranian regime. Should the Iranian regime then begin "eating around the edges" of the agreement—testing the international community, perhaps as part of readying a "creep out" strategy to develop nuclear weapon capability covertly or even as part of an overt "sprint to the bomb"—it may be very difficult to reestablish the existing sanctions and pressure regime in anything like a reasonable period of time. For this reason, part of any final agreement "resolving" the nuclear issue needs to be a prior agreement announced publicly and enshrined in a U.N. Security Council resolution, if possible, that both automatically reestablishes the existing sanctions/pressure regime and authorizes "all means necessary," including military force, in the event of any substantial violation of the agreement by Iran.

The sticking point, of course, will be who decides that a substantial violation has occurred. While risky, the best approach could be to develop a list of substantial violations (e.g., resuming nuclear weaponization research or other weaponization activities, enriching over 3.5 percent, failing to cooperate with the IAEA or throwing out its inspectors, opening any new enrichment or reprocessing facility, discovery of a covert nuclear facility) and include them in a U.N. Security Council resolution (although this virtually invites Iranian violations just short of this list). The application of the "all means necessary" clause must be automatic, not dependent upon either further IAEA action or another U.N. Security Council vote.

The basic bargain underlying the final agreement could draw substantially from this list of elements:

(1) The United States and the international community could agree that as the Iranian regime implements its responsibilities under this agreement and thereby reestablishes the confidence of the international community in its compliance with its Nuclear Nonproliferation Treaty obligations in a phased implementation process to be developed jointly by the two sides, matching "action for action," the United States and the international community would:

   a) Provide Iran diplomatic, financial, and engineering support in developing a truly peaceful civilian nuclear power program;

   b) Undertake a number of steps to resuscitate, revitalize, and reform the Iranian economy, including investment in Iran's dilapidated oil and gas infrastructure, assistance with food and oil subsidy reform, and technology transfers and financial support for Iran's struggling industrial sectors;

   c) Encourage businesses, universities, and charitable foundations to establish technical centers in Iran to train Iranian youth in the skills of the 21st century;

d) Establish robust exchange programs with Iranian students, business leaders, university administrators, and civil society leaders;

e) Commit to no new nuclear-related economic sanctions and gradually reduce existing nuclear-related sanctions as Iran meets its obligations under the phased implementation plan developed by the two sides;

f) Reestablish diplomatic relations over time;

g) Include Iran as a full partner in an international nuclear reprocessing and enrichment center located in the region but not in Iran (and without giving Iranian participants access to critical technology);

[h) Consider adding: After Iranian acceptance and implementation of the IAEA Additional Protocol and under full and intrusive IAEA inspection and monitoring, accept limited nuclear enrichment up to 3.5 percent at Natanz provided that excess 3.5 percent uranium beyond its own domestic needs is shipped out of the country. At no time, therefore, would Iran have more than 800 kg of 3.5 percent enriched uranium in its possession outside of nuclear fuel rods in Iranian domestic nuclear power reactors, and then only if under full IAEA monitoring and verification.]

(2) Consistent with the phased implementation process, Iran could agree that it would:

a) Forego nuclear reprocessing, disband all its existing facilities for that purpose, and agree not to construct, maintain, or operate any such facilities;

b) Forego enriching uranium beyond 3.5 percent (e.g. 20 percent) and give over to the IAEA all stocks of such enriched uranium;

c) Shut down and dismantle its uranium enrichment facility at Fordow [and Natanz, if subparagraph f is not added] and agree not to construct, maintain, or operate any unauthorized uranium enrichment facility overtly or covertly;

d) Accept and implement the IAEA additional protocol and full IAEA inspection and monitoring of all its nuclear activities;

e) Resolve past issues with the IAEA regarding its nuclear activities and agree that it will at no time undertake further nuclear weaponization research or other weaponization activities;

[f) Consider adding: After Iranian acceptance and implementation of the IAEA Additional Protocol and under full and intrusive IAEA inspection and monitoring, accept limited nuclear enrichment up to 3.5 percent at Natanz provided that excess 3.5 percent uranium beyond its domestic needs is shipped out of the country. At no time, therefore, would Iran have more than 800 kg of 3.5% enriched uranium in its possession outside of nuclear fuel rods in Iranian domestic nuclear power reactors and then only if under full IAEA monitoring and verification.

[g) If subparagraph f) is included: Agree to end its support for terrorist activities, cooperate with the international community in the struggle against terror, and respect the sovereignty and territorial integrity of its neighbors.]

Potential Benefits of Option 3:

- Would resolve the nuclear issue on terms acceptable to both sides and provide an effective mechanism for enforcement of the agreement;

- Would establish a framework of relations that could advance progress in dealing with the other grievances and concerns the United States and the international community have with the behavior of the Iranian regime, as well as the regime's concerns; and

- Would open opportunities for greater interaction between the international community and the Iranian people and other constituencies within Iran, which could enhance processes of political, social, and economic pluralism and openness in Iran.

Potential Costs of Option 3:

- Would dramatically draw down the leverage and incentives the United States and the international community have for changing the behavior of the Iranian regime, leaving little capital available for reaching agreements and understandings on the remaining grievances and concerns about the behavior of the Iranian regime;

- Acceptance of any uranium enrichment on Iranian soil could allow Iran to perfect its enrichment capability and would be seen by many as an abject capitulation by the United States and the international community (which have made suspension of enrichment until confidence has been restored in Iranian intentions, if not the total elimination of any Iranian enrichment and reprocessing capability, the touchstone of their position in the nuclear confrontation with Iran); and

- Would enhance the legitimacy of the Iranian regime and would not satisfy those who believe the problems with Iran stem from the nature of the current regime, and will not ultimately be resolved until that regime is changed.

Option 4: Establish De Facto Status Quo

This option aims to establish a de facto status quo acceptable to the United States and the international community based on a set of red lines. The purpose would be effectively to freeze the Iranian nuclear weapon program at its current level, preventing the expansion of Iranian capability to produce a nuclear weapon but without really rolling back the program. Under this approach, the United States and the international community would still have sufficient time to detect and respond to an Iranian covert or overt effort to "make a run for the bomb."

This approach could be adopted as an alternative to a negotiated settlement (especially if one believes the Iranian regime is too wedded to its hostility and opposition to the United States to accept any negotiated arrangement) or if negotiations break down for one reason or another. In either event, especially if the United States and the international community are unwilling to use military force, this Option 4 or Option 5 below (Long-Term Isolation and Pressure) would become the principal remaining options.

To be effective, the United States and the international community would have to make clear and credible that they would take action against the Iranian nuclear program if these red lines were crossed, either additional sanctions (described in Option 5 below) or military action (described in Option 6 or 7 below) or both. The approach could be the United States and the international community unilaterally declaring red lines about Iranian activity backed by the threat of force, or mutual, with either the United States and the international community declaring their willingness to respect presumed Iranian red lines or with Iran declaring its own red lines about U.S. and international community actions. The arrangement could be private between the two sides, public, or a mix of both (the most likely approach).

(1) For the United States and the international community, the red lines would be similar to the "substantial violations" described in Option 3 above, but with the addition of constraints on Fordow:

- Resuming nuclear weaponization research or other weaponization activities;

- Enriching over 3.5 percent;

- Failing to cooperate with the IAEA or throwing out its inspectors;

- Opening any new enrichment or reprocessing facility;

- Discovering a covert nuclear facility; or

- Iran's failing to freeze, if not cease, activity at Fordow.

(2) Any red lines declared by Iran are liable to be extreme, and the question will be whether the regime would accept a more limited set of red lines either explicitly or implicitly (i.e. by tacitly accepting a U.S./international community statement of the Iranian red lines they would be willing to respect). Such red lines might be:

- No new U.N. Security Council resolutions on the Iranian nuclear program;

- No new nuclear-related sanctions by the United States or any other member of the international community;

- Cessation of any clandestine actions within Iran; or

- The IAEA's dropping further efforts to resolve questions about past Iranian activities.

Even this list would likely be daunting for the United States and the international community to accept. To put into operation a mutual approach (with red lines on both sides), there might have to be secret contacts between representatives of the P5+1 and elements of the Iranian regime (such as, for example, a U.S. representative meeting clandestinely with Islamic Revolutionary Guard Corps (IRGC) head, Ghasem Soleimani).

This de facto status quo approach is likely to work (and be acceptable to the United States and the international community) only if Iran would accept very intrusive IAEA inspections and verification as part of the arrangement. This option would involve tacit acceptance of Iranian enrichment at 3.5 percent, but would try to freeze the Iranian nuclear program at its current level, short of a nuclear weapon capability.

In order to pressure Iran to accept this approach, the United States and the international community could speak more publicly about the additional sanctions they are capable of levying. These could include:

- Targeting front companies in Europe and Asia that supply Iran with dual-use components for the nuclear program;

- Targeting banks that process any financial transactions with the National Iranian Tanker Company;

- Targeting certain petroleum resource development joint ventures outside of Iran in which the Iranian government is a substantial partner or investor; and

- Blacklisting Iran's entire energy sector and labeling Iran a "zone of proliferation concern" to prohibit international businesses from dealing with Iran's petroleum sector.

Under this approach, the existing sanctions would remain in place to keep pressure on the regime to respect the red lines, but the United States and the international community would almost certainly have to give up the prospect of increasing those sanctions.

This option could also come into play after a use of military force, particularly a limited military strike under Option 6 below, which would have somewhat restored deterrence and made the U.S. setting of red lines more credible and hence more likely to be respected by the Iranian regime.

Potential Benefits of Option 4:

- Seeks to freeze the Iranian nuclear program at its current level short of achieving a nuclear weapon capability while allowing enough time to detect and take action if Iran were overtly or covertly to make a run to develop or obtain a nuclear bomb;

- Allows both the U.S. and the Iranian regime to bypass the domestic political costs associated with a formal negotiation process and to avoid the downsides of military action;

- Puts to the test the Iranian regime's claim that it does not seek a nuclear weapon, while providing the Israelis and the rest of the world with declared red lines as to when the United States would be willing to initiate military action against Iran.

Potential Costs of Option 4:

- If the de facto status quo arrangement does not include a freeze—if not a cessation—of activity at Fordow, it will not stop Iran from entering into the "zone of immunity" about which the Israelis have been so concerned.

- Because it is not the result of a formal negotiating track, it would be difficult under this approach to obtain U.N. Security Council authorization for military force in the event of Iranian violation of any of the red lines, and the United States would have to contemplate using military force without such authorization.

- This would leave Iran free to take action just short of U.S. red lines that could still contribute to improving its nuclear weapon capability (i.e., moral hazard).

Option 5: Intensify Long-Term Isolation and Pressure

Under this option, the United States and the international community would undertake a long-term isolation and pressure strategy toward the Iranian regime. The goal of this effort would be to get the Iranian regime either unilaterally to abandon its effort to obtain nuclear weapon capability (and verifiably dismantle the instruments of that effort, such as reprocessing and enrichment) or to engage in serious negotiations to resolve the dispute.

This option could be attractive if the United States and the international community were to decide that the Iranian regime is simply unable or unwilling to enter into a negotiated settlement, or in the event of an actual breakdown of negotiations. In either case, this approach could be viewed as an alternative to military action under Option 6 or 7 below (and an alternative to the de facto status quo approach of Option 4). This option could also be adopted after the execution of a military strike under Option 6 or 7, especially if such a strike did not result in a unilateral Iranian cessation of its nuclear efforts or the start of productive negotiations.

Under this approach, the existing vehicles of pressure and sanctions would have to be maintained and strengthened. Potential additional measures could include:

- Targeting front companies in Europe and Asia that supply Iran with dual-use components for the nuclear program;

- Targeting banks that process financial transactions with the National Iranian Tanker Company;

- Targeting certain petroleum resource development joint ventures outside Iran if the Iranian government is a substantial partner or investor;

- Blacklisting Iran's entire energy sector and labeling Iran a "zone of proliferation concern" to prohibit completely international businesses from dealing with Iran's petroleum sector;

- Joint military exercises with Gulf and regional allies;

- Expanded U.S. military assistance and cooperation with regional states; and

- Greater emphasis on interdicting arms and funding flowing to and from Iran.

At the same time, the United States and the international community would need to come up with creative ways to engage broader elements within the regime and Iranian society as a whole (including Iranian leaders in business, civil society, and the arts) in order to encourage rethinking the regime's policies both within the regime and the broader public.

It is hoped all these measures would cause debate, division, and even dissent within the Iranian regime and lead over time either to a change in its nuclear weapon policy or a transformation of the regime itself (which might aid resolution not only of the nuclear issue but also the other grievances and concerns the United States and the international community have with the current regime).

The time horizon for this effort, however, could be a long one, comparable potentially to the long struggle to isolate, pressure, and transform the Soviet Union in the Cold War period. In the interim (even should a favorable outcome ultimately emerge), not only would the regime be proceeding with its nuclear program but the United States and the international community would have to deter, prevent, and manage what are likely to be increasingly aggressive and dangerous efforts by the Iranian regime to "break out of the box" of increasing pressure and isolation. Such actions could include:

- Increasing financial and material support to terrorist organizations;

- Inciting violence through proxy groups in Iraq, Afghanistan, Syria, and Lebanon;

- Destabilizing international oil markets by attempting to close the Strait of Hormuz or taking other active measures to disrupt the flow of oil; and

- Increasing the threat to Israel.

Potential Benefits of Option 5:

- Avoids capitulation to the Iranian pursuit of a nuclear weapon capability;

- Offers the possibility of a positive resolution of the nuclear issue (and potentially other issues as well);

- Could encourage the ultimate transformation of the Iranian regime to one more cooperative with the United States and the international community (and one providing greater benefit to the Iranian people).

Potential Costs of Option 5:

- Would require an enormous U.S. and international commitment that may simply not be sustainable over the long term and may not succeed in any case;

- Would increase the risk of disruptive and dangerous behavior on the part of the Iranian regime, threatening U.S. and international interests in Israel, Lebanon, Iraq, Afghanistan, Syria, the West Bank, and potentially even the U.S. homeland;

- Would likely over time turn the Iranian people against the United States and the international community while the Iranian regime continued to advance its enrichment capability and could lead Iranian leaders to conclude the United States is really seeking regime change, thus prompting them to "go for" a nuclear weapon as a means of trying to guarantee regime survival.

Option 6: Conduct Limited Military Strike (Preferably a Clandestine Strike)

Military options could come under consideration in the event that:

(1) Negotiations break down;

(2) The Iranian regime violates an interim agreement (Option 1 or 2) or a final agreement (Option 3);

(3) If the Iranian regime, even in the absence of an agreement, were to take further steps towards a nuclear weapon capability;

(4) If the Iranian regime were to violate the terms of a de facto status quo agreement (Option 4) crossing U.S. and international community red lines; and/or

(5) As part of a longer-term strategy of putting increasing pressure on the regime to change its behavior (Option 5).

Depending on the circumstances, the objective of military action could be:

(1) To persuade the Iranian regime to return to negotiations;

(2) To induce the Iranian regime to return to compliance with the agreement(s) it has negotiated;

(3) To dissuade or prevent the regime from taking further steps towards a nuclear weapon capability;

(4) To enforce redlines; and/or

(5) To bring about a change over the longer term in the behavior and policies of the Iranian regime.

By its very nature, any military action would raise the stakes in the confrontation over the nuclear issue and risk setting off unforeseen and uncontrollable consequences. The downside of any military action is that it could actually increase the likelihood that the Iranian regime would move further toward a nuclear weapon capability, cause division within the United States on the Iranian issue, and erode international support for curbing Iran's nuclear weapon efforts after the strike. If possible, the result of any military strike should be just the opposite.

Any use of military force must be carefully prepared and undertaken in a context where it is viewed as a reasonable and necessary response to Iranian intransigence or unacceptable behavior. For this reason, it would be preferable if prior to any use of military force it could be established that:

(1) The negotiating track has been pursued to the point where it has clearly failed due to Iranian unreasonableness;

(2) Iran has violated an interim agreement (Option 1 or 2) expressly proscribing further Iranian steps toward developing nuclear weapons capability;

(3) Iran has violated a final agreement (Option 3) and an accompanying U.N. Security Council resolution authorizing "all means necessary" if the Iranian regime commits one of the listed "substantial violations" of the agreement; and/or

(4) Iran has violated a declared U.S./international community red line and thereby moved closer to a nuclear weapon capability.

To best achieve its objectives, any military action:

(1) Should be clearly focused on the nuclear issue and not be perceived as pursuing other objectives (such as regime change by force);

(2) Should limit as much as possible any collateral damage so as not to look like an attack on the Iranian people; and

(3) Should not be clearly attributable, as much as possible, either to the United States or its ally Israel in order to make it harder for the regime to justify publicly a military response, thus reducing the risk of Iranian retaliation and making it harder for the regime to use the attack as a rallying point.

A limited, clandestine, hard-to-attribute military action best meets these criteria. It could be focused on:

(1) Any new facilities or operations undertaken by the Iranian regime that violate any interim or final agreement and/or U.S./international red lines;

(2) The deeply buried enrichment facility at Fordow, but not the more vulnerable enrichment facility at Natanz (which would largely halt Iran's movement into the "zone of immunity" but still signal U.S./international willingness at least to consider limited nuclear enrichment at Natanz);

(3) The enrichment facilities at Fordow and Natanz and the heavy water reactor under construction at Arak (since these are the critical elements on the path to an Iranian nuclear weapon capability); and

(4) A very small number of facilities that provide critical support to these enrichment and reprocessing sites.

A word on "hard to attribute": It is not that a military strike would not be "detected" by the Iranians. Of course it would, and the Iranians would undoubtedly believe the United States or Israel was responsible. But the United States would want to conduct the strike in such a way as to make it as hard as possible for the Iranian regime to establish U.S. responsibility publicly. While U.S. officials would not publicly deny responsibility for the strike, they would not acknowledge it either. They would just refuse to comment. This is what was done by U.S. and Israeli officials with respect to the Israeli strike on the Syrian nuclear reactor in 2007. It allowed Syria's President Assad to decide not to retaliate and it is hoped would in this case make it harder for Iran to justify a major retaliation and give Iranian-supported groups like Hezbollah a reason to reject Iranian entreaties to conduct retaliatory terrorist attacks on U.S. or Israeli targets.

On balance, any resort to military force would be better undertaken by the United States than by Israel.

(1) Leaders of both U.S. political parties have made clear that an Iranian nuclear weapon capability would be unacceptable to United States—that such a capability is not just an Israeli problem that Israel must fix;

(2) The United States has been the leader of the international effort to deal with this problem, and with that leadership role comes the responsibility to take the hard decisions;

(3) The United States has the capability to conduct a military operation, whether overt or clandestine, that is superior to Israel's;

(4) The United States is a much harder target for any Iranian retaliation (and to protect Israel from any Iranian retaliation, the United States could privately inform Iran that Israel was not responsible for the strike, and Iran risks a major U.S. military response for any attack against Israel);

(5) An attack from the United States would likely generate somewhat less of a rally-round-the-flag effect within Iran than an Israeli strike;

(6) Israeli military action—particularly if viewed as defying international efforts to resolve the nuclear confrontation—would result in severe criticism of Israel and its diplomatic isolation; and

(7) A U.S. versus Israeli strike would make it easier to hold the "sanctions coalition" together post-strike.

If Israel refuses to defer to the United States and takes military action on its own, the United States would want to work with Israel to deter or prevent Iranian retaliation against Israel. For the United States to launch its own military action against Iran as part of that deterrence/prevention effort would be a separate and very serious matter, potentially involving the United States in a war with Iran.

The United States could use the prospect of a military strike to enhance the effectiveness of its diplomacy and increase the chances of a negotiated settlement if it would reveal publicly that it is both preparing the ground diplomatically and developing operational plans for a military strike should it become necessary (rather than its current approach of playing up the risks of military action while still keeping "all options on the table").

A limited military strike will need to be well prepared diplomatically and operationally so that it does not splinter or undermine international support for the current Iran policy. If a limited military strike is to have its desired effect of setting back Iran's nuclear program and making it harder for the Iranian regime to get the bomb, it must be followed by increased pressure on Iran (including additional sanctions), not international disarray and defections from the effort. This is especially true if the Iranian regime were to use the strike as a pretext to declare explicitly that it is pursuing a nuclear weapon capability.

A limited strike would send a message to the Iranian regime that the United States and the international community meant what they said, that they have the will and the capability to "prevent" (to use President Obama's words) the regime from obtaining a nuclear weapon, and the Iranian regime risks further military strikes if it continues to pursue those efforts.

Potential Benefits of Option 6:

- Would give credibility to the vow by the United States and the international community to prevent Iran from getting a nuclear weapon while reducing somewhat the likelihood of Iranian retaliation (both conventionally and asymmetrically through terror attacks by groups like Hezbollah).

- While giving the regime something with which to rally public support in the short run, in the longer term the limited strike could contribute to division and discord within the regime and the Iranian public about its nuclear weapon efforts and could result in a change in the regime's nuclear policy.

- Will buy additional time (2 to 5 years) on the Iranian nuclear clock, setting back the time at which Iran would enter the so-called "zone of immunity" about which the Israelis have in the past been so concerned and providing more time for negotiations or for pressure/sanctions to produce a change in Iran's nuclear policy.

Potential Costs of Option 6:

- Could push the Iranian regime to declare explicitly that it is pursuing nuclear weapons (while setting back the nuclear weapon program to only a limited extent) and cause the regime to do all it could to push up oil prices to economically damage the United States and its supporters.

- Would be controversial within the United States and could shatter or erode the international support for U.S. Iran policy and actually reduce post-strike international pressure and sanctions on Iran.

- Could rally Iranian public opinion around the regime and heighten public hostility to the United States and the international community, making it harder to resolve not only the nuclear issue but also other grievances and concerns over the policies of the regime.

Option 7: Conduct Major Military Strike (Necessarily Overt)

The logic of this option is that the risks and costs of any military action are so great that the objective of the strike should be to do maximum damage to Iran's nuclear program and set it back as long and as far as possible. A major military strike would have to be overt and, because of the force requirements, could only be conducted by the United States and not Israel. While such a strike would also have to be carefully prepared diplomatically and operationally, a major strike would almost certainly put greater pressure on the existing international support for a robust Iran policy; be more controversial and divisive within the United States; and engender a stronger reaction from the Iranian regime and the Iranian people.

A major military strike would most probably focus on:

(1)   All facilities associated with a potential Iranian nuclear weapon capability (but should spare strictly civilian nuclear power facilities like Bushehr);

(2)   Iranian air defense facilities (so as to reduce the risk to American planes and pilots); and

(3)   Iranian military aircraft, military airfields, and missile complexes (to reduce Iranian capability to retaliate against the United States, Israel, and U.S. friends and allies in the region).

But the diplomatic predicate for a major strike would be difficult to establish. It is likely that the mere failure of negotiations (as opposed to a clear effort by the Iranian regime to "get the bomb") would not be viewed by either the international community or the U.S. public as justifying a major military strike. Enormous advance preparations would be required to try to safeguard the regional oil infrastructure, de-salinization and water treatment plants, military installations, and population centers in the region from Iranian retaliatory strikes, terrorist attacks, and sabotage and to try to insulate the world economy from a major potential disruption in the oil and gas markets.

Potential Benefits of Option 7:

- Would send an even stronger signal of resolve and would set back the Iranian nuclear weapon program even further than a limited strike.

- Could raise questions in the mind of the Iranian regime about its own survival and thereby cause it to make a strategic shift in its nuclear policy toward compliance with the demands of the international community (and perhaps cause positive shifts on other issues as well).

- Does maximum damage to Iran's conventional retaliatory capability and could deter the Iranians from initiating an asymmetric response.

Potential Costs of Option 7:

- As opposed to a limited strike, probably makes it more likely the Iranian regime would explicitly declare its intention to seek nuclear weapons, and international support for the current Iran policy would shatter, reducing the post-strike pressure needed to try to prevent Iran from getting the bomb;

- Could strengthen public support for the regime and public hostility toward the United States and the international community, increasing the risk of even more extreme regime policies; and

- Poses increased risk of escalating into a full-fledged conflict based on either a conscious decision by the regime to go to war with the United States or the errant action of a rogue IRGC commander provoking a U.S. response (e.g. deciding to target a U.S. naval vessel).

Option 8: Acquiesce to a Nuclear-Armed Iran

If efforts to resolve the confrontation over the nuclear issue fail, and the United States and the international community either decide to forego the military option or find that it does not achieve their desired objectives, they could elect simply to accept an Iranian regime with a clear path to a nuclear weapon – and even with a nuclear weapon itself. This course of action would reflect a judgment that an Iran with nuclear weapons could nonetheless be "deterred" or "contained." The issue here, however, is what precisely is being "deterred" or "contained"? Iranian use of a nuclear weapon? The proliferation of nuclear weapons to other states that feel threatened by a nuclear Iran? The increased hegemonic behavior of an Iran with nuclear weapons? Its more aggressive support for terrorists and efforts to disrupt its neighbors? Or all of the above? One has to be skeptical that all of these effects can be successfully deterred or contained.

Under this approach the United States and the international community would:

(1) Rely on traditional deterrence-through-threat-of-retaliation to deter the Iranian regime from using a nuclear weapon against the United States, Israel, or any other country;

(2) Strengthen their military presence in the region and their defense relationships with, and the conventional military postures of, friends and allies in order to dissuade those states from seeking to offset Iran's nuclear weapon capability by developing their own (or, in the case of Israel, from resorting to military action against the Iranian nuclear capability); and

(3) Rely on intelligence sharing, cooperative interdiction under the Proliferation Security Initiative, and the threat to hold Iran responsible for the acts of any terrorists or other persons to whom it transfers nuclear weapon capability to prevent or deter the Iranian regime from sharing such capability.

Potential Benefits of Option 8:

- Could arguably lead to a more stable Middle East (see Kenneth Waltz in the July/August 2012 issue of *Foreign Affairs*);

- Could avoid the costs and uncertainties surrounding military action against Iran; and

- Could open the door to a more positive relationship with the Iranian regime and ultimately to a resolution of other grievances and concerns (especially if one believes that the "coercive" approach of the United States and the international community has been a barrier to reaching reasonable agreements with the Iranian regime).

Potential Costs of Option 8:

- Would be viewed in many circles as a dramatic defeat and loss of credibility for the United States and the international community;

- Would be viewed by many as a severe setback for the nuclear nonproliferation regime and could result in other states (both in the Middle East and elsewhere) pursuing at least their own nuclear enrichment capability and potentially the broader set of capabilities required for a nuclear weapon (including the weapon itself); and

- Might be viewed by Israel as an unacceptable outcome and could result in unilateral military action against the Iranian nuclear program, Israel's international isolation, tensions with the United States, and a military conflict between the United States and Iran.

Stephen Hadley is a principal at RiceHadleyGates LLC, an international strategic consulting firm founded with former Secretary of State Condoleezza Rice and former Secretary of Defense Robert Gates. Mr. Hadley previously served first as Deputy National Security Advisor and then as National Security Advisor in the administration of George W. Bush. Before joining the Bush administration, he was a partner in the Washington, D.C. law firm of Shea & Gardner and a principal in the Scowcroft Group, an international business advisory firm. Mr. Hadley served as the Assistant Secretary of Defense for International Security Policy under then Secretary of Defense Dick Cheney from 1989-1993 and in a variety of other capacities in the defense and national security field, including as Counsel to the Special Review Board established by President Reagan to inquire into U.S. arms sales to Iran (the "Tower Commission"), as a member of the National Security Council staff under President Ford, and as an analyst for the Comptroller of the Department of Defense. Currently, Mr. Hadley is a Senior Advisor on International Affairs at the United States Institute of Peace and a member of the State Department's Foreign Affairs Policy Board. He graduated magna cum laude and Phi Beta Kappa from Cornell University and received a J.D. degree from Yale Law School. He is a member of the Aspen Strategy Group.

"A bomb or be bombed? Both are realistic possibilities; either could occur without violating any laws of science and engineering or observed political behavior. But in my judgment, neither is likely. If required to answer yes or no: no bomb; no attack."

—GRAHAM ALLISON

Iran: A Bomb or Be Bombed?*

Graham Allison
Director, Belfer Center
John F. Kennedy School of Government
Harvard University

The mounting confrontation between Iran, on the one hand, and the U.S., Israel, and the international community, on the other, is the most urgent international challenge of the year ahead.[1]

If the U.S. acquiesces to an Iranian nuclear bomb, most analysts forecast a cascade of proliferation with Saudi Arabia, Turkey, and even Egypt following. It is hard to envisage a race for nuclear arms in a region this volatile without preemptive attacks and, ultimately, nuclear wars. Alternatively, if Israel or the U.S. conducts airstrikes on Iranian nuclear facilities, most analysts forecast that Iran will retaliate forcefully, launching ballistic missiles against Israel; using surrogates, including factions within Hezbollah and Hamas against Israel and Lebanon; and unleashing the Quds Force against American bases, interests, and individuals across the region and beyond. If the U.S. attacks Iran, some will note that this is the fourth Muslim-majority country to have been invaded or subjected to major air assaults by the U.S. in the past decade, lending credence to Islamic extremists' narrative that somebody out there does not like Muslims. Economic and political consequences following airstrikes will not be inconsequential. The likelihood of sustaining international sanctions will fall to zero.

Will Iran get a bomb or be bombed in 2012? The answer is, obviously, no one knows. As Yogi Berra observed, the great thing about the future is that it is uncertain. Recognizing that reality, politicians generally follow the advice of a former British foreign minister: never link a number and a date in a promise about the future. Intelligence officers have long taken their cue from the oracle at Delphi, formulating forecasts that allow multiple interpretations. Pundits are frequently bolder, exploiting newspapers' penchant for spotlighting them when they are right and forgetting quickly when they are wrong.

This chapter was presented to the Aspen Strategy Group in August 2012. The issue it addresses is obviously moving in real time, producing weekly changes in measurements like the number of centrifuges or the stockpile of enriched uranium. But the basic logic of the argument stands.

This essay is organized as brief answers to 10 key questions about Iran's nuclear challenge.

1. When will Iran get a nuclear weapon?

    My unambiguous answer is: it depends. Specifically, it depends on 1) Iran's decision to do so; 2) the path Iran chooses to a bomb; 3) the obstacles Iran faces along each path to a bomb; and 4) the costs and benefits to Iran of acquiring a bomb versus stopping at a base camp on the path to a bomb.

    Tables 1 to 4 present graphically three paths Iran could take to a nuclear bomb; the staircase to making a bomb; steps Iran has already taken up that staircase; and red lines or "unacceptable" developments stated by Israel and the U.S. that have been crossed and subsequently retired.

    When will Iran get a nuclear bomb? My personal best bet is: not in 2012, and not in 2013.[2]

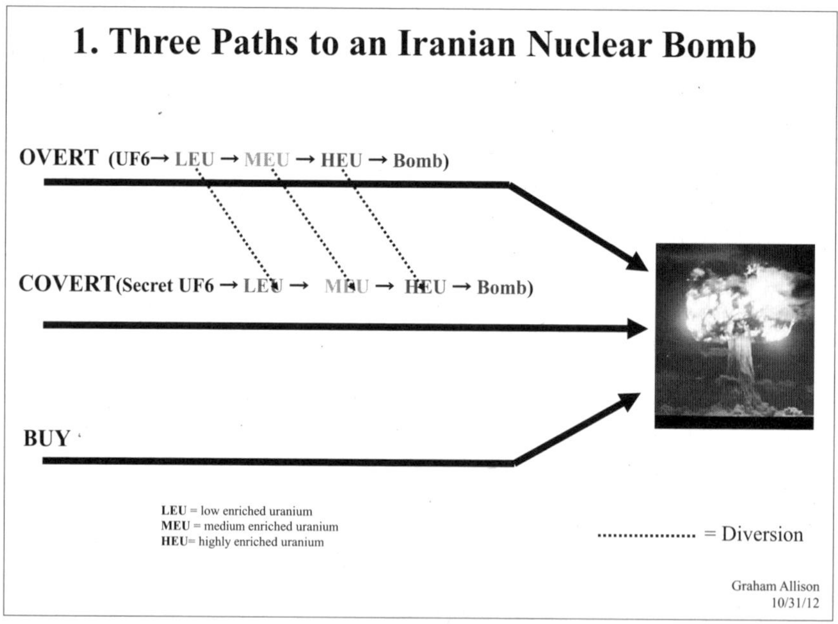

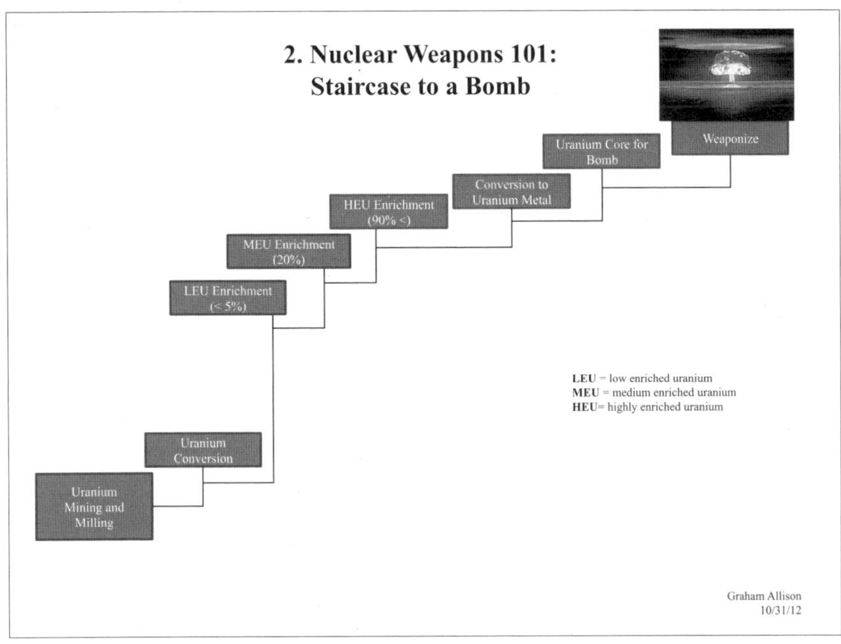
2. Nuclear Weapons 101:
Staircase to a Bomb
Weaponize
Uranium Core for Bomb
Conversion to Uranium Metal
HEU Enrichment (90% <)
MEU Enrichment (20%)
LEU Enrichment (< 5%)
Uranium Conversion
Uranium Mining and Milling
LEU = low enriched uranium
MEU = medium enriched uranium
HEU= highly enriched uranium
Graham Allison
10/31/12

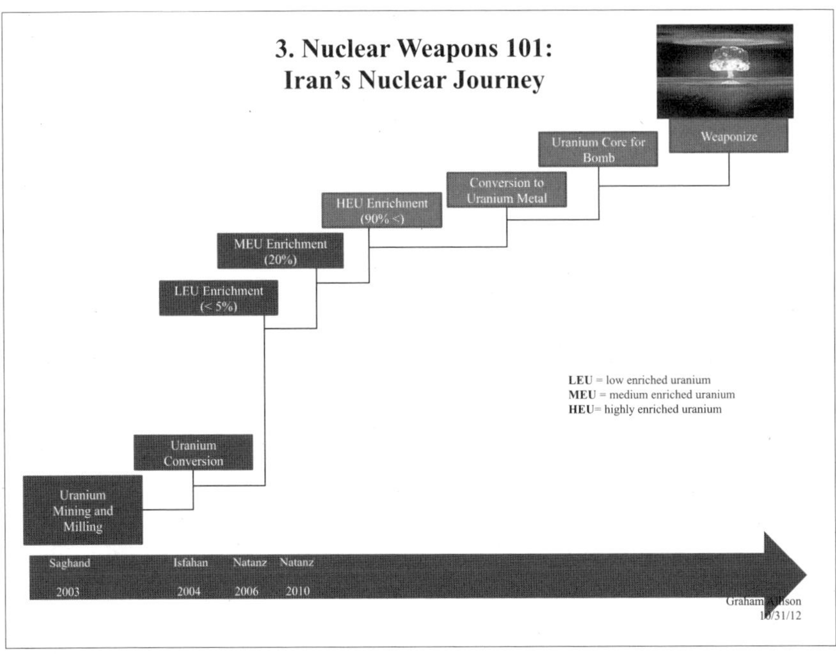
3. Nuclear Weapons 101:
Iran's Nuclear Journey
Weaponize
Uranium Core for Bomb
Conversion to Uranium Metal
HEU Enrichment (90% <)
MEU Enrichment (20%)
LEU Enrichment (< 5%)
Uranium Conversion
Uranium Mining and Milling
LEU = low enriched uranium
MEU = medium enriched uranium
HEU= highly enriched uranium
Saghand   Isfahan   Natanz   Natanz
2003   2004   2006   2010
Graham Allison
10/31/12

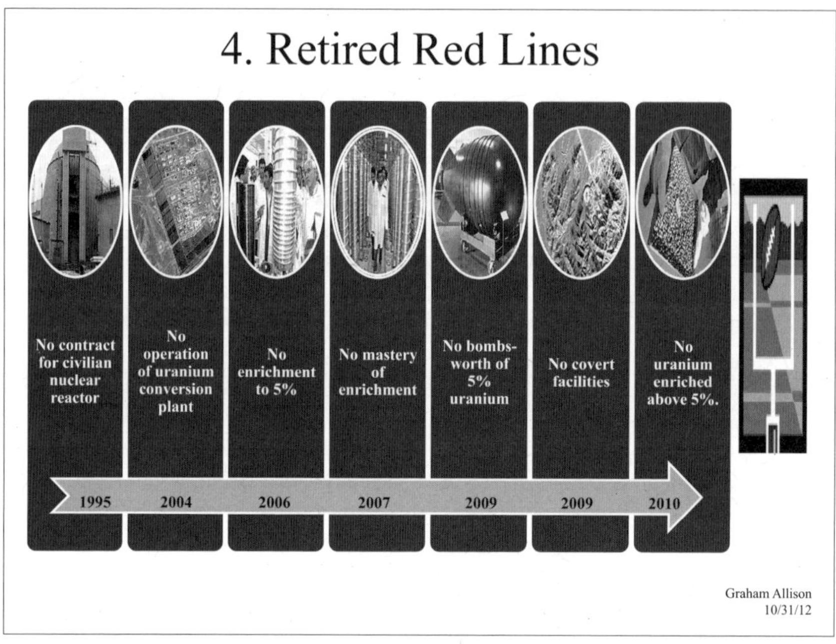

2. Where does Iran stand on the road to a nuclear bomb? How far has it advanced toward a bomb?

Table 3 reminds us that Iran has surmounted the most significant obstacle to making a bomb: it has mastered the technologies to enrich uranium indigenously. It has also operated production lines to produce a stockpile of low enriched uranium (LEU) that, after further enrichment, would provide the cores for six nuclear bombs. It has since 2010 been enriching uranium to a level of 20 percent (medium enriched uranium or MEU) and has thus done 90 percent of the work required to produce the highly enriched uranium (HEU) needed for an explodable nuclear bomb.

In a football metaphor, Iran has marched down the field into our red zone and now stands 10 yards away from our goal line (Table 5). As the graph of Iran's accumulation of enriched uranium demonstrates, despite a series of hostile attacks, which feed newspaper headlines and story lines, the trend line shows no significant breakpoints (Table 6).

Today, Iran has six bombs' worth of low and medium enriched uranium, and more than 10,000 centrifuges operating, producing an additional 360 pounds LEU and 22 pounds MEU monthly.

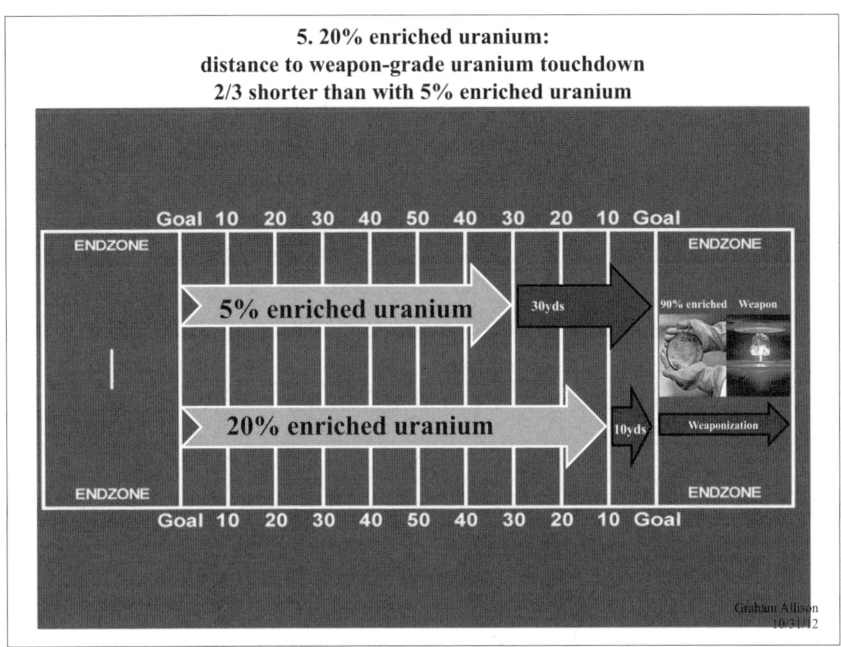

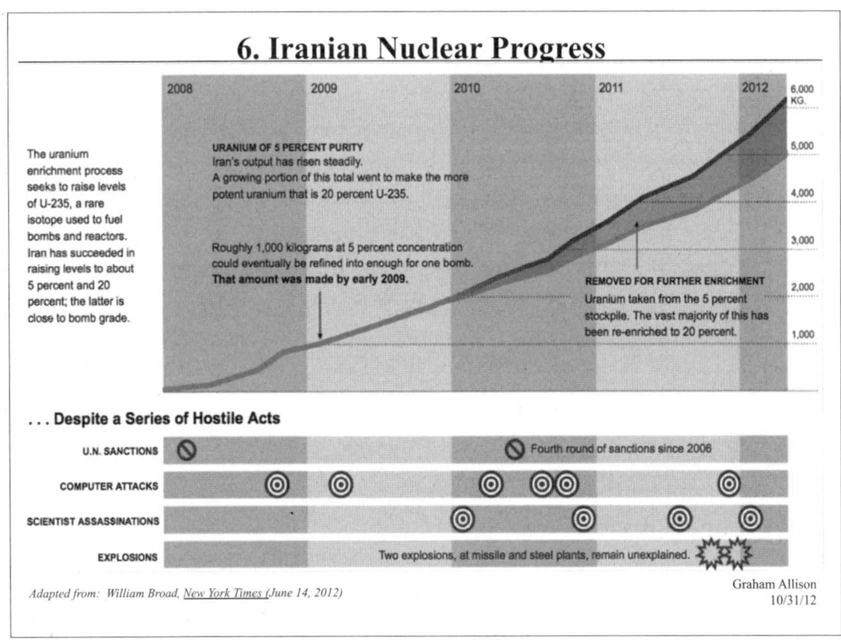

Adapted from: William Broad, New York Times (June 14, 2012)

Graham Allison
10/31/12

3. How has the U.S./West attempted to prevent Iran's acquiring nuclear weapons? What grade has the U.S./Western effort earned?

For the past decade, the principal strategy followed by Republican and Democratic American governments has been to declare our demands: Iran must not do A; Iran is not permitted to do B (after Iran has done A); Iran cannot do Z. Note the limits of a "strategy" that consists essentially of stating one's demands.

Elements of this strategy to date have included unilateral statements of demands; winning support in U.N. Security Council resolutions for statements of demands; winning support in the Security Council for resolutions imposing symbolic sanctions to support demands; working with a coalition of willing European allies to impose financial and oil sanctions; threats (usually vague) to act if Iran crosses the next red line. Sanctions have progressed from symbolic to nibbling to a qualitatively new phase in the past year, taking actions that are actually biting. If one believes what one reads in the papers, the program of sanctions has been complemented by a series of covert actions including cyberwar or cybersabotage, described by David Sanger under its label "Olympic Games," that included Stuxnet, Duqu, and Flame, assassinations of key scientists in the Iranian nuclear program, and unnatural explosions at key Iranian missile and steel plants.

Grading the decade of strategy for negotiations and diplomacy, it is hard to give the performance better than a C. The strategy has not created costs and benefits that make Iran's stopping more advantageous than proceeding. It has not offered terms of a deal that any Iranian government could plausibly accept. It has not engaged in sustained negotiations with Iran. As my colleague Nicholas Burns has pointed out, for 30 years there has been no sustained conversation between Iranian and American officials to explore the possibilities and limits for each of the parties. Contrast this with Henry Kissinger's conversations with Zhou Enlai in breaking the ice with China. The U.S. has not given Iran a godfather option: an offer Iran cannot refuse.

4. How difficult is it to identify the terms of a deal that would be better for both Iran and the United States than attack or acquiesce?

My answer is: not hard. Having been engaged in sustained conversations with U.S. government policymakers on this issue for most of the past decade, I can recall at least two occasions in which, viewed exclusively from the perspective of the recognized national interests of both parties, there seems to me to have been a zone of agreement. In 2003-2004, after the U.S. had toppled Saddam in three weeks without breaking a sweat, Iran appeared ready to accept an arrangement in which its enrichment activity would be constrained to a single cascade and subject to full transparency. Today, the U.S. and Iran are clearly circling around potential terms of an agreement that would cap all enrichment at 5 percent; stop expansion of facilities for enriching to 20 percent; swap current materials enriched to 20 percent for fuel assemblies for the Tehran Research Reactor (TRR); provide maximum transparency; and include (or imply) credible threats to impose catastrophic costs on Iran if the agreement were violated.

5. Why is it therefore hard to make a deal?

Failure has been more a function of confusion and division *within* the parties than *between* them. In my course at Harvard, I teach students that to make one deal in international relations requires three deals: first a deal within party A; then a deal within party B; and then sufficient overlap between each party's minimum requirements that diplomacy can reach agreement. When Iran was motivated to offer a deal that the U.S. should have found acceptable in 2003-2004, the U.S. was unwilling to accept it. When the U.S. was prepared to make a deal in 2009, Iran was too divided to accept it.

Imagine that this problem today were given to Metternich and Talleyrand in 1815, or Kissinger and Zhou Enlai in 1972. How hard would it be to solve?

6. When will we reach a point of no return, where a president will be forced to choose between attack and acquiesce?

As the draft of this paper presented in August 2012 predicted, Prime Minister Netanyahu has declared the negotiations to be ineffective and argued that, since the international community refuses "to draw a red line on Iran," it therefore has no "moral right to place a red light before Israel." He will continue to press his argument that we have come to a fork in the road where we must choose between attack and acquiesce. The U.S. government, key members of the Israeli national security establishment, and others will continue to argue (with considerable credibility) that sanctions and covert actions must be allowed more time to work, and that new sanctions and covert actions will be even more effective.

Netanyahu's demand for an unambiguous red line, short of a nuclear bomb that, if crossed, would trigger a U.S. attack on Iran, reveals deep frustration about the predicament in which he finds himself entangled. He also knows that Israel and the U.S. have been complicit in a process of drawing red lines they say Iran will never be allowed to cross, but then watching Iran cross those lines, after which they retreat to the next operational obstacle on the path to a bomb and declare it to be the real red line, only to stand by again as Iran crosses it.

Since 1996, Netanyahu has been sounding the alarm, warning that the "deadline for preventing an Iranian nuclear bomb is getting extremely close." Since then, Israeli politicians and officials have repeatedly raised the alarm about "last chances" and "points of no return." In 2003, the head of the Israeli military intelligence forecast that Iran would soon cross the "point of no return" at which "it would require no further outside aid to bring the program to fruition." A year later, Prime Minister Ariel Sharon warned that Iran would cross this point if it were allowed to develop a "technical capability" for operating an enrichment facility. As Iran approached that capability, Defense Minister Shaul Mofaz described the tipping point not as the capability, but as the "enrichment of uranium" itself. Simultaneously, the head of the Mossad, Meir Dagan, warned that Iran would reach this technological point of no return by the end of 2005. After Iran began enriching uranium, Prime Minister Ehud Olmert drew a new line in 2006 as enrichment "beyond a limited number of cascades."

As Iran has crossed each red line, Israel has retreated to the next and, in effect, hit the repeat button. From conversion of uranium, to production of low enriched uranium (less than 5 percent) that can be used as fuel for civilian power plants, to a stockpile of low enriched uranium sufficient (after further enrichment) to make one nuclear bomb, to a stockpile sufficient for a half dozen bombs, to enrichment beyond 5 percent to 20 percent medium enriched uranium, to operation of centrifuges enriching to 20 percent at the deep underground, formerly covert facility at Fordow, to achievement of a "nuclear weapons capability," Israel's warnings have grown louder, but with no more effect.

This does not mean that all Israeli warnings of "points of no return" are unfounded. Recall that in the children's story about the boy who cried wolf, in the end the wolf actually appears.

Later this year or in early 2013, expect Netanyahu to reject the Obama administration's (and much of his own security establishment's) arguments and press vigorously for a U.S. attack, threatening to act unilaterally otherwise. At that point, look for a more intense explanation of options short of attack for slowing or stopping Iran's nuclear progress. I have identified at least three such options, and have no doubt there are others. Watch this space.

7. What will trigger an Israeli attack on Iran's nuclear facilities? What will be the key drivers?

My answer is *internal* factors will be as important as external factors. The hard truth is that there will be little *material* change in the risks Israel faces from Iran as Iran continues its current, careful, cautious, deliberate but steady advance toward the nuclear goal line. The number of centrifuges enriching at Fordow will increase. The best disguised and least noted important fact, however, in the International Atomic Energy Agency's September 2012 report on Iran's nuclear program is that Iran's stockpile of MEU hexafluoride, the form in which it could most easily be re-enriched for bombs, actually *decreased* from May to August 2012. Iran has chosen to divert half of its MEU stockpile to fabricate fuel for the TRR. Moreover, despite claims about installation or operation of centrifuges at Fordow crossing the line to the "zone of immunity," there will be little *material* change in the impact Israeli airstrikes can have upon Iran's nuclear facilities in the months between today and January 1, 2013. As an historical reminder, consider the principal trigger of Prime Minister Menachem Begin's decision to attack Iraq's nuclear facility at Osirak in 1981. It was fear that he would no longer be prime minister, that he would be succeeded by Shimon Peres, and that Peres would not have what it took to do what was required when it was necessary.

8. What would trigger a U.S. attack on Iran's nuclear facilities?

Were the U.S. to discover unambiguous evidence that Iran was in the process of breaking out or sneaking out on a timetable that could be thwarted by an American attack, an attack would become likely. But, aware of this threat, Iran is highly unlikely to take such an action.

A more likely trigger of U.S. airstrikes would be an Israeli airstrike that prompted an Iranian response that threatened U.S. interests, including attacks on Saudi Arabian oil exports.

A third possible scenario for attack could occur in 2013 if Romney wins the presidency. A new president powerfully influenced by "my friend Bibi" will be at risk of what presidential scholar Richard Neustadt called a "transition error" to which all new presidents are highly prone in their first year as they try to understand their new job.

9. What is most likely future for 2012: a bomb or be bombed?

My best bet is that Iran will proceed cautiously, carefully, steadily. I do not believe Iran has yet decided to cross the goal line. I agree with Israeli Chief of Staff Benny Gantz's assessment that Iran is "going step by step to the place where it will be able to decide whether to manufacture a nuclear bomb. It hasn't yet decided whether to go the extra mile." In my view, the U.S. will pursue every alternative to attack, recognizing the costs and risks of an attack.

As expected, we have witnessed a drum roll and intensifying threats of attack from Netanyahu as he sees what he appears to believe is the most important "zone of immunity" closing. For him, that is not Defense Minister Ehud Barak's concern about a material change in Iranian nuclear facts on the ground or the impact of an Israeli attack upon those facts. Rather, it is his concern about a zone of political immunity prior to the elections: were Israel to attack, even over the objections of President Obama, the president would have no option but to support our ally. Netanyahu's position at home has been gravely undercut, however, not only by the revolt of the security barons, but also by his own head of state, President Peres, who has warned publically that "we cannot [attack Iran] on our own." After elections, if Obama is reelected, Bibi must worry that the U.S. might reach a deal that Israel would find extremely uncomfortable, or that if Iran were to continue on its path, the president might find some way to waffle.

A bomb or be bombed? Both are realistic possibilities; either could occur without violating any laws of science and engineering or observed political behavior. But in my judgment, neither is likely. If required to answer yes or no: no bomb; no attack. If forced to bet, my estimate of the probability of a bomb or an attack in 2012 is 25 percent. That means I am prepared to bet $3 against $1 that on January 1, 2013, Iran will not have a nuclear bomb, and Iran will not have been the target of military airstrikes by Israel or the United States.

10. Why could I be wrong?

After having heard, or himself made, a convincing argument for a conclusion, America's greatest secretary of state, George Marshall, would frequently conclude with "just one more question." His question: "Why could I be wrong?"

In addressing questions like the one posed by this paper, analysts learn to assess alternative futures. While the future is strictly unknown and therefore uncertain, some features are much more easily predictable than others. The probability that the sun will rise, or that Ajax Mountain remains a prominent feature in the landscape of Aspen, Colorado, this time next year, is highly likely.

In contrast, bets about whether Israel will attack Iran before the end of this year turn fundamentally on choices made by one individual. Regardless of the strong opposition from his military and security establishment, and his own president, and the fact that 76 percent of Israelis oppose a unilateral attack without U.S. support, given current distribution of power, and assuming that he can persuade enough of his "security cabinet," if Bibi Netanyahu decides to attack Iran, he can. His decision will be powerfully influenced by the facts of the case, the views of his colleagues in the government, his relationship with the American president, the presidential challenger, and other influential Americans, his memories of his father and of the history of his people.

His decision about attacking or postponing an attack will be purposive and rational in the sense that it reflects his calculation of the costs and benefits of alternatives. But either answers—attack or postpone—are plausible conclusions a rational actor could come to, confronting the complexities of the challenge of Iran's nuclear ambitions. Imagine being assigned to make the case why Bibi may choose to attack before November 6; or between November 6 and January 20; or after January 20; or not attack. Those of us watching intently should find little difficulty in producing a credible case for each.

Betting therefore about outcomes that can be determined by one person's calculations of an uncertain future is thus inherently vulnerable to error. But I am prepared to bet. As one extends the timeline into 2013, my crystal ball becomes hazier. But if forced to wager, I would bet that it is more likely than not (51 percent or more) that in 2013 Iran does not get a bomb, and Iran is not bombed.

Graham Allison is Director of the Belfer Center for Science and International Affairs and Douglas Dillon Professor of Government at Harvard's John F. Kennedy School of Government. As "Founding Dean" of the modern Kennedy School, under his leadership, from 1977 to 1989, a small, undefined program grew twenty-fold to become a major professional school of public policy and government. Dr. Allison has served as Special Advisor to the Secretary of Defense under President Reagan and as Assistant Secretary of Defense for Policy and Plans under President Clinton, where he coordinated DOD strategy and policy towards Russia, Ukraine, and the other states of the former Soviet Union. He has the sole distinction of having twice been awarded the Department of Defense's highest civilian award, the Distinguished Public Service Medal, first by Secretary Cap Weinberger and second by Secretary Bill Perry. He served as a member of the Defense Policy Board for Secretaries Weinberger, Carlucci, Cheney, Aspin, Perry and

Cohen. He currently serves on the Advisory boards of the Secretary of State, Secretary of Defense, and the head of the CIA. His first book, *Essence of Decision: Explaining the Cuban Missile Crisis* (1971), was released in an updated and revised second edition (1999) and ranks among the all-time bestsellers with more than 450,000 copies in print. His latest book, *Nuclear Terrorism: The Ultimate Preventable Catastrophe*, now in its third printing, was selected by *The New York Times* as one of the "100 most notable books of 2004." Dr. Allison is a member of the Aspen Strategy Group.

[1] This is an issue about which I have been writing for a decade, attempting to advance the analysis. For more relevant articles on the topic, go to http://belfercenter.ksg.harvard.edu. Advances include: providing a framework for thinking about the Iranian nuclear challenge as a Cuban missile crisis in slow motion in which protagonists are moving to a confrontation at which an American president will be forced to choose between attack and acquiesce, as President Kennedy was forced to do when Khrushchev attempted to sneak nuclear-tipped missiles into Cuba 50 years ago this fall in October 1962 ["The Nightmare This Time" (2006)]; critiquing the first Bush administration's policy of "no engagement, no carrots and no serious sticks," and later "mindless maximalism" in setting preconditions for negotiations ["Bush's U-turn towards Common Sense" (2008)]; suggesting how lessons from the Bush-Cheney-Bolton strategy toward North Korea of "threaten and neglect" that left the administration at its end with a score of Bush 0, Kim Jong-il 8 should inform U.S. policy toward Iran ["Blocking Iran's Nuclear Bomb" (Senate testimony, 2008)]; demanding recognition of the ugly reality that Iran had lost its nuclear virginity: having passed the brightest red line on the road to a bomb by acquiring the capability and know-how to enrich uranium indigenously ["A New Red Line on Iran's Nuclear Program" (2009)]; explaining the significance of 20 percent enrichment versus 5 percent enrichment—demonstrating that this takes Iran to our 10-yard line rather than the 30-yard line (where they arrived when they were enriching uranium to 5 percent) ["Obama should test Iran's nuclear offer" (2011)]; identifying "sneak out" as Iran's most likely path to a nuclear bomb in the near term ["Slinking towards the bomb" (2012)].

[2] For perspective, recall the U.S. intelligence community's most famous (or notorious) National Intelligence Estimate of December 2007, which assessed "with moderate confidence that the earliest possible date Iran would be technically capable of producing enough HEU for a weapon is late 2009, but that this is very unlikely" and argued that "Iran probably would be technically capable of producing enough HEU for a weapon sometime during the 2010-2015 time frame. (INR [the State Department's Bureau of Intelligence and Research] judges Iran is unlikely to achieve this capability before 2013 because of foreseeable technical and programmatic problems.) All agencies recognize the possibility that this capability may not be attained until after 2015." While this assessment was wrong about when Iran achieved the technical capability to produce enough HEU for a weapon, it was correct about when Iran would actually produce enough HEU for a bomb. It compares favorably to forecasts made by many in the U.S. and Israel that an Iranian bomb was less than a year away.

Part 5

TRADE, AID, AND INVESTMENT:
BUILDING AN ECONOMIC RECOVERY

CHAPTER 8
Middle East and North Africa:
Historic Context, Current Situation, and Possible Implications of the "Arab Spring"

Kito de Boer
Director, Middle East
McKinsey & Company

"Two years ago, no one could have imagined where we are today. Two years from now it is even more likely we will be facing a reality scarcely imaginable today. If there is one lesson from this, it is that this is not the time for incremental thinking. The potential range of outcomes is far greater than many might wish to believe."

—KITO DE BOER

Middle East and North Africa:
Historic Context, Current Situation, and Possible Implications of the "Arab Spring"

Kito de Boer
Director, Middle East
McKinsey & Company

Context

The Middle East and North Africa (MENA) is a "noisy neighborhood," a region characterized by substantial economic progress as well as economic volatility and political instability. In order to understand where the region might be going, it can be helpful to examine the journey it has made up to this point.

Compared to those living in the West, the past 50 years has been a very different experience for people living in MENA. The pace of socio-economic and political change has been materially very different. In the West, the 1960s was the era of "Mad Men," the Rolling Stones, and the space mission. Although there has been rapid socio-economic progress since then, the landscape of the 1960s is still readily recognizable to the current generation.

In contrast, for many of the current generation in MENA the 1960s appear to be an alien land. The past 50 years have taken the region on a steep trajectory characterized by volatility and turbulence.

MENA's Rapid Economic Progress

The pace of progress in the region has been truly exceptional. The U.N. Development Index (which has tracked countries' development since 1980) lists four MENA countries among the top 20 in the world in their rates of improvement (Morocco, Egypt, Tunisia, and Algeria). The U.N. Development Report places Oman and Saudi Arabia among those countries that have achieved the most rapid improvement in the conditions of their people (in descending order the top five are Oman, China, Nepal, Indonesia, and Saudi Arabia).

These improvements are reflected in increased average life expectancy. In 1960, life expectancy in the large MENA countries was 45 years. Today it is 73, an increase of 28 years. This is rapid even by the standards of the most rapidly improving countries. Indonesia, for instance, started at the same point and has increased life expectancy by 24 years. During the same period, the U.S. increased average life expectancy by eight years, from 70 to 78.

Education and literacy have also seen substantial progress. Primary school enrollment in MENA increased from 64 percent in 1971 to 96 percent today. Whereas the literacy level in Saudi Arabia was barely 10 percent in 1960, it now exceeds 80 percent. Female literacy has improved at an even faster rate than male literacy, albeit from a lower base. These improvements are the result of substantial investment. Saudi Arabia currently spends more on education as a proportion of GDP than most developed countries (Saudi Arabia, 6.8 percent, U.S., 5.7 percent, Indonesia, 3.5 percent). The provision of education is also outward looking. Saudi Arabia currently has 130,000 students sponsored to study in international universities, half of whom are in the U.S. and one-third of whom are women.

In absolute terms, however, the nature of this progress should not be overstated. Education attainment levels in Saudi Arabia are still within the bottom quartile of global rankings. Only one percent of Saudi students who took the recent Program for International Student Assessment tests scored above the average of Singapore, and MENA primary school expenditure is 30 percent below that of the U.S. (on a relative spend basis). In Saudi Arabia, only five percent of children go to pre-school, compared to over 90 percent in most OECD counties.

Another dimension of the pace of change experienced in the region is the rapid rate of urbanization. Between 1980 and 2005, the level of urbanization in Algeria increased from 44 percent to 63 percent, in Morocco from 41 percent to 55 percent, in Tunisia from 51 percent to 65 percent, in Lebanon from 74 percent to 87 percent, in Oman from 48 percent to 72 percent, and in Yemen from 17 percent to 29 percent. This pace of urbanization disrupted not only traditional relationships and ways of life but also concentrated populations. This proximity, in turn, helped increase demands upon essential services, raised awareness of inequalities within societies, and eventually enabled mass political mobilization. Twitter usage grew in Saudi Arabia 3,000 percent in June 2012. Over the past 12 months, the growth has been 1,200 percent, which makes it the world's fastest growing market for Twitter.

The petrochemical industry has supported much of the region's progress. Saudi Arabia, in particular, continues to invest to retain global leadership as an oil producer. The country plans to spend $125 billion on upstream and downstream expansion over the next five years. This follows nearly a decade of investing $40 billion a year in bringing on 4.25 million barrels per day. These capacity additions alone are greater than the total capacity of any other OPEC producer. The Khurais field, which entered production in June 2010 with a capacity of 1.2 million barrels per day, is the largest single addition in Saudi history. The Manifa field, due to go on stream in 2014, will produce a further 0.9 million barrels per day.

MENA's Volatility and Instability

Despite its substantial material improvement, the region has undergone a roller coaster ride characterized by political instability, economic volatility and underlying structural challenges.

MENA has seen more violent conflicts during the past 50 years than any other region apart from sub-Saharan Africa (in excess of 100 compared to more than 120 in sub-Saharan Africa). The conflicts include the Algerian and Lebanese civil wars, the overthrow of the Shah of Iran, the Iran-Iraq war, two Gulf wars and multiple conflicts with Israel. The recent and current civil wars in Libya and Syria, as well as the disturbances in Tunisia, Egypt, and Yemen represent a significant uptick in stress. In terms of the levels of violence, however, the current experience falls within the bounds of "normality" for many MENA citizens.

The region's volatility is not helped by the socioeconomic consequences of seesawing oil prices. Real oil prices (at constant 2005 US$) were $73 barrel in 1980; they then dropped to $22 in 1995 before rising again. By 2010, prices were back close to where they started in 1980 at $71. This volatility had direct consequences for the oil exporting countries of the Gulf Cooperation Council (GCC). In 1980, the GDP per capita of the GCC was the equivalent of Texas: at $18,000 per capita it was higher than the OECD average ($16,000) and three times greater than East Asia ($6,000). By 2005, GCC GDP per capita had declined by 30 percent to the level of Mexico City ($12,000), while the OECD had increased GDP per capita by 50 percent ($24,000) and East Asia by 90 percent ($11,000). Only Venezuela's and Zimbabwe's performances were worse.

Not only is the region of MENA vulnerable to fluctuations in oil prices; many MENA countries are also susceptible to changing food prices. The share of household expenditure spent on food in the non-oil exporting MENA countries ranges from 35 percent in Tunisia to 43 percent in Algeria. Like oil prices, food prices have fluctuated wildly in recent years. In the decade from 1990 to 2000, the Food and Agriculture Organization Food Price Index declined from 100 to 90. In the seven years from 2004 to 2011, it doubled from 100 to 200. Clearly, price increases on this scale hit household expenditures hard.

In addition to oil dependence, the economies of the region also suffer from severe structural problems. MENA unemployment levels are twice the global average. Youth unemployment is four times higher than the global average. The female labor force participation rates are among the lowest in the world (15 percent in Algeria, 17 percent in Saudi Arabia, 25 percent in Egypt, Tunisia and Yemen and 44 percent in the UAE, whereas the rate is 51 percent in Indonesia and 58 percent in the U.S.)

The region's public sector is also oversized by world standards. In MENA, the public sector accounts for nearly 30 percent of total employment (in Kuwait, the proportion exceeds 90 percent for nationals, and in Saudi Arabia it is nearly 80 percent). The world average for public sector employment, excluding China (where it is 36 percent), is 18 percent, while for the OECD and Latin America it is around 13 percent. In Saudi Arabia, only 6 percent of the national population works in the private sector; this compares to 30 percent in Malaysia.

Not only is the level of public sector employment high by international standards, but so is its cost burden. In Saudi Arabia, in the period from 2003 to 2009, government wages increased by 76 percent and the number of public servants by 26 percent, yet government services as a proportion of GDP increased by only 18 percent, indicating a sharp decline in productivity. This relatively poor performance is echoed throughout the region where the overall performance of public administration is very poor by international standards. According to a 2005 World Bank report on reform in the Arab world, "Of greater concern [than the business environment] is the level of progress on governance. The area of public sector accountability is the worst in the world."

Private business continues to struggle to play its full role throughout the region, although the business environment has improved somewhat since 2005. According to the World Bank's Ease of Doing Business ranking, during this time Saudi Arabia moved from 38 to 10, Egypt from 141 to 108, and Tunisia from 58 to 40. Nonetheless, the business environment remains poor overall. According, again, to the World Bank in 2005, "MENA's progress on reforming the business environment has been the weakest in the world, and on average MENA countries rank in the bottom third." The countries mentioned as being in the bottom third included Algeria, Egypt, Lebanon, Libya, Qatar, Saudi Arabia, Syria, and Yemen.

MENA is Heterogeneous

MENA is as much a cartographical convenience as it is a reflection of a coherent reality. While language and religion are important unifying features, the very distinct differences among the countries is greater than in many other regions of the world.

These differences are evident within short geographical distances. Yemen and Qatar are a similar distance apart as Boston and Chicago—800 miles—but the differences between the two MENA countries could hardly be greater. Yemen has a population of 25 million, 15 times larger than that of Qatar (25 million versus 1.7 million), but the size of Yemen's economy is less than a third that of Qatar's (Qatar's GDP is $130 billion compared to Yemen's $35 billion). According to the International Monetary Fund, Qatar's per capita GDP is second only to Luxembourg and double that of the U.S. while Yemen ranks 140 places lower, just above Mauritania. Looking at this wealth gap another way, each Qatari has a per capita GDP 75 times that of a Yemeni. Nor are their prospects in any way similar. In 2011, Qatar was the fastest growing country in the world, with a growth in GDP of 18.7 percent (see CIA *World Fact Book*), whereas Yemen ranked 183 out of 185 countries, facing a decline in GDP of -2.5 percent. The $200 billion Qatar plans to invest in preparation for hosting the soccer World Cup is twice the budget of Yemen's government over the next decade.

Demographics show similar disparities. The nation with the oldest population within the region is twice as old as the youngest. The median age of MENA's population ranges from 16 in Yemen (fourth lowest globally, a notch above Mali) to 30.8 in Qatar, the highest in the region (although Qatar is closely trailed by Bahrain, UAE, Tunisia, and Lebanon). The world average median age is 28. The youngest populations of the region include those of Saudi Arabia (22) and Syria and Jordan (21). In Europe, the difference between the oldest population—Italy (44)—and the youngest population—Ireland (35)—is only 30 percent.

In the area of human development, of the 14 MENA countries indexed by the UN, the UAE ranks the highest at number 30. Middle-ranked countries include Qatar, Bahrain, Saudi Arabia, and Kuwait. The lowest ranked country is Morocco at 130 (other low-ranking countries include Syria, Egypt, and Tunisia). Life expectancy in the region varies by 17 years, from 79 in the UAE (in the U.S. it is 78) to 62 in Yemen. By comparison, in the Americas life expectancy varies by 15 years, ranging from Canada (80) to Bolivia (65).

Gross capital formation is the rate at which countries invest in fixed assets, and for most of the major economies in the region the investment rate clusters around 19 to

23 percent of GDP. The two extremes are Qatar (40 percent) and Yemen (12 percent). Algeria (38 percent), Morocco (31 percent) and Lebanon (32 percent) are all at the upper end.

Private sector gross capital formation is a useful indicator of the role of government in the total economy. In the oil-rich economies such as Qatar, Saudi Arabia, Kuwait, and Libya, the private sector barely registers as a component of capital formation. In contrast, in the following five countries the private sector is a material investor: Lebanon (30 percent), Morocco (25 percent), Tunisia (20 percent), Jordan (19 percent), and the UAE (15 percent).

The region's current account balances in relation to GDP vary dramatically. MENA contains some of the fiscally strongest economies in the world, which possess large surpluses (according to 2011 data), including Kuwait (42 percent), Qatar (28 percent), Saudi Arabia (24 percent), and the UAE (9 percent). At the other extreme, two MENA countries are comparable to Greece (-10 percent) in terms of how far they are in the red: Lebanon (-14 percent) and Jordan (-10 percent). Tunisia and Morocco also have problematic balances (-7 percent).

Likewise, the strength of the national balance sheets varies enormously. Cumulatively, the following five countries in the region have a total of approximately $2 trillion in national savings (either as foreign exchange reserves and/or sovereign wealth funds): Saudi Arabia, the UAE, Kuwait, Algeria, and Qatar. The same five countries also have low levels of national debt (below 20 percent). At the other end of the spectrum, the countries with high debt/GDP levels include Lebanon (140 percent), Egypt (76 percent), and Jordan (70 percent). Two countries within the region have low levels of foreign exchange reserves. They are Egypt ($15 billion) and Tunisia ($6 billion).

The region is not strongly integrated economically. Overall, intra-MENA trade is just 4 percent of GDP. For Morocco and Algeria it is just 1 percent; for Kuwait, Libya, and Saudi Arabia it is 2 to 3 percent. The 2 countries with the highest intra-MENA trade are Jordan (18 percent) and the UAE (7 percent). Some 60 to 80 percent of the region's trade is with Europe.

While MENA's share of world trade is just 4 percent, its cross-border labor demands are highly significant at the world level. MENA is the source of 16 percent of global wage remittances and 10 percent of global wage receipts.

Impact of the Arab Spring

The wave of revolutionary demonstrations and protests that began on December 10, 2010 has since spread throughout much of the Arab world. To date, rulers have been forced from power in Tunisia, Egypt, Libya, and Yemen. Civil uprisings have erupted in Bahrain, and there is an ongoing civil war in Syria. More limited protests have occurred in many other countries, including Saudi Arabia, Oman, Jordan, and Morocco.

The first-order financial impact of the Arab Spring is likely to be in the range of $40 to $50 billion. This first-order effect is the result of the rapid slowdown in growth due to the impact of the revolution, which has turned MENA growth rates into the slowest among the emerging markets. Second-order effects caused by increased subsidies, government wages, and increased interest payments on debt as well as devaluation will also need to be considered in due course.

The cost of the Arab Spring is being borne primarily by a small number of the revolutionary countries. The economic impact on the oil-producing GCC has been markedly different from that on the oil-importing MENA countries.

In 2010, the IMF forecast 4.8 percent GDP growth during 2011 for the oil-importing MENA countries. The actual growth achieved was 2.2 percent. The expected growth for 2012 is estimated to be 2.7 percent, with 3.6 percent predicted for 2013. This compares to the 2010 forecast for this period of above 4 percent. It is, therefore, not unreasonable to conclude that the first-order financial impact of the Arab Spring is a cumulative 5 percentage points of GDP, or approximately $40 to $50 billion.

Among the oil importing countries, three saw significant slowdowns. Tunisia's GDP growth dropped from 3.1 percent in 2010 to -0.8 percent in 2011, Lebanon's from +7.0 percent to 1.5 percent, and Egypt's from +5.1 percent to 1.8 percent.

In contrast, most of the oil-exporting countries achieved strong economic performance during 2011 based on the rising oil price, which increased from $79 a barrel in 2010 to $104 a barrel in 2011. Two countries, however, saw massive GDP declines. Libya's GDP growth collapsed from 2.5 percent in 2010 to -61 percent in 2011, and Yemen's shrank from +7.7 percent in 2010 to -2.5 percent in 2011.

Egypt's performance in 2011 is representative of the turbulence caused by the Arab Spring. GDP growth is expected to be 1.5 percent in 2012. Its international reserves declined by more than 50 percent, from $36 billion to below $15 billion, sufficient to pay for just five months' imports, and its stock markets fell by 50 percent (although it has bounced back in 2012). Foreign holdings of Egyptian debt were reduced by 95 percent, dropping from $5 billion to $280 million. During this period, the cost of its debt rose from 11 percent to 16 percent. Credit default rates, which had declined from around 400 BPS (basis points) in 2009 to below 200 BPS in mid-2010, rose to over 600 BPS. Perhaps not unexpectedly, the income from tourism (which accounts for approximately 10 percent of GDP in Egypt) declined by 30 percent during this period, having increased 16 percent the previous year. Unemployment in Egypt has increased from 9 percent to 10.5 percent. Subsidies have been increased by the equivalent of 1 percent of GDP. Government wages increased by 15 percent and fuel subsidies by 30 percent.

Looking at MENA as a whole, Foreign Direct Investment (FDI) has dropped by more than 50 percent, from above $20 billion to below $10 billion. Net capital flows have also declined by more than 90 percent, as foreign banks have repatriated funds to reduce risk and strengthen their domestic positions. Bond issues declined from $3 billion in 2010 to below $1 billion in 2011.

As in Egypt, tourism in the region in 2011 was down by 9 percent (while globally it increased by 5 percent). Egypt, Tunisia, Syria, and Lebanon have been the hardest hit, each showing declines in excess of 25 percent. Likewise, the region's stock markets fell in aggregate by 15 percent in 2011 (compared to the 2.5 percent increase globally in emerging markets). In contrast, remittances from overseas workers have held up, in part, because the GCC performance has been strong. Morocco's remittances increased by 10 percent and Egypt's by 4 percent. Those for other countries were flat or down by 1 to 2 percent.

Numerous governments in the region have responded to the pressures arising from the street protests by increasing subsidies or reducing taxes. Jordan, for example, has tripled subsidies for oil and food. Overall, in the MENA countries outside the GCC, government spending has increased by 30 percent. Measured as a proportion of GDP, these subsidy increases represented 5 percent of Jordan's and 4 percent of Yemen's economies. In 2011, Saudi Arabia launched programs with an estimated cost of $140 billion. These included salary increases, an additional two months' pay awarded as a bonus to government employees, the introduction of unemployment benefits, and a major low-cost house-building program.

As mentioned earlier, the pressure on government finances has led to a worsening in the fiscal balance as a proportion of GDP in a number of countries. For some the situation is acute, most particularly in Lebanon (14 percent), Jordan (10 percent), Tunisia (7 percent), and Morocco (7 percent). In addition, Yemen (-3.5 percent) and Egypt (-2.0 percent) are both facing substantial fiscal pressures.

Immediate Prospects

On the assumption that the region's politics remain relatively stable, a surface reading of the macroeconomic data suggests the following: the oil-importing countries will consolidate during the remainder of 2012 and begin the path back toward the pre-Arab Spring growth rates of around 4 to 5 percent, which they are likely to achieve by 2014. North African countries such as Morocco and Tunisia will face greater headwinds due to the fact that historically 70 to 80 percent of their exports are tied to Europe. The oil exporters will continue to grow at around 5 percent, with a strong bounce-back from Libya following its 50 percent decline in GDP in 2011. There is also some evidence of the financial markets rebounding after the problems of 2011. Broadly, the region's citizens also appear relatively optimistic about their medium-term future.

Beneath this surface reading, however, there are concerns about the longer-term economic sustainability and health of many countries within the region. Whereas politics drove economics in 2011, in 2013 and beyond economics is likely to drive politics.

There are two major reasons to be concerned about the medium-term prospects of the oil-importing nations.

First, the global economic context makes life difficult for them. Not only are oil and food prices likely to remain elevated, but European economic prospects also look bleak, and European growth is critical to the North African countries, as it is their primary export market. In addition, the global banking and financial system is still under stress and demonstrates a low-risk appetite, which will make private funding of capital more difficult and expensive. This is critical; the IMF estimates that the oil-importing countries will require close to $100 billion in gross financing through 2013.

Second, in 2011 politics drove economics in a way that will likely increase the pressure for economic reform. Subsidies were increased, taxes reduced, and capital expenditure cut. In the short term, this government stimulus will help counter the negative impact of instability. In the longer term, the impact of rising fiscal deficits is unsustainable. A number of countries in the region are likely to need bilateral and multilateral support. Devaluations are anticipated in some countries: Egypt, Jordan, Yemen, and Lebanon all look particularly vulnerable. Morocco and Tunisia are also stressed and exposed to Europe.

The best-case scenario is for a long, drawn-out economic recovery accompanied by fundamental economic reform that is likely to be unpopular in the short term.

The IMF describes the MENA's challenge as one of "[m]oving from stabilization to transformation: stabilization is an immediate need. But at the same time countries need to make tangible progress on transforming and modernizing their economies."

Enabling this transformation will require the countries of the region to take steps in four areas:

1. Economics: The countries will need to develop a path toward sustainable government finances. This should be based on improved tax and revenue collection, as well as a reduction in subsidies (or at least more effective targeting) and the move toward a system of needs-based social support.

2. Entrepreneurialism: The region needs to modernize its business, financial, and legal environments in order to better attract and develop the private sector. This will require reforming financially important sectors such as banking and insurance, retail, real estate, and health care.

3. Employment: The Arab world has twice the level of unemployment relative to its peers. Youth unemployment is acute, with an estimated annual opportunity cost of $50 billion, higher than the total cost of the Arab Spring. Given the region's demographics, if nothing is done this situation will deteriorate further. Vocational training, targeted at making the unemployed employable, will be critical. Expenditure on vocational training is currently 30 to 40 percent that of peer-group countries. This will need to be increased.

4. Education: Currently the education systems in the region ill-serve their populaces. There is a strong need for education programs better able to address both the quantitative and qualitative dimensions of learning. The quantitative dimension requires filling the structural gaps that exist in many of the systems. Pre-schooling is entirely absent in many countries, as are polytechnics (vocational schools). Pre-schools play an important role in shaping how children learn. Polytechnics are vital in teaching the less academic and more vocational skills crucial to most economies. The qualitative dimension will require focusing on the hard and soft skills demanded by employers. This includes inculcating capabilities such as critical thinking and developing a productivity-oriented mindset, as well as improving skills in English and information technology and strengthening the basics of numeracy and literacy.

Increased investment will be central to creating a sustained economic revival. MENA's governments are likely to have to lead this, because the private sector is weak and defensive throughout the region. As yet, there does not appear to be any credible initiative within the region to address the scale of the economic challenges ahead.

For the oil-producing economies, their economic strength provides them with the means to continue to power their economies. These countries have also demonstrated a willingness to support their neighbors in the region. If they are to anchor the region's revival, which they have the fiscal ability to do, they will need to build credible institutional capability—an analogue to the European Bank for Reconstruction and Development, for example, which was founded in response to the fall of the Berlin Wall. The current support offered to the region by the oil-producing nations is well-intentioned but is currently insufficient to address the scale of the funding and policy-reform gap.

The private sector, particularly foreign capital, has been in rapid retreat within the region. Domestic private capital is currently highly risk averse. Although there are some signs of recovery, albeit from a very low base, the general mood is still one of concern. Consumer and retail businesses are holding up quite well because governments have increased salaries and handouts. Other private sector "engines" have stalled. Telecom is becoming saturated, real estate has pockets of growth but is facing a "boom days" hangover, and banking is in a defensive repair posture.

Geopolitical uncertainty also casts a cloud that increases the perceptions of risk, particularly in the minds of the providers of foreign capital. Within the region, however, the view on the major oil exporting countries is generally more positive. Iraq is big and growing at double-digit rates. Personal security risks are the primary concern here. Libya is emerging as a positive story. The UAE also looks strong, with Dubai beginning to recover from its real estate crash.

Among the leading nations of the region, Saudi Arabia is likely to be stable for the next decade. At the top, succession appears well ordered; at the bottom, the fiscal strength exists to help meet the population's economic needs. There are, however, two issues the Kingdom must address.

First, it needs to develop more effective mechanisms for transferring national wealth to individuals. The two primary mechanisms in place at present—subsidies and the provision of government jobs—are blunt instruments. The level of subsidies, particularly fuel subsidies, is very high and risks becoming counterproductive. Fuel subsidies already cost in excess of $50 billion a year. As a consequence, over the past 20 years Saudi Arabia's energy intensity (the number of barrels of oil consumed per $1000 GDP) has increased from five to 10 times the global average. Likewise, the public sector is already saturated, providing more jobs than it can realistically sustain. This "unnatural" job creation is depressing productivity. Saudi Arabia's productivity has declined since 2000, while Egypt's has improved by one percent a year, Turkey by six percent a year, and China and India by eight percent a year.

The second issue Saudi Arabia needs to face is reducing the government's increasing dependency on oil revenues. One way to think about its oil dependency is in terms of the break-even cost of running the government expressed as the net revenue per barrel of oil (the oil price at which government costs will be covered). In 2000, the government's break-even cost was about $12 per barrel. Today it is about $85. It will reach $100 within the next five years. By 2030, at current trends, one forecast suggests that the break-even price will be over $300 per barrel.

In summary, the next 15 to 20 years for Saudi Arabia are likely to be an unrepeatable "golden age." The country needs to act today in order to prepare for the time when the present fiscal feast returns to famine. There is hope that it might do so. Many in the country vividly recall the difficult times, lasting nearly 20 years (from 1983 to 1999), when Saudi Arabia regularly ran budget deficits and debt soared to 120 percent of GDP. This experience brings a sense of perspective to the present.

As for the non-oil producing countries within the region, both their economics and politics are in flux. In many countries, the downside risks appear greater than the upside opportunities.

Egypt's fiscal position is fragile; over the next three to five years it will have to navigate between the Scylla of fiscal reality and the Charybdis of citizen expectations. The outcome of Syria's civil war is important politically. The current trajectory suggests that the existing regime is likely to collapse before a viable alternative emerges. The specter of sectarian strife, ethnic cleansing, and the potential use of chemical weapons, with the civil war's inevitable spillover into Lebanon, will have ramifications in Israel and Jordan and is of major concern internationally.

SYRIA: BACK TO THE FUTURE?

The concept of a united Syria is a fairly recent one. After the First World War, the territories now known as Lebanon and Syria became a French mandate (lasting from 1920 to 1946). The French regime had a preference to divide and rule based along religious lines. The Alawite territory centered on Latakia was created during the period 1920-36. When the state of Syria was created, the Alawite state remained separate. Its inhabitants did not join the Arab nationalist movement against French rule, and they prospered in the French-sponsored military. Today there are 1.3 million Alawites. One million live in Syria, where they comprise 12 percent of the population; 75 percent live in Latakia.

Yemen does not register on most investors' radar screens, and it runs the risk of being ignored or viewed mainly as a security risk. Yemen has a population of 25 million Arabs, which is bigger than the Arab population of either Saudi Arabia or Syria. It is a major humanitarian and potential political disaster in the making. Accordingly to *Foreign Policy*'s Failed State Index, Yemen rates eighth, next to Haiti. Yemen's median age is the equivalent of a junior in high school. Its starting position is one of the weakest in the region, and its citizens face a future with rapidly declining oil revenues and water resources.

In summary, while private capital will hesitate to invest in the region at present and will wait until the clouds on the political horizon clear, public capital (outside the oil-exporting countries) is going to be increasingly scarce and costly. In these circumstances, "business as usual" is not a viable option, and muddling through is unlikely to be an adequate response. A fit-for-purpose response demands regional leadership.

Despite the present challenges, the majority of citizens appear more positive than economists about recent developments. According to recent polls by the Arab American Institute and Oxford, the majority of those in Egypt, Morocco, and Saudi Arabia believe life will be better in five years. In the case of Egypt, there has been a 120 percent increase in the number holding a positive outlook since 2009. Likewise, some 80 percent of Libyans and 90 percent of Syrians expect their lives to be better in five years.

There are also early indicators of economic progress. The financial markets have halted the decline of 2011 and are now showing early signs of recovery from a low base. The Egyptian EGX30 is up 35 percent in 2012; having started the year at 3600, it is now near 4900 (having hit 5500 in March), making it one of the best performing markets. Tunisia's market is up about 10 percent (although Morocco is down 10 percent because of its strong ties to Europe). The investment banking market in H1 2012 was worth $14 billion, a 140 percent rise over H1 2011. Similarly, private equity has doubled volumes from $240 million in H1 2011 to $480 million in H2. Nonetheless, these are very small volumes by the scale of other markets and are just a quarter of their size in 2007.

Early indicators also suggest that industrial production is up in 2012. In Egypt, electricity consumption has increased 12.5 percent versus H1 2011. Industrial production in Tunisia, Morocco, and Jordan is also up by between four and five percent. Likewise, imports in Q1 2012 are up in Egypt by 27 percent, in Jordan by 24 percent, and in Tunisia by 14 percent. Exports are also up around 15 percent, which suggests increased economic activity but also a worsening trade deficit.

The currency situation is more complicated. Egypt's foreign reserves had dropped by 50 percent from June 2011, when they stood at $27 billion, to $15 billion in May 2012. At one stage, reserves were declining by more than $1 billion per month. This decline has been reversed over the past three months. The markets, however, are anticipating that Egypt's currency, which has been stable to date, will see a 20 percent devaluation by the end of the year.

Social and Political Transformation

During the Arab Spring, the spotlight of much of the world's media focused on the role social media played in the uprisings. Undoubtedly, such technology was important in enabling communication and coordination, but its role should not be overestimated.

Social media such as Twitter and YouTube are buoyed by the level of mobile phone penetration within the region, which stands at 124 percent (i.e. 124 phones for every 100 people), higher even than in the US (where it is 103 percent). In 2011, the use of Arabic grew by 2,200 percent, making it the fastest growing language on Twitter. In June 2011 traffic grew by 3,000 percent.

In contrast to the level of mobile penetration, Internet penetration is modest. In Yemen, penetration is three percent, in Algeria 18 percent, in Egypt 19 percent, and in Morocco and Syria 22 percent, while in Saudi Arabia it is significantly higher at 48 percent. Satellite TV plays an important role throughout MENA, following more than a decade of rapid growth. In 1996, there was only one regional broadcaster. Today, there are nearly 300. Al Jazeera and MBC/Al Arabiya have developed as influential sources of news coverage.

However high profile it may have been, technology was an enabler of the Arab Spring but not its cause. The underlying forces driving the uprisings were primarily socio-economic.

The region's demographics are an unstoppable force. In the space of one generation (from 1975 to 2005), the population of MENA has more than doubled. On an absolute basis, during this time MENA has added more people than the combined populations of the U.S. and the main European countries. Since 1970, the countries of the GCC have increased their populations seven-fold (rising from 6 million to 43 million). MENA has grown four-fold (from 103 to 428 million). The U.S., by contrast, has grown 50 percent (from 205 to 310 million).

The economies of MENA performed well during the 1960s and 1970s. Arab nationalism was effective in mobilizing the machinery of state. GDP per capita grew by an average of 6 percent a year, the fastest rate globally. Between 1970 and 1980, GDP per capita increased by 85 percent, rising from $2,000 to $3,900. The period 1980 to 2004, in contrast, was characterized by a marked slowdown in growth. GDP per capita grew by just 6.4 percent in 25 years, one of the worst performances on the planet. After 1980, it took nearly 25 years to reach what had been achieved every year during the previous decade.

The countries of the GCC have had a particularly volatile journey. In 1970, GDP per capita (in 2005 $) was $10,000. By 1980, it had more than trebled to $36,000. Thirty years later, in 2010, GDP per capita remains 20 percent lower at $28,000.

Taking a longer-term perspective, it can be seen that the growth in MENA's economies has barely been able to keep pace with population growth. Relative to the rest of the world, the countries in the region have fallen behind. This slow pace of economic expansion, combined with one of the world's fastest rates of population growth, has resulted in high unemployment levels. Overall, the official figures show that unemployment in MENA is 15 percent, double the global average, and that youth unemployment is four times the global average.

In reality, many of the statistics on unemployment are unreliable and probably understate the real situation. They are unreliable because they do not reflect the fact that labor participation rates in most MENA countries are structurally lower than elsewhere. The participation rate in the U.S. is 64 percent and in Indonesia 68 percent. Few MENA countries approach these levels (the exceptions are Bahrain, where it is 70 percent, and Kuwait, where it is 68 percent). Most MENA countries have participation rates below 50 percent. (Saudi Arabia, Morocco, and Egypt all have a labor participation rate of 50 percent; in Jordan it is notably low at 41 percent).

Recent experiences in Saudi Arabia illustrate the difference between official statistics and reality. The official data suggest that unemployment stands at 450,000 people. When the new Hafiz unemployment benefits program was launched earlier this year, some two million people registered for the benefits, of which 700,000 passed the screening criteria defining their eligibility.

Such discrepancies are echoed throughout the region. This underlines the serious nature of the challenge unemployment presents to progress and stability. The employment creation problem can be illustrated by calculating how long it will take to find jobs for all those in the current "pipeline" of job seekers. For example, in the U.S. there are currently 60 million people below the age of 15; if the labor participation rate remains stable (the current U.S. workforce is approximately 155 million), this would mean 40 million jobs are needed for this cohort. Broadly speaking, the U.S. has 60 years to create the number of jobs currently in existence, matching the pipeline to the current job supply. The demands are even lower elsewhere in the OECD. For instance, because its population is in decline, Germany has 100 years to match the pipeline. In contrast, Saudi Arabia has just 20 years and Egypt 30 years to do what the U.S. has 60 years to accomplish.

Not only is the scale of job creation a challenge, but so also is creating jobs of the right quality. Throughout the region, well-paid, white-collar jobs are hard to find. As a result, in most countries nationals have a strong preference for government jobs. Across MENA, 30 percent of all employment is in the public sector, twice the level in the U.S. or the OECD. The global average (excluding China) is 18 percent. In Kuwait, 93 percent of nationals are employed in the public sector; in Saudi Arabia it is 80 percent and in Libya 66 percent. In most of the oil-producing countries in the region, the local population has little experience of, or exposure to, working in the private sector.

The Silatech-Gallup polls of 16,000 15-to-29-year-olds provide a valuable resource for glimpsing the mindsets and attitudes of young Arabs in the region. The surveys were conducted in 2009 and 2011. The data highlight a number of key points:

Saudi youth provide consistently high scores and are among the most optimistic in the region. Some 89 percent of Saudi women believe they can progress in their careers; this figure is similar to the majority of Arab countries, though lower scores were recorded in Egypt (71 percent) and Jordan (78 percent). In Saudi Arabia, 60 percent of youth believe the present economic conditions to be good, compared to 20 percent in Egypt and 34 percent in Jordan. Likewise, 52 percent of Saudi youth believe it is a good time to get a job, a proportion two to three times greater than in most other countries in the region (in Yemen only 10 percent believe this, in Egypt 15 percent, and in Jordan 22 percent).

The youth of Egypt and Jordan show considerable dissatisfaction. Their perceptions about the economic conditions and their job prospects are 10 to 20 points below peer groups.

Three areas highlighted by the Silatech-Gallup polls are most revealing:

- Some 60 percent of respondents prefer to work for the government. This percentage is fairly constant across all major countries in the region.

- The majority of respondents say they wish to live in their own country and do not want to migrate abroad. The figure wishing to stay put is notably high in Saudi Arabia at 89 percent, compared to 54 percent in Jordan, 51 percent in Tunisia, 59 percent in Algeria, and 72 percent in Egypt.

- The most pressing concern for Arab youth appears to be that of affordable housing, and it is this area that has seen the sharpest fall in satisfaction between 2009 and 2011. The satisfaction levels in Jordan during this period dropped from 54 percent to 27 percent. They also declined sharply elsewhere. In Egypt they fell from 42 percent to 25 percent, in Tunisia from 75 percent to 43 percent, and in Saudi Arabia from 57 percent to 47 percent.

Housing is emerging as a major issue. In Arab societies, marriage, jobs, and housing are all closely linked. With youth unemployment increasing and housing supply lagging behind demand (and, as a consequence, house prices rising), it is taking longer for young people in the region to arrive at the financial stability they require in order to get married.

The situation in Egypt illustrates the social impact of this linkage. While the population has grown by 50 percent since 1985, the number of marriages has increased by only 25 percent. Concomitantly, Egypt's marriage rate (the number of marriages per 1000 population) has declined from 9.3 per 1000 in 1970 to 7.2 in 2006.

The delay in household formation is most pronounced among the better-educated urban citizens who are prepared to wait longer in order to obtain a good job. Research (Assaad in 2009) indicates that an employed man has three times the chance of getting married within a three-year period than does an unemployed one. Furthermore, a young man with a "good job" has three times the chance of getting married than does a young man with an ordinary job. In short, the streets of the region are being filled with unemployed young men and women who are unable to get married and move on with their lives.

In the final analysis, employment and its corollary of unemployment are the clearest lenses through which to study the root causes of the Arab Spring. Creating sufficient employment is fundamental to the future of the region. The employment narrative leads to housing and marriage in one direction, to education and vocational training in another, and to economic policy and the creation of a thriving private sector in another. Employment creation remains central whichever direction one turns. To address its current challenges, the region requires employment creation on an unprecedented scale. Without it, the Arab Spring might well turn into a winter of discontent.

A Personal Postscript

As an institution McKinsey does not involve itself in matters of politics. As an individual, based in the region since 1999, I am frequently asked my view on where the region is headed. My response has four components to help people come to their own view:

1. No one knows.

    Two years ago, no one could have imagined where we are today. Two years from now it is even more likely we will be facing a reality scarcely imaginable today. If there is one lesson from this, it is that this is not the time for incremental thinking. The potential range of outcomes is far greater than many might wish to believe.

2. Listen to the street more than the elite.

    The region is being shaped by a generation of people, many of whom we are unfamiliar with or do not understand, and who make many of us uncomfortable. The current pace of change is very rapid. It places a premium on building networks with young Arabic- and Persian-speaking Muslims who cannot only take the pulse of the street but are also integral to what is happening on it.

3. Think "path" not forecast.

> Forecasts have little validity in times of fundamental uncertainty. In contrast, an appreciation of history, coupled with understanding of the fundamentals, can help outline the potential paths of evolution.

> Three important fundamentals have to be dealt with. First, the majority of the region's population is comprised of conservative and devout Muslims. Second, substantial minority groups are currently fearful and need to be protected. Third, the military in the region are often a key political force.

> Given these fundamentals as a starting point, it is possible to define paths of success and failure. The path of success leads to Turkey, Indonesia, and Malaysia. It took 30 to 50 years for them to evolve from "strong man" states to possessors of effective and representative governments. The path is long, the journey hard, but these countries point in the direction where the sun shines.

4. Focus on the minorities.

> The history of the region and the heartbeat of democracy are defined by the dignified treatment of "minority" groups. Look closely at the Palestinians in Jordan (whom many believe are now the majority), the Copts in Egypt (the region's largest "minority" population), the Shia in Saudi Arabia (comprising 10 to 15 percent of the population), the Alawites in Syria (10 percent of the population), almost everyone in Lebanon, and the 30 million Kurds spread across Turkey, Iraq, Iran, and Syria.

> The Arab Spring faces two paths for these "minorities": engage and empower or separate and defend. The former will require compromise and tolerance; the latter will result in Balkanization and civil strife.

Kito de Boer is a Director of McKinsey & Company in the Middle East. He currently leads the Public Sector Practice across Europe, the Middle East and Africa (EMEA). The central theme of Mr. de Boer's work with Government clients has been reform. He has helped to support the region's leaders create the modern institutions and policies required by forward-looking governments. Specifically, Mr. de Boer has worked on issues related to labor market reform, economic reform, education reform and healthcare reform. Mr. de Boer joined McKinsey in London in 1985 and in 1993 moved to New Delhi to help launch the India practice. In 2000, he moved to Dubai to lead the formation of the Middle East practice of which he was Managing Director until 2008. Since founding the Middle East office, Mr. de Boer has also been one of the leaders of the McKinsey Center of Government, and has served clients across the Middle East, North Africa and South-Asia (MENASA). Mr. de Boer received a B.S.C. from Loughborough University of Science and Technology and an M.B.A. from Cranfield University.

Part 6

CHAPTER 9

Revising U.S. Strategy in Light of the Arab Uprisings

Colin H. Kahl
Professor
Georgetown University

"In a perfect world, we would be able to design a strategy that advances all of these interests simultaneously, and there would be no need to prioritize our objectives or accept trade-offs among them. But in the real world, advancing some U.S. interests in the MENA region will produce tensions with others, and policymakers will have to make difficult decisions."

—COLIN H. KAHL

Revising U.S. Strategy in Light of the Arab Uprisings

Colin H. Kahl
Professor
Georgetown University

The Arab revolutions have brought the United States to a turning point in the Middle East and North Africa (MENA). Longstanding dynamics within and between states in the region are in flux. To date, given the scale and velocity of turmoil sweeping the Arab world, the United States has understandably adopted a largely reactive approach, attempting to adjust its policies to a rapidly changing environment.

As the new realities of the region take shape, however, it is time to take a step back, assess the landscape, and begin to craft an overarching strategy. The United States continues to have vital national interests at stake in the Arab world. Yet it will be difficult to advance all of America's interests and objectives simultaneously. This essay describes a number of broad strategic choices available to policymakers, while highlighting some of the difficult trade-offs they entail. The goal is not to prescribe a particular course for U.S. policy in the years ahead. It is, rather, to map the regional context, identify key U.S. interests, highlight a number of tensions involved in pursuing these interests simultaneously, and outline competing strategic options for navigating the hard choices now confronting Washington.

The Regional Context

Any discussion of strategy must begin with an assessment of regional dynamics.

The Arab uprisings. The popular uprisings sweeping the MENA represent the dominant driver of regional events.[1] On December 17, 2010, the self-immolation of Mohamed Bouazizi, a fruit vendor driven to despair by the profound corruption and daily indignities of Tunisian dictatorship, started a process that lit the entire region on fire. Tunisians took to the streets en masse, ending the twenty-three-year rule of President Zine El Abidine Ben Ali in a mere twenty-eight days. Although, in many respects, Tunisia was a peripheral country on the margins of the Arab world, events there quickly set in motion a cascade of revolutionary protests across the region.

From Tunisia, the uprisings spread to Egypt, where hundreds of thousands demonstrated in Cairo's Tahrir Square and elsewhere throughout the country. Hosni Mubarak's decades-old reign came to an end over the course of eighteen days in January and February 2011. The Supreme Council of the Armed Forces oversaw a contentious year-long democratic transition, culminating in the election of a parliament dominated by Islamist parties and a new president, Mohammed Morsi, from the once-banned Muslim Brotherhood.

Given Egypt's status as a traditional Middle Eastern and North African powerhouse, the most populous Arab state, and the cultural hub of the Arab world, Mubarak's fall ensured the further spread of revolutionary fervor. Mass protests challenged regimes in Bahrain, Yemen, Libya, and Syria, but the results were uneven. In Bahrain, the Sunni Al Khalifa monarchy held on, using repression and outside assistance from Saudi Arabia to crush demonstrations by the island nation's Shiite-majority population. In Yemen, protests, tribal violence, and foreign pressure combined to force a transition of power from President Ali Abdullah Saleh to his vice president. In Libya, Muammar Gaddafi's threat of genocidal violence against the rebel stronghold of Benghazi sparked a NATO-led intervention that ended his rule (and his life).

In Syria, Bashar al-Assad's regime, which initially felt immune from the turmoil besetting fellow dictators, saw a diffuse protest movement morph into a violent nationwide insurgency in response to the regime's brutal crackdown.[2] As of this writing, the conflict in Syria has devolved into a grinding civil war, producing tens of thousands of casualties and refugees, with no clear resolution in sight. It remains conceivable that Assad's regime will barely survive, emerging severely weakened but propped up by Iranian and Russian patrons. It is also possible that the opposition, perhaps enabled by more assertive Western and Arab state intervention, will defeat Assad's forces. What would follow from such a victory remains deeply unclear, however. Perhaps a rebel victory would usher in a more inclusive state, but it could also lead to a failed state consumed by battling warlords harboring al-Qaeda linked extremists. Alternatively, the current stalemate may persist, producing escalating civil strife and a deepening regional proxy conflict pitting Iran, Lebanese Hezbollah, and Russia against Qatar, Saudi Arabia, Turkey, and the United States, with profoundly destabilizing consequences for all of Syria's neighbors, especially Lebanon, Jordan, and Iraq and possibly Israel.[3]

The simultaneous revolts across the Arab world demonstrated that the apparent stability of dictatorship in the MENA was a house of cards built on a pile of sand. There is no going back to the status quo ante. Given the dramatic rise in popular activism empowered by twenty-first-century satellite television, modern communications technology, and social media, one thing seems clear: *long-term* stability in the region will require meaningful steps by all governments toward genuine political and economic reform. At the same time, in the *near term*, the defining feature of the current strategic landscape will be uncertainty: uncertainty about the success of ongoing democratic transitions and the ability of new governments in Egypt, Libya, and Yemen to tackle severe economic and governance challenges; uncertainty about what other regimes will fall and what parties will rise to take their place; uncertainty about the intensity, duration, and regional consequences of violence in places like the Sinai, Syria, and Yemen; and uncertainty about the strategic orientation of key states like Egypt, including the willingness of newly empowered Islamist parties to cooperate with the United States and other Western countries in pursuit of common objectives. The anti-American protests that swept the region in September 2012 in response to a YouTube video defaming the Prophet Muhammad, and the uneven governmental responses to the crisis, were symptomatic of the kind of underlying turbulence that is likely to complicate U.S. policy in the region for years to come.

Iran's nuclear and regional ambitions. Iran's aspirations to become a nuclear power and a local hegemon are another primary driver of regional events.

In recent years, Iran has made significant progress in developing its nuclear capabilities, producing widespread concern in Washington, Jerusalem, and numerous Arab capitals. If Iran were to acquire nuclear weapons, many fear that Tehran would be emboldened to increase its support for militancy, terrorism, and subversion in the Levant, Iraq, and the Gulf, further destabilizing an already tumultuous Middle East.[4] Iranian nuclearization could also incentivize other regional states, especially Saudi Arabia, to seek their own nuclear deterrents, potentially setting off a volatile arms race and increasing the prospects that regional crisis could escalate to nuclear war.[5] In the absence of a diplomatic resolution to Iran's nuclear challenge, Israeli or U.S. leaders may decide to launch a preventive military strike to set back the program, potentially triggering widespread Iranian retaliation and the possibility of a wider war in the Levant or Persian Gulf. In an effort to deter Iranian aggression and be prepared for any contingency, the United States maintains some 50,000 forces in the Gulf, including robust naval, air force, ground, and ballistic missile capabilities.[6]

Although Iran has not yet acquired a nuclear weapon, the Iranian regime is putting all the pieces in place to develop a bomb at some point in the future should Ayatollah Ali Khamenei, Iran's supreme leader, decide to do so. According to the International Atomic Energy Agency (IAEA), Iran currently has sufficient quantities of low-enriched uranium (LEU) that, if further enriched to weapons-grade level (above 90 percent purity), could produce half a dozen nuclear weapons. Should Iran's supreme leader decide to dash for a bomb, credible estimates suggest it would take Iran a few months to enrich the fissile material for a single nuclear device and, when additional weaponization requirements are factored in, about a year total to produce its first crude nuclear weapon; it would take another couple of years for Iran to produce a sophisticated enough warhead for a ballistic missile. Importantly, however, none of these decisions are likely to be made in the near-term since Iran's nuclear facilities are under IAEA inspection, and efforts to divert LEU and enrich to weapons-grade level would be detected. Fearing any such move would produce a devastating response by the United States or other countries, Iran's leadership is unlikely to rush for a nuclear weapon until they can dramatically reduce the timeline to build a bomb or construct one in secret—which could be years off.[7]

Iran's nuclear ambitions have produced considerable anxiety, but their nuclear behavior and destabilizing activities have also generated considerable international pushback, leaving Tehran more diplomatically and economically isolated than at any time since the 1979 revolution. The George W. Bush administration gained support for several UN Security Council Resolutions (UNSCRs) calling out Iran for its failure to meet its international obligations under the Nuclear Non-Proliferation Treaty. The Obama administration substantially expanded on these efforts, producing UNSCR 1929 in the spring of 2010, putting in place the most comprehensive set of sanctions ever targeted at Tehran. UNSCR 1929 provided a framework for follow-on unilateral measures passed by the U.S. Congress and steps by like-minded states in Europe, Asia, and elsewhere, producing unprecedented economic pressure on Iran's financial, transportation, and energy sectors. The United States has sanctioned Iran's Central Bank (greatly complicating its ability to facilitate oil sales), the European Union has ceased importing Iranian oil, and major customers in Asia have also curtailed their purchases. As of this writing, Iran has largely been cut off from the global financial system, Iranian oil revenues had been cut nearly in half, the Iranian currency (the *rial*) had been significantly devalued, and inflation was rampant.[8]

Moreover, in many respects, the Arab Spring has increasingly become a Persian Winter.[9] Throughout the Arab uprisings, the Iranian regime has tried (unsuccessfully) to cast the demonstrations sweeping the region as an "Islamic Awakening" inspired by Iran's own 1979 revolution. For the most part, Iran's narrative has been met with scorn and ridicule in the Arab world.[10] The widely held perception of Iranian meddling has decimated Iran's "soft power" since the Arab revolutions began. Iran's support for Syria's brutal crackdown, following on the heels of Tehran's own repressive response to the 2009 Green Path Movement protests, has been especially damning to the regime's credibility in the region.[11]

Iran's struggles to exploit the Arab uprisings are likely to persist. As Arab publics increasingly look to their own governments to represent their interests, Iran's ability to leverage regional discontent to influence the Arab street will continue to wane. Emerging political actors vying for influence and votes in an increasingly populist landscape will be keen to brandish their Arab nationalist credentials and reluctant to forge close alliances with Tehran.

The rise of the Muslim Brotherhood in Egypt presents a particular challenge. The country is already asserting a more independent and assertive foreign policy.[12] This policy will not always square with American interests, but a democratic Egypt, whether dominated by Sunni Islamist or secular parties, is likely to emerge as an important counterweight to Iranian leadership in the region.[13] Egyptian President Morsi's trip to Tehran in August 2012 to attend a Non-Aligned Movement summit provides a useful illustration. Morsi's visit was the first by an Egyptian head of state since the 1979 Iranian revolution and, as such, it was widely criticized by Western commentators. But instead of kowtowing to Tehran, Morsi embarrassed his hosts by giving a speech expressing Egypt's "solidarity with the struggle of the Syrian people against an oppressive regime that has lost its legitimacy."[14] Likewise, despite the fact that Tehran is a major supplier of weapons to Hamas and other Palestinian militants, it was Cairo, not Tehran, that brokered the ceasefire that ended the November 2012 Gaza-Israel conflict.[15]

The biggest threat to Iran's regional influence is the potential fall of Assad's regime, Iran's only Arab-state ally and an essential conduit for supporting militancy in the Levant. Indeed, the uprising in Syria has produced a major problem for the integrity of the entire "resistance camp" in the region that Iran claims to lead. In Lebanon, Hezbollah's leadership has felt compelled to rhetorically and materially back Assad, a key patron and major source of the organization's weapons. This support has exposed Hezbollah as a self-interested, Shiite-sectarian movement, badly damaging its Arab nationalist and resistance credentials at home and abroad.[16] Meanwhile, Hamas, another card-carrying member of the resistance camp, has moved its foreign headquarters from Damascus and is increasingly drifting into the orbit of Egypt, Qatar, and even Turkey.

As the resistance camp weakens, and especially if Assad falls, Iran may attempt to compensate by doubling down in Iraq. But this will be a difficult bet to win. To be sure, U.S.-imposed regime change, sectarian conflict, and the rise of a Shiite-led government in Baghdad have all provided Iran with fresh avenues for influence in Iraq. The susceptibility of Iraq's government to Iranian hegemony, however, is widely exaggerated. Iraqi nationalism is profound, and local distrust of Iran, a country against which Iraq waged the bloodiest war of the late twentieth century, runs deep, even among the country's Shiite population. Iraqi leaders across the ethno-sectarian spectrum also continue to desire a long-term strategic partnership with the United States and improved relations with Turkey and Iraq's Arab neighbors—objectives that are ultimately incompatible with Iranian domination. As Iraq's oil wealth and military strength grow over time, one can expect the country to chart its own course. Iran will likely have more influence with Baghdad than many in Washington and elsewhere are comfortable with, but Iraq will not be a puppet dangling at the end of Tehran's strings. Even if it were, Iraq could not replace Syria as an Iranian gateway to the Levant.

Balancing in the Gulf. The political revolts sweeping the Arab world have combined with concerns over Iran's nuclear and subversive activities to produce profound anxiety among Gulf Cooperation Council (GCC) states. As a consequence, in a classic example of balance of power politics, the GCC has significantly increased its arms purchases from the United States and other countries, while deepening intra-GCC security cooperation. To insulate the region's monarchies from the contagion effects of the Arab Spring and strengthen the anti-Iranian bloc, the GCC have also invited two non-Gulf kingdoms, Jordan and Morocco, to join the club.[17]

These efforts have been spearheaded by Saudi Arabia, Iran's principal rival for regional and ideological influence. The geopolitical contest long pre-dates the Arab Spring. Saudi Arabia backed Saddam Hussein during the Iran-Iraq war, and, over the past decade, Riyadh and Tehran have funneled support to competing factions in the fractured polities of Iraq, Lebanon, and the Palestinian territories. Similarly, since the Arab uprisings began, the Kingdom and Islamic Republic have supported rival proxies in Syria and Yemen. And, in March 2011, Saudi Arabia's perception that Iran was behind widespread protests against the Al Khalifa monarchy produced an ill-advised Saudi-led GCC intervention into Bahrain. In the face of Iran's continued nuclear and hegemonic ambitions, Saudi Arabia and other GCC states can be expected to keep circling the wagons.[18] This balancing behavior, in turn, will keep Iran somewhat in check, albeit at the expense of deepening Sunni-Shiite sectarian polarization in the region.[19]

Al Qaeda under stress. A decade after 9/11, al Qaeda "central" remains active in Pakistan and, in and around the MENA, al Qaeda affiliates operate in the Maghreb, the Horn of Africa, the Levant, Iraq, and the Arabian Peninsula. The instability, expansion of ungoverned spaces, and preoccupation of local security forces with regime survival resulting from the Arab uprisings have increased the tactical freedom of maneuver for al Qaeda affiliates and other violent extremists in Libya, Yemen, Syria, and the Sinai.[20] As America's old autocratic allies are replaced by new governments that are more skeptical of Washington, it is likely that the quantity and quality of counterterrorism cooperation in some places will degrade.

Yet, as a consequence of aggressive counterterrorism activities that began under President George W. Bush and were expanded by President Barack Obama, al Qaeda has also been badly damaged. Osama Bin Laden is dead and scores of leaders and operatives in Afghanistan, Pakistan, Iraq, Somalia, and Yemen have been taken off the battlefield. As a result, the capability of the al Qaeda-related groups to carry out large-scale attacks against the United States homeland has been sharply degraded.[21]

More broadly, al Qaeda has seen its standing in the MENA greatly diminished in recent years. Even before the Arab Spring, polling across the Arab world suggested al Qaeda's appeal had plummeted. As a result of the political change sweeping the MENA, al Qaeda's ideology and prospects for long-term viability have suffered a major blow. Despite pushing for violent revolution against regional despots for decades, the Arab uprisings were not in any meaningful sense inspired by al Qaeda or its ideology. Instead, they were driven by demands for expanded political and economic opportunity, an end to corruption, and advances in basic human dignity. Most protests began peacefully, even if some eventually evolved in a more violent direction; none began with al Qaeda's call for violent jihad. Protesters across the region demanded a twenty-first-century version of democracy, not a seventh-century caliphate. To be sure, elections have empowered Islamists in Tunisia and Egypt, but few share al Qaeda's vision for the future or seek to align with the terrorist organization.[22]

Israeli-Palestinian impasse. No summary of regional dynamics, past or present, would be complete without a discussion of the Arab-Israeli conflict. Arab-Israeli tensions no longer represent the central cleavage or primary driver of events in the MENA, but as the recent Gaza war demonstrates, the conflict retains its power to suddenly recapture the regional agenda. The failure to reach an Israeli-Palestinian accord continues to pose a fundamental challenge to both Israel's security and regional stability. In the absence of a two-state solution, the geographic reality of expanding Israeli settlements and continued occupation in the West Bank will inevitably collide with the demographic reality of an expanding Palestinian population, making it difficult for Israel to maintain its identity as both a Jewish and democratic state.[23] Meanwhile, Palestinian disenchantment with both the peace process and their own leadership could produce a third intifada, a "Palestinian Spring," or both.[24] In the context of rising populism across the Arab world, either of these outcomes would risk deepening Israel's isolation and exacerbating regional conflict.

Despite the high priority President Obama gave the Israeli-Palestinian issue immediately upon taking office, the administration's early efforts to push both sides back into meaningful and sustained negotiations failed to overcome the powerful forces pushing against peace.[25] The rightward drift in Israel politics—including the adoption by many religious Israelis and right-leaning immigrants of the settler community's view that the entirety of the West Bank is Israeli land—has lessened the political appetite and urgency for achieving a two-state outcome.[26] And even though the Arab Spring arguably makes achieving a peace deal more important than ever for Israel's long-term security, Israeli leaders have instead chosen to "hunker down" in the face of upheaval in Egypt and Syria, the possibility of instability in Jordan, and the growing threat from Iran.[27] For their part, Palestinian leaders remain deeply divided between the Fatah-led leadership in the West Bank and the Hamas-dominated Gaza Strip, and the Palestinian Authority (PA) lacks the popular legitimacy and political control to take the risks necessary to move the peace process forward. Recent attempts by the PA to reconcile with Hamas and attain non-member observer status in the United Nations reflect a growing sense among Palestinians that the Israeli government is unwilling to stop settlement activity (the PA's precondition for resuming peace talks) and a belief that the United States is unwilling to put sufficient pressure on Israel to do so.[28] Meanwhile, many Israelis criticize the Palestinians for failing to take advantage of the 2009-2010 settlement freeze and blame the peace process impasse on Palestinian "rejectionism," especially the refusal of the PA to recognize Israel as a Jewish state.[29] As a consequence, while the peace process is not dead, it is barely on life support.

U.S. Interests and Objectives

With this context in mind, it is possible to take stock of U.S. interests and objectives in the MENA. This is important because, after all, strategies are designed to advance interests. While the MENA region is experiencing unprecedented political and geopolitical change, nothing has changed about the importance of the region to the United States.

First and foremost, Washington has an interest in *protecting the U.S. homeland against threats that may emerge from the MENA*, especially those emanating from weapons of mass destruction and terrorism. As such, a major objective of U.S. policy in the region will remain preventing Iran from acquiring nuclear weapons. Continuing to disrupt, dismantle, degrade, and (where possible) defeat al Qaeda affiliates and other international terrorist organizations (including Iranian-backed groups) that target the United States homeland is another imperative.

Second, the United States continues to have a vital interest in *ensuring the free flow of commerce and energy resources* in the region. The combination of new sources of oil and natural gas, biofuels, and energy efficiency could make the United States much less dependent on imported oil in the years ahead.[30] Nevertheless, worldwide demand for oil and gas will continue to increase and key countries in Europe and Asia will remain dependent on Middle East supplies. Because energy markets are global, serious disruptions and price shocks resulting from turmoil in the MENA will continue to pose a significant threat to the U.S. and global economies for the foreseeable future.[31] As a result, promoting regional stability will remain an important objective for U.S. policy. Of particular importance is working to ensure that key energy producers, such as Saudi Arabia or Iraq, do not disintegrate, or that strife in Syria, Yemen, or elsewhere do not spill over and produce regional conflagrations. Preventing Iran from militarily dominating the Persian Gulf, keeping critical "sea lines of communication" open (especially the Strait of Hormuz, through which 20 percent of the world's tradable oil flows), and ensuring adequate U.S. military freedom of action within the region are also crucial for energy security.

Third, the United States has a longstanding interest in *ensuring the security and survival of the State of Israel*. Steps to counter Iranian threats and promote regional stability advance this interest, as do continued close defense and intelligence ties, security assistance to ensure Israel's unrivaled self-defense capabilities, and blunting international efforts to delegitimize the Jewish state. Ensuring Israeli security also requires support for a two-state solution, encouraging continued Egyptian and Jordanian adherence to their peace treaties with Israel, and working overtime to build a comprehensive regional peace that includes agreements with Lebanon and Syria and the normalization of Israel's relationship with the Arab world.

American policy in the MENA has attempted to advance these three core interests for decades, and nothing about the rapidly changing political landscape alters their importance. However, in light of the Arab uprisings, a fourth vital interest should now be added to the list: *advancing the dignity and prosperity of the region's people.* Development, reform, and good governance in the MENA are not only consonant with deeply held American values, but they are absolutely essential to long-term stability in the region. Advancing these interests will likely require consolidating democratic transitions in Egypt, Libya, Tunisia, and Yemen; adopting power-sharing agreements to buttress Iraq's fragile democratic experiment; nurturing ongoing reform efforts in Jordan and Morocco; encouraging evolutionary steps toward more representative and accountable government in the Gulf states; and ending the bloodshed in Syria to enable a more inclusive, post-Assad political order. Throughout the region, it will require sustained support for human rights, the rule of law, women's empowerment, and the growth of civil society.

Strategic Dilemmas and Choices

In a perfect world, we would be able to design a strategy that advances all of these interests simultaneously, and there would be no need to prioritize our objectives or accept trade-offs among them. But in the real world, advancing some U.S. interests in the MENA region will produce tensions with others, and policymakers will have to make difficult decisions.

Tensions are particularly acute in four areas:

First, containing Iran's ambitions and maintaining the free flow of oil and gas may require a sizable forward U.S. military presence in the Persian Gulf and robust security ties with Gulf regimes. Yet this increases U.S. strategic dependence on the least democratic governments in a democratizing region. This dependence, in turn, makes it difficult to prioritize political reform in Gulf states. It undermines U.S. "soft power" with the Arab street by continuing to align U.S. policy with autocratic governments, and it may inadvertently contribute to the emerging Sunni-Shiite cold war in the region.

Second, and similarly, a forward U.S. operational presence throughout the region and close ties with partner governments' security services may be essential for combating terrorism. But this very American military presence in the Arab world continues to provide al Qaeda and other extremists with valuable propaganda and recruitment opportunities.

Third, tilting toward Israel's position in their conflict with the Palestinians may be essential to reassure Israeli leaders of Washington's commitment to their security and encourage them to take risks for peace. The perception that we lack a "balanced" approach to the peace process, however, complicates our credibility with Arab partners and undermines our ability to engage new Islamist governments and the Arab street.

Finally, in light of the Arab uprisings, it is more important than ever to prioritize political and economic reform. Yet assertively pushing reform complicates ties with key autocratic partners, may provoke accusations of interference and a nationalist backlash in some democratizing states, could worsen short-term instability in some countries, and risks empowering Islamist groups less inclined to cooperate with Washington.

Although it is impossible to maximize the pursuit of all U.S. interests and objectives simultaneously, highlighting these four key dilemmas clarifies the hard choices confronting Washington policymakers. Figure 1 reframes each of the dilemmas as a question and uses the answers to identify four basic strategic options for the MENA region moving forward.

FIGURE 1: STRATEGIC OPTIONS

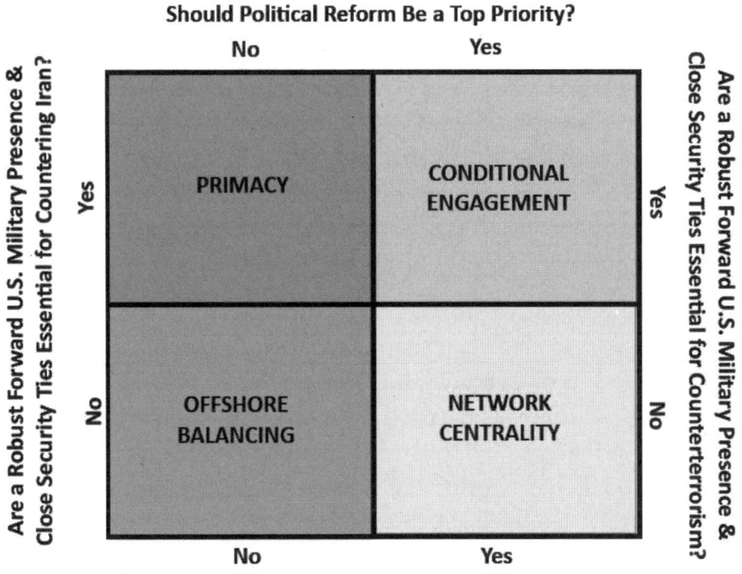

Primacy: Proponents of this approach start from the premise that the United States has abdicated its leadership role in the MENA in recent years by withdrawing troops from Iraq, drawing down its forces in Afghanistan, engaging in "naïve" diplomacy with Tehran, creating "daylight" between the United States and Israel on the peace process and the Iranian nuclear issue, favoring multilateral approaches to Libya and Syria, reducing defense budgets, and signaling a "rebalancing" of U.S. foreign policy to the Asia-Pacific. As a result, these critics charge, friends and enemies alike doubt Washington's commitment to defending vital U.S. interests in the region. Instead of "leading from behind," the goal of a primacist strategy would be to re-assert and re-establish U.S. dominance in the region.[32]

A primacist strategy would maximize the objectives of countering Iran, maintaining a robust presence in the Persian Gulf to reassure U.S. allies and guarantee the free flow of oil and gas. It would seek to ensure operational military access across the region for counterterrorism and other military contingencies.

The approach highly values military instruments as demonstrations of U.S. power and resolve. It would favor U.S. military intervention in Syria, including more lethal assistance to Syrian insurgents and the establishment of safe havens and no-fly zones to better enable the opposition to topple the Assad regime. It would also take a skeptical view of nuclear diplomacy with Tehran and would be more inclined to use force to degrade Iran's nuclear infrastructure.

Furthermore, a primacist strategy would prioritize efforts to maintain good relations with key partner states over political reform imperatives and Arab popular sensitivities when there is a tension among these objectives. For this reason, it would tilt heavily toward Israel in the peace process and, more broadly, it would not involve significant U.S. pressure on friendly states. Supporting democratic change would take a back seat to protecting other vital interests and maintaining America's "relative dominance" in the region.[33]

Of course, neoconservative proponents of this approach would disagree, arguing instead that a primacist strategy can and should include robust American democracy promotion efforts.[34] But, by necessity, this strategy could not place the same priority on political reform as some other approaches. Indeed, while neoconservatives back muscular military action intended to produce democratic regime change in *adversarial* states like Syria and Iran,[35] a primacist strategy would require maintaining large numbers of forwardly deployed U.S. forces in the region and a very close working relationship with Gulf monarchies. This strategic dependence on friendly autocratic regimes is difficult to reconcile with an assertive approach to promoting political reform in those same states, and the resulting perception of hypocrisy among Arab publics would undermine the credibility of U.S. democracy promotion efforts more broadly. Moreover, although neoconservatives speak passionately about democracy, in practice they often back away when doing so risks empowering the "wrong" parties (e.g., Islamists) through elections. By advocating a decisive tilt toward Israeli positions on the Palestinian issue, the approach favored by many neoconservatives would inevitably complicate Washington's ability to engage with many emerging populist democratic and Islamist actors in the Arab world.

Conditional engagement: A conditional engagement strategy would also put a significant emphasis on satisfying the security requirements for countering Iran and terrorist threats. But, compared to the primacist approach, conditional engagement would place greater priority on consistently and credibly promoting political and economic reform, accepting some risk of strained relations with allies and short-term uncertainty for the sake of long-term stability.

A conditional engagement strategy would attempt to leverage U.S. security, economic relationships, and assistance to actively push political and economic reform, identifying key benchmarks and calibrating assistance accordingly. It would endeavor to use a mix of incentives and persuasion to promote reform, but, when necessary, it would also use explicit conditions on U.S. assistance as leverage to pressure resistant governments. In Egypt, for example, it would make security assistance, economic aid, and U.S. support for multilateral assistance packages conditional on government reforms, as well as a continued Egyptian commitment to abide by the country's peace agreement with Israel.[36]

The approach would also make arms sales—including both advanced weaponry and technology that could be used for internal repression—to GCC states and Iraq conditional on moves toward more representative and accountable government and commitments to restraint in the face of domestic opponents. Moreover, conditional engagement would place more emphasis on security sector reform with the aim of improving respect for human rights, civilian control, and the rule of law.

In terms of the U.S. military posture in the region, conditional engagement would capitalize on the drawdown from Afghanistan to reposition some forces out of the Persian Gulf, removing those forces supporting the Afghan war while leaving sufficient numbers for a possible contingency with Iran. The goal would be to reduce the enduring U.S. presence while maintaining access and the ability to rapidly scale up in the event of a major armed conflict. The strategy would also seek to diversify the presence both inside and near the MENA region to reduce military "over-dependence" on any one country (e.g., the over-reliance on naval facilities in Bahrain for the U.S. Fifth Fleet). By reducing military over-dependence on Gulf states in particular, the strategy would seek to increase leverage to push remaining autocracies toward reform by making a threat to remove remaining assistance more credible. Reducing and diversifying the American military presence would also lessen U.S. exposure to instability events or the loss of military access in any one country. At the same time, the approach assumes that continued common interests between the United States and GCC states in countering Iran, combating terrorism, and ensuring the free flow of oil and gas from the region would provide a hedge against the possibility of a complete rupture in security relations. That said, the approach clearly runs the risk that cooperation will degrade or that partner states will turn to alternative suppliers for security assistance.[37]

Conditional engagement would also prioritize democratic change in adversarial states, but it would do so with more caution than the primacist approach. In Syria, the conditional engagement strategy would likely entail more assertive support for the opposition, although the depth of direct U.S. military intervention in the conflict would hinge crucially on judgments about the associated costs and risks. The strategy would also highlight Tehran's atrocious human rights record and aggressively sanction violators.[38] It would remain committed to defending U.S. partners against Iranian aggression and leave the option of the use of force against Tehran's nuclear program "on the table." But, compared to the primacist approach, it would be much more committed to nuclear diplomacy and would not rush to employ the military option, since doing so risks further destabilizing the region, sparking a wave of anti-Americanism, and solidifying popular support for the Iranian regime, while only setting back the Iranian program for a few years.[39]

Finally, conditional engagement would emphasize a balanced approach to the Middle East peace process, both as a means of promoting an Israeli-Palestinian accord and to enhance U.S. credibility and soft power with the newly empowered Arab street. This would not entail "throwing Israel under the bus" or tilting toward the Palestinian position in negotiations. Washington's commitment to Israel's security would remain sacrosanct. At the same time, however, U.S. policy would recognize that both Israel and the Palestinians have legitimate claims and aspirations. Consequently, Washington would actively serve as an honest broker, seeking to bridge differences and locate areas for compromise that preserve Israeli identity and security while fulfilling Palestinian aspirations for dignity and sovereignty. The United States would press both sides, as well as other regional states, to make difficult choices and support them when they take risks for peace.[40]

Network centrality: The goal of this strategy would be to establish the United States as the central node in multiple networks of influence in the region.[41] Promoting reform and enhancing U.S. soft power in an increasingly populist region would be the major priorities. In MENA countries undergoing democratic transitions, the approach would emphasize expanding connections with civil society and emerging political actors, including moderate Islamists. In friendly autocratic states, the strategy would also seek to cultivate societal connections, building indigenous support and capacity to push reform from the bottom up. In adversarial states, the approach would support democratic regime change by forging connections with opposition networks. Lastly, to enhance U.S. credibility with the newly empowered Arab street across the region, it would adopt a balanced approach to the Middle East peace process.

A network centrality approach contends that the United States can protect its interests and exert significant influence in the region without large-scale U.S. military involvement. The strategy would rebalance U.S. aid to the region by shifting much of Washington's security assistance budget toward economic, civil society, and democracy assistance programs. It would then focus remaining security assistance on building capacity in friendly states for external defense and coalition activities (as opposed to internal defense capabilities that might facilitate repression). Direct U.S. military involvement would be limited to providing unique military capabilities and "key enablers" to assist partner nations defending against common external threats like Iran. The United States would seek to be the critical integrating node in regional air and ballistic missile defense systems, shared early warning, maritime task forces, and counterterrorism activities, but it would do so with the smallest possible military footprint.[42] The goal would be twofold: to maintain a small forward operational ability presence to achieve U.S. military objectives (although clearly much less than the previous two strategies would), and, by intentionally fostering among partners a number of critical security dependencies on niche U.S. military capabilities, Washington would seek to maintain leverage that could be used to push states toward greater cooperation and reform.

The strategy would thus aim to make the United States essential to both nongovernmental and governmental networks. But, in the end, it would privilege connections to civil society over traditional state-based relationships when and if the two conflict. For this reason, the strategy would have to absorb a short-term risk of fraying relations with some Arab governments—both democratizing and autocratic, that will likely bristle at American "interference" in their societies—and it may also empower anti-American social groups to make the same charge. By contributing to the perception that the United States was pulling back militarily from the region and building relationships with new populist and Islamist actors, this strategy would also likely produce significant strains in the U.S.-Israeli relationship.

Offshore balancing: In one way or another, the previous three approaches envision some form of active, forward U.S. regional engagement. In contrast, offshore balancing would seek to advance American interests by taking a step back. Whereas a primacist strategy attempts to reassert U.S. primacy by maintaining a robust military presence in the MENA, advocates of offshore balancing contend that such an approach actually undermines U.S. power by contributing to military and fiscal overstretch. Offshore balancing would instead reduce U.S. strategic commitments in the MENA and use retrenchment as a means of addressing and managing the military and economic causes of America's relative decline, conserving U.S. resources for use in those rare instances when vital national interests are truly at stake (e.g., if regional oil supplies are threatened by an aggressor state). The United States would not seek to dominate the MENA region, but rather would work indirectly "by, with, and through" U.S. allies and partners to maintain a balance of power favorable to American interests. By pulling back, it would prevent partner states from free riding on the United States, forcing them to take on more of the regional security burden.[43]

Proponents of an offshore balancing approach believe it is possible to achieve core U.S. security interests in the MENA with a much lighter U.S. military footprint. They contend that a smaller American presence in the Persian Gulf, for example, would ease Tehran's security anxieties, lessening the regime's incentives to acquire nuclear weapons. Should that fail, they believe the United States could rely on deterrence to neutralize the most harmful consequences of a nuclear-armed Iran. In the counterterrorism domain, the offshore balancing approach would eschew the kind of large-scale military deployments that arguably radicalize local populations and motivate attacks on U.S. interests. Instead, the strategy would rely heavily on local security forces to go after common enemies and use long-range U.S. strike capabilities, drones, and small numbers of Special Operations Forces to target groups that imminently threaten the U.S. homeland.[44]

Needless to say, this approach would avoid ambitious nation-building efforts and would not bank on transforming states in the region into functional democracies. Moreover, because this approach requires working through partner states to advance America's hard security interests in the region, it would by necessity take a much lighter touch in pushing controversial reforms that could alienate partners and complicate security cooperation.

Finally, although some advocates of offshore balancing are highly critical of America's special relationship with Israel,[45] in practice the approach would likely have to rely on—and work indirectly through—Israel to help uphold a balance of power favorable to U.S. interests in the region. For this reason, it would be difficult for Washington to press Israel to accommodate Palestinian concerns. The sense among Israeli leaders that the United States was stepping back from active military involvement in the region might also make them less inclined to take the security risks required to produce a two-state solution.

Conclusion

As the United States grapples with the dramatic events unfolding in the MENA, this essay has sought to provide a framework that identifies key questions in lieu of providing all the answers. The four strategies outlined above are ideal types. In the real world, policy makers may pursue elements of them in combination or in sequence, or come up with alternatives not considered here. But no strategy in isolation or combination is likely to achieve all U.S. interests in the region simultaneously. The MENA region may be in great flux, but the requirement for policy makers to make tough choices, accepting risks in some areas for gains in others, remains unaltered.

Colin H. Kahl is an associate professor in the Security Studies Program at Georgetown University's Edmund A. Walsh School of Foreign Service and a Senior Fellow at the Center for a New American Security (CNAS) focusing on Middle East security and defense policy. From February 2009 to December 2011, Dr. Kahl served as the Deputy Assistant Secretary of Defense for the Middle East. In that capacity, he developed and implemented the U.S. Defense Department's strategy and policy toward Bahrain, Egypt, Iraq, Iran, Israel and the Palestinian territories, Jordan, Kuwait, Lebanon, Oman, Qatar, Saudi Arabia, Syria, the United Arab Emirates and Yemen. During his tenure, he played a lead role in: designing and overseeing the responsible drawdown and transition strategy in Iraq; shaping the Pentagon's efforts to counter Iran's nuclear weapons ambitions and destabilizing activities; promoting unprecedented defense cooperation with Israel; building a Regional Security Architecture in the Gulf; and crafting the Department's response to the Arab Awakening. In June 2011, Dr. Kahl was awarded the Secretary of Defense Medal for Outstanding Public Service by Secretary Robert Gates. Dr. Kahl has published widely on U.S. defense strategy in the Middle East, including articles in *Foreign Affairs*, *Foreign Policy*, *International Security*, *The Los Angeles Times*, *Middle East Policy*, *The National Interest*, *The New York Times*, and *The Washington Post*. Dr. Kahl received a B.A. in political science from the University of Michigan in 1993 and a Ph.D. in political science from Columbia University in 2000.

1   Marc Lynch, *The Arab Uprising: The Unfinished Revolutions of the New Middle East,* (New York: PublicAffairs, 2012).

2   For excellent surveys of the events surrounding the Arab revolutions, see Fouad Ajami, "The Arab Spring at One," *Foreign Affairs*, March/April 2012, http://www.foreignaffairs.com/articles/137053/fouad-ajami/the-arab-spring-at-one?page=show; and Lynch, *The Arab Uprising.*

3   Tony Karon, "Five Reasons Why the Assad Regime Survives," *Time*, August 30, 2012, http://world.time.com/2012/08/30/five-reasons-why-the-assad-regime-survives/.

4   Colin H. Kahl, Melissa Dalton, and Matthew Irvine, "Risk and Rivalry: Iran, Israel, and the Bomb," Center for a New American Security, June 2012, http://cnas.org/riskandrivalry.

5   Eric S. Edelman, Andrew F. Krepinevich Jr, and Evan Braden Montgomery, "The Dangers of a Nuclear Iran," *Foreign Affairs*, January/February 2011.

6   Thom Shanker, "In Kuwait, Panetta Affirms U.S. Commitment to the Middle East," *The New York Times*, December 11, 2012, http://www.nytimes.com/2012/12/12/world/middleeast/in-kuwait-panetta-affirms-us-commitment-to-middle-east.html?_r=0.

7   William C. Witt, et al., "Iran's Evolving Breakout Potential," Institute for Science and International Security Report, October 8, 2012.

8   Alireza Nader, "Smart Sanctions," *Foreign Policy* (online), September 25, 2012, http://www.foreignpolicy.com/articles/2012/09/25/smart_sanctions.

9   Dalia Dassa Kaye and Frederic Wehrey, "Arab Spring, Persian Winter," *Foreign Affairs*, July/August 2011, http://www.foreignaffairs.com/articles/67942/dalia-dassa-kaye-and-frederic-wehrey-michael-scott-doran/arab-spring-persian-winter.

10 Robert F. Worth, "Effort to Rebrand Arab Spring Backfires in Iran," *New York Times*, February 2, 2012, http://www.nytimes.com/2012/02/03/world/middleeast/effort-to-rebrand-arab-spring-backfires-in-iran.html?pagewanted=all.

11 Colin H. Kahl, "Supremely Irrelevant," *Foreign Policy* (online), January 25, 2012, http://www.foreignpolicy.com/articles/2012/01/24/supremely_irrelevant?page=full.

12 "Egypt's Foreign Policy: Independent—Or Not?" *The Economist*, September 1, 2012, http://www.economist.com/node/21561898.

13 Giorgio Cafiero, "Can Egypt Chart Its Own Course?" *Middle East Post*, September 18, 2012, https://middleeastpost.com/giorgio-cafiero-can-egypt-chart-its-own-course-washington-dc-foreign-policy-in-focus-september-17-2012/; and Nader, "Smart Sanctions."

14 "Morsi Criticizes Syria at Tehran Meeting," *Al Jazeera*, August 30, 2012, http://www.aljazeera.com/news/middleeast/2012/08/20128308579560767.html.

15 Peter Baker and David D. Kirkpatrick, "Egypt Leader and Obama Forge Link in Gaza Deal," *New York Times*, November 21, 2012, http://www.nytimes.com/2012/11/22/world/middleeast/egypt-leader-and-obama-forge-link-in-gaza-deal.html?pagewanted=all&_r=0.

16 Thanassis Cambanis, "How the Arab Spring Killed Hezbollah," September 20, 2012, http://www.tnr.com/blog/plank/107543/how-the-arab-spring-killed-hezbollah#.

17 Suleiman al-Khalidi, "Analysis—Arab Dynasties Lure Jordan, Morocco into Anti-Iran Bloc," *Reuters*, May

13, 2011, http://www.reuters.com/article/2011/05/13/us-gulf-alliance-idUSTRE74C29W20110513.

[18] F. Gregory Gause, III, "Is Saudi Arabia Really Counter-Revolutionary?" *Foreign Policy* (online), August 9, 2011, http://mideast.foreignpolicy.com/posts/2011/08/09/is_saudi_arabia_really_counter_revolutionary; and F. Gregory Gause, III', "The Gulf Regional System and the Arab Spring," *The Montréal Review*, March 2012, http://www.themontrealreview.com/2009/The-International-Relations-of-the-Persian-Gulf.php.

[19] For example, while there is no compelling evidence that protestors in Bahrain were actually taking direction from Tehran, the GCC intervention and the regime's crackdown had the self-fulfilling effect of further radicalizing the country's Shiite majority, pushing them closer to Iran and worsening regional sectarian tensions.

[20] Bruce W. Jentleson, et al., "Strategic Adaptation: Toward a New Strategy in the Middle East," Center for a New American Security, June 2012, pp. 17-18.

[21] For a good overview, see Brian Michael Jenkins, *Al Qaeda in Its Third Decade: Irreversible Decline or Imminent Victory*, (Santa Monica, CA: The Rand Corp., 2012).

[22] Peter Bergen, "Time to Declare Victory: Al Qaeda is Defeated," *CNN.com*, June 27, 2012, http://security.blogs.cnn.com/2012/06/27/time-to-declare-victory-al-qaeda-is-defeated-opinion/; and Jenkins, *Al Qaeda in Its Third Decade*, pp. 5-6.

[23] Akiva Eldar, "Israel's New Politics and the Fate of Palestine," *The National Interest*, July/August 2012, pp. 5-15.

[24] Khaled Elgindy, "Why Palestinians Protest," *Foreign Affairs*, September 20, 2012, http://www.foreignaffairs.com/articles/138131/khaled-elgindy/why-palestinians-protest.

[25] Scott Wilson, "Where Obama Failed in Forging Peace in the Middle East," *Washington Post*, July 14, 2012, http://www.washingtonpost.com/politics/obama-searches-for-middle-east-peace/2012/07/14/gJQAQQiKlW_story.html.

[26] Eldar, "Israel's New Politics and the Fate of Palestine."

[27] For a summary of Israeli concerns regarding the Arab uprisings, see Efraim Inbar, "Israel's National Security Amidst Unrest in the Arab World," *The Washington Quarterly*, Vol. 35, No. 3 (Summer 2012), pp. 59-73.

[28] Daniel Kurtzer, "Reviving the Peace Process," *The National Interest*, January/February 2012, pp. 38-46.

[29] See, for example, Yosef Kuperwasser and Shalom Lipner, "The Problem is Palestinian Rejectionism," *Foreign Affairs*, November/December 2011, pp. 2-9.

[30] Tim Mullaney, "U.S. Energy Independence Is No Longer Just a Pipe Dream," *USA Today*, May 15, 2012, http://usatoday30.usatoday.com/money/industries/energy/story/2012-05-15/1A-COV-ENERGY-INDEPENDENCE/54977254/1.

[31] Bruce W. Jentleson, et al., "Strategic Adaptation," p. 19; and Rex W. Tillerson, "The New North American Energy Paradigm: Reshaping the Future," Council on Foreign Relations, June 27, 2012, http://www.cfr.org/united-states/new-north-american-energy-paradigm-reshaping-future/p28630.

[32] See, for example, Charles Krauthammer, "Collapse of the Cairo Doctrine," *Washington Post*, September 20, 2012, http://www.washingtonpost.com/opinions/charles-krauthammer-collapse-of-the-cairo-doctrine/2012/09/20/72fb7f62-035f-11e2-91e7-2962c74e7738_story.html; and Lee Smith, "Obama in Retreat,"

The Weekly Standard, July 2, 2012, http://www.weeklystandard.com/articles/obama-retreat_647776.html?nopager=1.

[33] Robert Kaplan, "Good Mideast Dictators," *Stratfor,* July 25, 2012, http://www.stratfor.com/analysis/good-mideast-dictators-robert-d-kaplan.

[34] William Kristol, "Obama's Moment in the Middle East – and at Home," *Washington Post,* February 23, 2011, http://www.washingtonpost.com/wp-dyn/content/article/2011/02/22/AR2011022203763.html; and Jamie M. Fly, "Obama is Unwilling to Lead the U.S. Response to the Arab Spring," *U.S. News & World Report,* September 27, 2012, http://www.usnews.com/debate-club/has-obama-properly-handled-the-arab-spring/obama-is-unwilling-to-lead-the-us-response-to-the-arab-spring.

[35] See, for example, Jamie M. Fly and Gary Schmitt, "The Case for Regime Change in Iran," *Foreign Affairs,* January 17, 2012, http://www.foreignaffairs.com/articles/137038/jamie-m-fly-and-gary-schmitt/the-case-for-regime-change-in-iran.

[36] See the contribution of Michèle Flournoy and Melissa Dalton in this volume.

[37] The overall discussion of conditional engagement in this section draws from Jentleson, et al., "Strategic Adaptation," pp. 27-33. See also Lynch, *The Arab Uprising,* chap. 8.

[38] Sarah Morgan and Andrew Apostolou, "Why Obama Should Highlight Iran's Human Rights Abuses," *Foreign Affairs* (online), November 7, 2011.

[39] See, for example, Kahl, "Not Time to Attack Iran."

[40] Jentleson, et al., "Strategic Adaptation," pp. 33-35.

[41] Although the strategy has not been explicitly applied to the MENA, this section draws heavily on Anne-Marie Slaughter, "A Grand Strategy of Network Centrality," in Richard Fontaine and Kristin M. Lord, eds., "America's Path: Grand Strategy for the Next Administration," Center for a New American Security, May 2012, pp. 43-56.

[42] To some extent, this goal is already reflected in U.S. Central Command's "Regional Security Architecture," but CENTCOM envisions a much larger enduring U.S. presence in the Middle East. See Gen. David Petraeus, Remarks to the 6th International Institute for Strategic Studies Regional Security Summit (The Manama Dialogue), December 12, 2009, http://www.iiss.org/conferences/the-iiss-regional-security-summit/manama-dialogue-2009/plenary-sessions-and-speeches-2009/fifth-plenary-session/fifth-plenary-session-general-david-petraeus/.

[43] Christopher Layne, "The Global Power Shift from West to East," *The National Interest,* May/June 2012, pp. 30-31; Harvey M. Sapolsky, Benjamin H. Friedman, Eugene Gholz, and Daryl G. Press, "Restraining Order: For Strategic Modesty," *World Affairs Journal,* Fall 2009, pp. 84-94; and Stephen M. Walt, "The End of the American Era," *The National Interest,* November/December 2011, pp. 13-15.

[44] Sapolsky, Friedman, Gholz, and Press, "Restraining Order," pp. 89-91; and Joseph M. Parent and Paul K. MacDonald, "The Wisdom of Retrenchment," *Foreign Affairs,* November/December 2011.

[45] Walt, "The End of the American Era," pp. 14-15.